Microsoft Dynamics AX 2012 R3 Financial Management

Boost your accounting and financial skills with
Microsoft Dynamics AX 2012 R3

Mohamed Aamer

BIRMINGHAM - MUMBAI

Microsoft Dynamics AX 2012 R3 Financial Management

First published: November 2013

Second edition: February 2015

Production reference: 1090215

Published by Packt Publishing Ltd.
Livery Place
35 Livery Street
Birmingham B3 2PB, UK.

ISBN 978-1-78439-098-3

www.packtpub.com

Credits

Author
Mohamed Aamer

Reviewers
Marco Carvalho
János Molnár
Wendy Rijners
Syed Muhammad Sajid

Commissioning Editor
Usha Iyer

Acquisition Editor
Subho Gupta

Content Development Editor
Ritika Singh

Technical Editors
Krishnaveni Nair
Rikita Poojari
Humera Shaikh

Copy Editors
Shivangi Chaturvedi
Deepa Nambiar
Vikrant Phadke

Project Coordinator
Judie Jose

Proofreaders
Simran Bhogal
Ameesha Green
Paul Hindle
Joanna McMahon

Indexer
Monica Ajmera Mehta

Graphics
Sheetal Aute

Production Coordinator
Conidon Miranda

Cover Work
Conidon Miranda

About the Author

Mohamed Aamer is a Microsoft Dynamics AX Support Engineer for the EMEA region with Microsoft, Egypt. In 2013, he was awarded Microsoft Dynamics AX MVP, and he was the first AX MVP in the Middle East and Africa. His main focus is on implementing Microsoft Dynamics AX to fit customers' needs. He uses his time to help and support Microsoft partners to answer their complex questions and tackle obstacles they might face; he understands customer business cycles and solves customer business problems through a combination of business process reengineering and utilization of Microsoft Dynamics AX functionalities. He is a Microsoft Certified Professional (MCP) specialized in financial management and supply chain management. In addition to this, he has been a Microsoft Certified Trainer (MCT) for 5 years.

Mohamed has varied consultation experience in dealing with Microsoft Golden Partners and Microsoft customers. He has worked as a consultant in many industries, such as retail fashion, retail electronics, cement manufacturing, trading, and ready mix. He has carried out multiple implementations of Microsoft Dynamics Retail Management System and Microsoft Dynamics AX in numerous capacities, such as project manager, solutions architect, and lead consultant. His consulting skills are complemented by his business, management, and interpersonal skills.

He is also a columnist of AX Excellence at the MSDynamicsWorld.com community, an official blogger at Microsoft Dynamics Community, and has his own blog (www. blog.mohamedaamer.com). He delivers evangelizing sessions to Microsoft Student Partners (MSPs) to introduce Microsoft Dynamics AX and Microsoft Dynamics Sure Step to them. He has been ranked in the top 100 influential people at www. dynamicsworld.co.uk for 2 consecutive years. He has obtained other badges from Microsoft, such as Microsoft Community Contributor (MCC) and Microsoft Dynamics Community Expert.

Mohamed authored *Microsoft Dynamics 2012 Financial Management* and reviewed *Customer Success with Microsoft Dynamics Sure Step*, both by Packt Publishing.

When not working on complex business processes, he attends live Sufi shows and music concerts.

Acknowledgments

My sincere thanks go to all people who directly/indirectly taught, guided, supported, and advised me to build my personal profile; I am doing my best to improve myself. The following acknowledgments are for people who had a massive impact on my career; I'd like to thank all of them, though I cannot thank them enough.

I dedicate this book to the memory of my father and my Uncle, Hamza; both of them invested seed of concepts and beliefs in my brother and me, and now we are harvesting the fruits of this. My father always told me, "I believe in you; when you say you can do, you achieve more than what you target. Just focus." My uncle, Hamza, told me after my graduation, "You just met your lifetime teacher who will guide you through your entire life."

My older brother, Ramy, who inspired me, gave me more than his time, efforts, tons of daily advice, coaching, and led me to the right path. He always supports and encourages me. He is my mentor; Ramy put me on the Information Technology track and gave me the chance to choose the right field to pursue. He helped me finish college and convinced me to attend the first e-commerce seminar in the Middle East; this was the first spark. I consider Ramy as my source of energy.

I would like to thank my mother for her support and prayers.

I would also like to thank my wife, who has given up so much of our personal life during the development of my career; I cannot thank her enough for that.

Thanks to Dr. Salah ElKashef, who is a training and e-learning consultant and founder of ElKashef E-Learning University. Salah is my first instructor who introduced e-commerce to me in 2002 and helped me to become a certified e-commerce consultant before my graduation. He helped me by directing my career to Information Technology management.

I would like to thank Shaimaa Farid, who is an IT administrator at the Alexandria Trust. I have worked with Shaimaa as an application consultant for Microsoft Dynamics RMS; she is the one who provided me with information about the Microsoft Dynamics AX scholarship in 2008. Shaimaa has given me a lot of support and encouragement to focus on my career as a consultant. She is one of the best customer-oriented people I have worked with.

Thanks to Mohamed Samy, who works as a solution architect. He is the one who introduced me to the community as a speaker for Cairo Code Camp; I used to deliver sessions with him as a copresenter, evangelizing Microsoft Dynamics AX and Microsoft Dynamics Sure Step to the Egyptian community. He predicted that I will become an AX MVP. Mohamed is a very talented IT geek with unique creative solutions; I enjoy our community activities together.

I would also like to thank Ahmed Kazem, cofounder and CTO of Lamartica. Ahmed is an artistic developer; he can learn any technology in a very short time. He develops, maintains, and supports my blog technically. I have never met a smart and gifted developer like him.

Thanks to Ahmed Aboulmagd, who is a technical evangelist at Windows Phone Microsoft. Ahmed used to manage and schedule the Microsoft Dynamics AX and Microsoft Dynamics Sure Step sessions with Microsoft Student Partner (MSPs); I believe we did a good job, especially when we saw some students joining that field.

Thanks to Dr. Nezar Samy, Director at Information Systems Department, Nile University. Nezar was my instructor for Information Technology Management Professional Certificate at American University in Cairo: he taught me the role of IT as a business enabler and gave me a chance to improve my presentation skills.

I would also like to thank Chandru Shankar, Manufacturing Industry Director at EMEA MBS Microsoft. Chandru has given me a lot of motivation and support in my career; he is always available to give advice and share ideas; I am very proud to have met a person like him and have him as a family friend. Chandru is my role model.

Thanks to Jason Gumpert, who works as an editor at `MSDynamicsWorld.com`. I have been working with Jason since 2012 as an author for a feature column for the MSDynamicsWorld community. Jason gave me a chance to develop my writing techniques and style from blogs to articles; I believe my pieces reached more people through his community. He is an open-minded person, who is always open to new initiatives.

I would also like to thank Ashraf Abusen, Group Chief Financial Officer at ASEC Cement. I consider Abusen as my coach who taught me to utilize logical thinking and understand how to build up a practical solution for complex business requirements and streamline this solution with all business divisions. Abusen is a charismatic leader; he has the best skills to build the road map of the ERP solution.

Thanks to Ashraf Aly, Senior Global ERP Director at Ascom. Ashraf is a talented manager who can manage and drive complex ERP implementation; he spotted my skills and gave me the opportunity to utilize my abilities. Ashraf has unique, flexible techniques to deal with stakeholders of any project and achieve the objectives of that project.

Thanks to Julie Gale, who works as a project manager with Microsoft. She helped me learn more about Microsoft Dynamics Sure Step. She also supported me in community activities.

I would also like to thank Microsoft EMEA Global Business Support (GBS). I am very proud to be part of this world-class team; they have always given me a lot of support. I cannot thank them enough for their ongoing support and guidance from management and colleagues. Special thanks to Eva Del Pino Ramirez, Dynamics AX Support Manager at Microsoft, for her continuous encouragement and feedback, which helped me develop my abilities.

Thanks to Microsoft Dynamics Academic Alliance Team and Lyndsey Creamer, program manager/project manager of the Microsoft Dynamics Academic Alliance Team at Microsoft, Jane Birkegaard, senior program manager at Microsoft Dynamics, and Ashley Pecoraro, former program manager for Academic Alliance Team at Microsoft; Lyndsey, Jane, and Ashley gave me a lot of support to be involved in DynnA activities to share my knowledge and experience with DynnA members. They are very open to new ideas and they are willing to help as much as they can.

I would also like to thank Microsoft Dynamics Community Team and Nick Hoban, Sr. Release Manager ECIT at Microsoft; Nick guided me in the right direction to help me share my blog posts with the Dynamics Community.

Thanks to Microsoft Dynamics AX MVPs. They enrich the community with their experience and knowledge on Microsoft Dynamics AX. Special thanks to Brandon George, Microsoft MVP and Director of Business Intelligence at Sunrise Technologies; Antonio Gilabert, Microsoft Dynamics AX MVP and founder of AX3; and former AX MVPs, Fred Chen, technical architect at Microsoft, and Arijit Basu, senior solution architect at Microsoft. They give me a lot of support and encouragement as an AX MVP.

About the Reviewers

Marco Carvalho has been programming since the age of 12. He has a lot of experience working in different industries, ranging from private investments to security and management consulting. He has been architecting and developing solutions with a mindset that "anything is possible."

Currently, Marco is a consulting manager at Junction Solutions and is a Gold Partner who specializes in multichannel retail as well as food and beverage industry, where he serves as a technical lead on projects.

He is the author of *Microsoft Dynamics AX 2009 Administration* and reviewer of *Implementing Microsoft Dynamics AX 2012 with Sure Step 2012*, both by Packt Publishing.

> I would like to thank my fellow authors and Packt for considering me. I look forward to many more publications!

János Molnár is an experienced Dynamics AX senior developer from Hungary. János has gained a wide angle of expertise through many international AX 2012 implementation projects in the heavy equipment Caterpillar business at a Hungarian Microsoft Gold Partner DAX developer company. He was involved in projects in USA, Australia, Singapore, India, and New Zealand, where he took roles as an onsite development coordinator working with Microsoft directly on the implementations. This time, as a lead developer, János gained experience in technical leadership and gained deeper understanding of business and functional processes. He is a Microsoft Certified Professional for AX and BI.

> I would like to thank the author and Packt Publishing for letting me be a reviewer for this book. The review process helped me match my technical skills with my functional knowledge.

Wendy Rijners is a consultant at Abecon. Over the past few years, Wendy has worked for several customers who use Dynamics ERP solutions. Since 2011, she has been focusing on retail in combination with Dynamics AX and has been involved in a Microsoft Dynamics AX 2012 R2 + POS implementation. Wendy is part of the Product Management Retail team that provides customer's needs to the Abecon Retail standard to make sure that every retailer can cover their processes in AX.

Syed Muhammad Sajid is a respected and self-motivated professional with more than 12 years of experience in the software industry.

He has more than 4 years of experience as a software quality assurance engineer/lead and years of experience in project management with Microsoft on AX 2012 and other client projects. He is currently working as project manager and senior functional consultant on AX 2012 R2 and R3 with different clients, managing multiple projects simultaneously. He has extensive experience in managing large-scale projects with a large team from the requirement-gathering phase to completion. He is highly skilled in tracking details, communicating deadlines, and following up with internal and external partners to ensure on-time completion within budget.

He has experience in different domain applications such as the public sector, health care, education, retail, mortgage, real estate, and online shopping malls (B2B and B2C).

He also worked with the Microsoft Dynamics AX Global Development team. He has worked as a test manager in the development of Financials, HRM, Payroll, and Budgeting modules of Microsoft Dynamics AX.

He was part of the successfully completed Microsoft Dynamics AX 5.0, which was released by Microsoft in 2008. He was also part of the successfully completed Microsoft Dynamics AX 6.0, which was released by Microsoft in 2011, with public sector functionalities (US).

www.PacktPub.com

Support files, eBooks, discount offers, and more

For support files and downloads related to your book, please visit www.PacktPub.com.

Did you know that Packt offers eBook versions of every book published, with PDF and ePub files available? You can upgrade to the eBook version at www.PacktPub.com and as a print book customer, you are entitled to a discount on the eBook copy. Get in touch with us at service@packtpub.com for more details.

At www.PacktPub.com, you can also read a collection of free technical articles, sign up for a range of free newsletters and receive exclusive discounts and offers on Packt books and eBooks.

https://www2.packtpub.com/books/subscription/packtlib

Do you need instant solutions to your IT questions? PacktLib is Packt's online digital book library. Here, you can search, access, and read Packt's entire library of books.

Why subscribe?

- Fully searchable across every book published by Packt
- Copy and paste, print, and bookmark content
- On demand and accessible via a web browser

Free access for Packt account holders

If you have an account with Packt at www.PacktPub.com, you can use this to access PacktLib today and view 9 entirely free books. Simply use your login credentials for immediate access.

Instant updates on new Packt books

Get notified! Find out when new books are published by following @PacktEnterprise on Twitter or the *Packt Enterprise* Facebook page.

Table of Contents

Preface

The essential foundation of the Enterprise Resource Planning (ERP) implementation is the financial part that is considered as the backbone of the implementation. The implementation team from the partner side and customer side should ensure that the financial module is well structured and designed. This book provides a broad guide to Microsoft Dynamics AX Financial Management fundamentals for parties involved in the implementation project, with considerations of the business rationale behind functions, basic setups, configurations, transactions in action, and examples of real-life scenarios.

What this book covers

Chapter 1, Getting Started with Microsoft Dynamics AX 2012, explains the ERP concept, integration of modules, the financial posting mechanisms in Microsoft Dynamics AX 2012 R3, the role of consultant in implementation team, Microsoft Dynamics Sure Step implementation methodology, Microsoft Dynamics Lifecycle Service, and the Microsoft Dynamics AX 2012 R3 user interface.

Chapter 2, Understanding the General Ledger, explains the usage of main accounts, control points, and the Microsoft Dynamics AX 2012 R3 shared financial data concept. It also gives you a practical insight on opening balance tips and month-end closing procedures.

Chapter 3, Understanding Cash and Bank Management, will help you understand the cash and bank management module integration, controls, the bank reconciliation process, and then cover the bank facility function.

Chapter 4, Understanding Accounts Payable, focuses on integrating Accounts payable with other modules, the vendor transactions, invoices, payment, and prepayment, in addition to vendor controls and basic master data.

Chapter 5, Understanding Accounts Receivable, focuses on integrating Accounts receivable with other modules, the customer transactions, sales invoices, free text invoices and its correction, in addition to customer controls and basic master data.

Chapter 6, Exploring Fixed Assets, focuses on the integration of fixed assets with other modules and their transactions.

Chapter 7, Functioning of Cash Flow Management, focuses on the integration points between cash flow management and other modules in Microsoft Dynamics AX, provided with basic setups, configuration, and cash flow transaction.

Chapter 8, Working with Cost Management, covers the inventory costing model in Microsoft Dynamics AX 2012 and provides information about inventory cost setups and configuration, inventory reconciliation with general ledger, recalculation, and closing.

Chapter 9, Exploring Financial Dimensions, focuses on financial dimensions model in Microsoft Dynamics AX 2012, its practical utilization, and its reporting.

Chapter 10, Exploring Financial Reporting and Analysis, will help you to find out the reporting needs at early stages of the implementation project and what sides you should consider during the project's life cycle. It also explores Microsoft Dynamics AX inquiry forms and SQL Reporting Services (SSRS) reports.

What you need for this book

All examples were performed using a virtual machine of Microsoft Dynamics AX 2012 R3 Image from the Microsoft partner/customer source.

Who this book is for

This book is intended for application consultants, controllers, CFOs, and other professionals who are involved in the Microsoft Dynamics AX implementation project. Basic knowledge of financial terms, concepts, and Microsoft Dynamics AX terminology is required.

Conventions

In this book, you will find a number of text styles that distinguish between different kinds of information. Here are some examples of these styles and an explanation of their meaning.

Code words in text, database table names, folder names, filenames, file extensions, pathnames, dummy URLs, user input, and Twitter handles are shown as follows: "In the voucher line, select the **Account type** value as **Vendor**, select the vendor ID, enter 1000 in the **Credit** side amount, and select the **Offset account** value."

New terms and **important words** are shown in bold. Words that you see on the screen, for example, in menus or dialog boxes, appear in the text like this: "The user can arrange the order of modules by clicking on the **Navigation Pane Options**...."

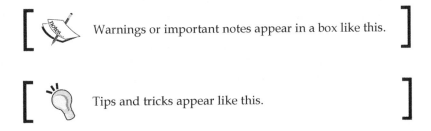

Warnings or important notes appear in a box like this.

Tips and tricks appear like this.

Reader feedback

Feedback from our readers is always welcome. Let us know what you think about this book—what you liked or disliked. Reader feedback is important for us as it helps us develop titles that you really get the most out of.

To send us general feedback, simply e-mail to feedback@packtpub.com, and mention the book's title in the subject of your message.

If there is a topic that you have expertise in and you are interested in either writing or contributing to a book, see our author guide on www.packtpub.com/authors.

Customer support

Now that you are the proud owner of a Packt book, we have a number of things to help you to get the most from your purchase.

Errata

Although we have taken every care to ensure the accuracy of our content, mistakes do happen. If you find a mistake in one of our books—maybe a mistake in the text or the code—we would be grateful if you could report this to us. By doing so, you can save other readers from frustration and help us improve subsequent versions of this book. If you find any errata, please report them by visiting http://www.packtpub.com/submit-errata, selecting your book, clicking on the **Errata Submission Form** link, and entering the details of your errata. Once your errata are verified, your submission will be accepted and the errata will be uploaded to our website or added to any list of existing errata under the Errata section of that title.

To view the previously submitted errata, go to https://www.packtpub.com/books/content/support and enter the name of the book in the search field. The required information will appear under the **Errata** section.

Piracy

Piracy of copyright material on the Internet is an ongoing problem across all media. At Packt, we take the protection of our copyright and licenses very seriously. If you come across any illegal copies of our works, in any form, on the Internet, please provide us with the location address or website name immediately so that we can pursue a remedy.

Please contact us at copyright@packtpub.com with a link to the suspected pirated material.

We appreciate your help in protecting our authors and our ability to bring you valuable content.

Questions

If you have a problem with any aspect of this book, you can contact us at questions@packtpub.com, and we will do our best to address the problem.

1
Getting Started with Microsoft Dynamics AX 2012

The **Enterprise Resource Planning** (**ERP**) application is a must for companies irrespective of whether it is a small or big enterprise; it is a tool that gives visibility to management regarding the enterprise's performance on all levels. People should be familiar with the ERP concept irrespective of who implements the solution or uses it (definitely, the level of detail varies between the user and the consultant, but the core is common). This chapter covers the following topics:

- Understanding the ERP characteristics
- Discovering the ERP implementation team
- Exploring the key intentions of ERP implementations
- Understanding the ERP module's integrations
- Exploring ERP and reporting
- Posting types in Microsoft Dynamics AX
- Exploring the common terms used in ERP implementations
- Exploring Microsoft Dynamics Implementation Methodology – Sure Step
- Exploring Microsoft Dynamics **Lifecycle Services** (**LCS**)
- Looking at the Microsoft Dynamics AX user interface

Understanding the ERP characteristics

The ERP is a mission-critical application for the business, as the day-to-day activities rely on this application where the end users enter the transactions, and the management is able to monitor the business performance on a daily basis and take decisions within a proper time period. The main characteristic that differentiates the ERP from other applications, as mentioned in the Wikipedia definition of the ERP, is as follows:

> "*A business management software – usually a suite of integrated applications – that a company can use to collect, store, manage, and interpret data from many business activities.*"

From this definition, the ERP is an integrated application. In the past, each business area had its own application, and this lead to creating isolated islands for each department in the same organization, which cost organizations a lot of time, effort, and money. This leads to lack of accurate information which directly affects management decision making, because of unavailability or redundancy of information; for example, the customer account in accounts receivable is different from the customer code in the sales department, so the management could not identify the balance of this customer. With the ERP, the data is unified, controlled, and classified. This gives the company the ability to transform this data into information that helps in the decision-making process.

Discovering the implementation team

It is important for companies that want to implement the ERP to understand that its implementation is not an easy task and it requires a professional partner. For example, **Value Added Reseller** (**VAR**), which has a consulting team experienced in implementing the ERP, preferably has a partner that is an expert in the customer industry. There is a high level of engagement between customers' top management, key users, and end users in the implementation life cycle. The implementation team is considered as the key success factor for the ERP implementation.

The following diagram illustrates the ERP implementation team that consists of **Subject Matter Experts** (**SMEs**) and **key users** from customer- and partner-side applications, and technical consultants. This team works together closely during the implementation, where the customer representatives (SMEs and Key users) deliver the business requirements (that is, what they are expecting from the ERP), with the consulting team that bridges the gap between the business requirements and the implemented application. The implementation deliverables comes through several workshops from analysis, design, development, and testing.

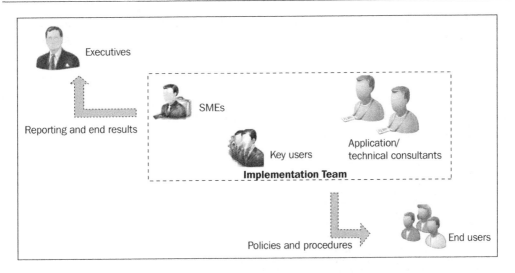

The implementation team should focus on two types of internal clients: business executives and end users. Each client has a different perspective of the ERP implementation, and the implementation team should consider their requirements during the implementation lifecycle. The executives' management focuses on reporting and end results, and the implementation team delivers policies and procedures to end users who then operate the final product, which is the ERP application.

Responsibilities and motivation of an ERP consultant

Application consultant, Functional consultant—the job title differs from one company to another, but whatever the title is, the application consultant is considered as a middle man between the ERP and the customer, where the application consultant is specialized in the ERP application and is able to understand the business requirements and adopt it to the ERP software. The application consultant can start their career after graduating from university; they can major in business administration, finance, or information systems, if it covers subjects related to business.

Alternatively, the application consultant can start working in other fields. Some people start out as an accountant, procurement agent, commercial agent, or even sales representative. I do not consider it a career shift; I consider it as an advance in one's career path. In other words, it is capitalizing on previous experiences.

Traditionally, consulting skills are divided into two main areas: the **business side**, which is known as a functional consultant, and the **technical side**, which is known as a technical consultant. Then, there is a more general **soft skills** set that all application consultants need, as they spend most of their time in discussions, workshops, and training, related to business.

Some of the key skills a company should look for in an application consultant are highlighted in the following diagram:

Business side	Technical side
• Business knowledge in business domains Vertical or Horizontal • Understanding business process cycles • Understanding business integration	• Understanding application flow of information • Understanding ERP integration • Understanding ERP implementation life cycle
Soft skills	
Communication skills Presentation skills Business writing skills	Leadership skills Project management skills Technical writing skills

The application consultants have a very important role in the implementation of the project, as they are involved in implementation tasks and activities. Microsoft Dynamics Sure Step has defined the application consultant role during implementation phases. It is a long and broad list of tasks, and this range of tasks is what I believe keeps most application consultants motivated and satisfied with their jobs. The challenges are always changing and the career path offers many opportunities to develop new skills.

Exploring key intentions of ERP implementations

Enterprises that intend to implement Microsoft Dynamics AX ERP pursue a variety of common benefits from the ERP, but in most of the projects, there wasn't any well-defined benefits that the organization's management agreed on, and no roadmap to help them accomplish those intentions. It is vital to plan the ERP implementation carefully. In the sections that follow, we will take the key objectives of ERP implementation.

The organization can have a legacy system and manual business processes, and they need to be unified by one single integrated application to manage, operate, and control the business areas and deliver reports to management, as shown in the following diagram:

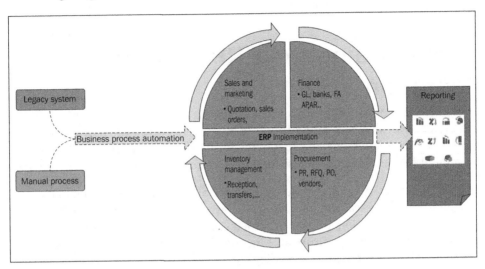

Enterprises that have decided to implement ERP should be coordinating together with a consulting partner specialized in Microsoft Dynamics AX. The customer and partner should plainly outline the objectives of the ERP solution as early as possible in the diagnostic phase. They can replace the legacy system and reduce manual business processes by automating the business processes using the ERP solution in the organization's departments. Samples of ERP implementation intentions are as follows:

- **Business process**: This comprises the following:
    - Business process automation
    - Streamlined business process in cross-function operations
    - Unified business process across holding and subsidiaries
    - Single point of contact for reducing the redundant data within departments

- **Controlling**: This comprises the following:
    - Segregation of duties and data access privileges
    - Advanced workflow and managerial approval matrix and its ceiling of expenditure amounts
    - Tracking the actual costs against budgeted
    - Inventory tracking and cost control

- **Decision support**: This comprises the following:
  - Real-time and ad hoc reports for all organization levels
  - Dynamic and dimensional reports
  - **Key Performance Indicators (KPIs)** and indicators dashboard

Understanding the ERP module's integration

The core objective of running a business is to make a profit, which requires making revenue that cover the costs and adding the margin to secure the profit. This is the core role of management to achieve this profit; the ERP application gives the management the necessary business insights to monitor the business performance.

Microsoft Dynamics AX manages and controls day-to-day transactions that occur in the company; these transactions are transformed into financial information that represents the key component of the financial statements (balance sheet and income statement), which are expenditure and income; in other words, cash out and cash in. All these are shown in the following diagram:

The cash-to-cash cycle entails the core two cycles, which are commonly known by Procure to pay and Order to cash. The first cycle covers the expenditure part (cash out), that is, every aspect related to vendor management, procurement management, purchasing management, product reception, and vendor invoices, payment, and settlement. The second cycle covers the revenue part (cash in), that is, every aspect related to customer management, sales management, product delivery, customer invoices, collection, and settlement.

Microsoft Dynamics AX enables the module's integration that relates transactions to each other, and can automatically inherit information from one and pass it to another after adding additional information, along with generating automatic financial entries in the general ledger and control points to monitor the transactions. There is integration between Microsoft Dynamics AX 2012 R3 modules, where production modules are integrated with the warehouse management module and sales and marketing module, in addition to the procurement and sourcing module.

The project module is integrated with the inventory module, sales and marketing module, Accounts receivable modules, procurement and sourcing modules, and Accounts payable module. This book focuses on the integration of the financial module.

Accounts payable

The Procure to Pay cycle linked the following business functions that are accountable for company expenditure:

- Operations
- Procurement
- Purchasing
- Warehousing *Product Reception*
- Financial
    - ◦ Accounts payable
    - ◦ Bank management

The Procure to Pay cycle manages and controls the business processes of procuring the needed materials, receiving them, and paying to the vendor. There are specific documents to handle these business processes.

The related financial transactions to this cycle are the product receipt, vendor invoice, payment, and settlement.

Product receipt

The product receipt represents the physical reception of products in the company warehouse. This increases the physical quantities in the inventory and reduces the quantity of the remainder in the purchase order, in addition to changes in the inventory value according to the inventory valuation method.

Invoice

The vendor sends the purchase order invoice either along with product reception or after product reception. Recoding the vendor invoice to reflect the company's liabilities to the vendor results in an increase in the open vendor balance. Microsoft Dynamics AX supports a company's internal control in vendor invoices by matching the invoice with the purchase order and the invoice amount.

It can be a three-way match for a product when comparing the purchase order quantity against the product receipt, and the purchase order invoice against the invoice amount. It is a two-way match for services when comparing the purchase order amount against the invoice amount. For the service invoices that are not related to purchase order, such as cleaning services, just issue an invoice to the vendor against delivered services. This reflects the company liabilities to the vendor.

Payment

The vendor payment processing reduces the company liability to vendors. The payment can be an advanced one, attached to a specific purchase order and independent of other purchase orders; it is usually the responsibility of the accounts payable section in the finance department.

Settlement

The settlement processing involves settling the open invoices against payments. This process affects vendor statements by decreasing open vendor invoices and, increasing closed vendor invoices.

Accounts receivable

The Order to cash cycle joined the following business functions that are accountable for a company's revenues:

- Sales
- Warehousing *Product Issuance*
- Finance
    - Accounts receivable
    - Bank management

This cycle manages and controls the business processes of sales activities, customer orders, delivering goods, and collection from the customer. There are specific documents to handle these business processes, which are sales order, issuing process by packing slip, and finally the invoice document.

The related financial transactions to this cycle are packing slip, invoice, collection, and settlement.

Packing slip

The packing slip represents the physical issuance of products from the company warehouse. This decreases the physical quantities in the inventory and reduces the quantities remaining in the sales order.

Invoice

After the delivery of goods or services to the customer, the sales team issues a customer invoice, increasing the customer open invoices. This affects the customer statement and customer aging, in addition to the revenue recognition and the cost of goods sold.

Collection

The customer collection process represents the transaction of the required amount of money from the customer whether it is against an open invoice or advanced collection.

Settlement

The settlement process settles the open invoices against collection. This process affects the customer statement, reducing the number of open customer invoices and increasing the number of closed customer invoices and aging.

Exploring ERP and reporting

The main principles of reporting are reliability of business information and the ability to produce the right information at the right time for the right person. Reports that analyze the ERP data in a meaningful way represent the output of the ERP implementation; it is considered as the cream of the implementation, the next level of value that the solution owners should aim for. This ideal outcome results from building all reports based on a single information source, the ERP solution where the business is recording all transactions on a daily basis.

As shown in the following diagram, the organizational reporting levels are divided into the following three main layers:

- Operational management
- Middle management
- Senior management

Each level has a different perspective of report usage, irrespective of whether it is tactical/short-term usage or strategic/long-term usage, and a different opinion on a report's complexity.

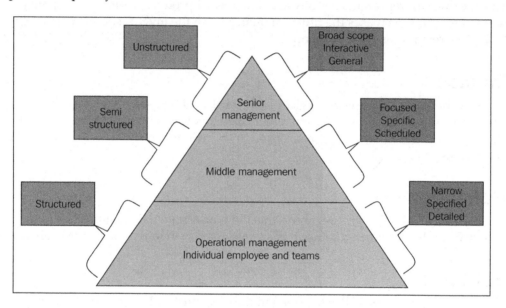

The dimensional characteristic of information is divided into two dimensions; the first is scope of information and the second is types of decision making.

The scope of information defines the required level of detail for each managerial level. Typically, the scope can be described as follows:

- **Narrow, specified, and detailed**: This is the first layer of the information scope for operational management level. Managers in this level, typically, receive information relevant to their particular subunit. They require narrow scope of reports, with details to the lowest level of information (transactional level) and specific to the daily operational work.

- **Focused, specific, and scheduled**: This is the second layer of the information scope for managerial level. Managers in this level, typically, receive summarized information. They require the reports with a scope focused on aggregate and summarized transactional information. These reports cover specific periods: weekly, monthly, quarterly, half yearly, and yearly.

- **Broad, interactive, and general**: This is the third layer of the information scope and is the highest level for top management. They require reports with a broader scope to get more comparisons, actual versus budget, period comparisons, and KPIs, in addition to the aggregated reports that cover specific monthly, quarterly, half yearly, and yearly performance.

The type of decision making used by an organization is another dimension of reporting analysis. Typically, decision-making styles can be described as follows:

- **Structured**: This is a repetitive and routine decision-making style and is best used in the operational layer. This style requires reports that are considered as static.

- **Semi-structured**: This is a mix between the structured and unstructured decision-making style and is best used in the middle management layer. This style requires reports that are considered as static or dynamic.

- **Unstructured**: This style is used by the decision makers at the executive level, who must provide judgment, evaluation, and business insight to evaluate the overall business performance. This style requires reports that are considered as dynamic.

Posting types in Microsoft Dynamics AX

In Microsoft Dynamics AX, there are two ways to post transactions to general ledger accounts. The first type is through the posting profile that represents the integration point between general ledger and subledgers, and it generates the entries automatically according to the posting profile setup. The second type is journal entries that post directly to ledger accounts. The two ways are explained in detail as follows:

- **Posting profile**: This is the integration point between the subledgers (fixed assets, payables, inventory, banks, receivables, project, and production) and the general ledger. It is a set of ledger accounts that are used in generating the automatic ledger entry in which a transaction occurred. It is possible to select different ledger accounts for each type of subledger transaction. Microsoft Dynamics AX offers flexibility in posting profile setups.

- **Journal posting**: The journal model in Microsoft Dynamics AX is a journal header that contains voucher lines, in which the default data in the journal name (header) is copied into voucher lines such as currency and sales tax, which can be changed in the voucher line. Every subledger has its own journal name based on the transaction type.

The voucher line can be a ledger account, vendor account, customer account, fixed asset, bank, or project. If the selected account is an option other than the ledger account, the subledger posting profile will directly post to the ledger account.

Exploring the common terms in ERP implementations

There are some common terms that are used in all the phases of the ERP implementation. These terms describe a specific task or activity during the implementation lifecycle, and they are as follows:

- **Installation**: This process is the first step to have the application on your server and client machines. This process examines the installation prerequisites and makes the application ready to be used.

- **Configuration**: This process identifies which options will be activated (checked) according to customer requirements and this will be followed in the day-to-day business (module parameters).

- **Setup**: This process sets up the data within the application, identifying how to group the data according to customer requirements, vendors, items, and chart of accounts.

Microsoft Dynamics AX gives flexibility to be adopted into business needs by personalizing the application, modifying it, or customizing it. This is described as follows:

- **Personalization**: The personalization or enhancements are small changes that occur in the application to fit customer requirements, such as rearrangement of form fields, or it can be company-wide enhancements or can be user based on preferences. The purpose of enhancements delivers more usability to operational *data entry* users.

- **Modification**: The modifications are medium to large changes that occur in the application to fit customer requirements, such as changing a field's property to make it mandatory, setting a default value for a checkbox in a transaction form instead of making the user select it every time, and developing file validations. It can also be company-wide modifications. The purpose of these modifications is to have more control on application options and behavior rather than modules' parameters.

- **Customization**: The customizations are the largest changes occurring in the application to fit customer requirements, such as changes in an application's business logic and calculations, changes in modules integration concepts and posting profile, and developing new module that are not covered in the standard application modules. Although customization is not recommended in ERP implementation, the purpose of customization is to cover a critical business need to be handled by the application.

Exploring Microsoft Dynamics Implementation Methodology – Sure Step

Veteran ERP consultants understand how to execute an implementation project. They can call on their years of experience to design a new project that will have a good chance at success. When the next generation of consultants joins the team, these practices will be passed along, even if there is no process in place to manage the knowledge transfer. Many implementation consultants can probably recall their own experience learning as *the way it was always done* in their previous jobs.

Consulting companies can apply their own implementation methodology based on previous projects, and there is no problem with this as long as the company achieves its objectives and satisfies its customers. The company should also be committed to continuously improving its own methodology and building on it by experience.

However, there is a range of problems with an implementation methodology based on transferring the senior consultant's knowledge and experience to the next class of junior consultants. Such informal or small-scale approaches will lead to variances in implementation approach between different consultants, even in the same company, and it can create differences from one project to another, even for the same consultant. To add to the risk, a consulting firm that depends on consultants to provide an implementation methodology is exposed to a loss creditability with their customers if the consultant is changed and the new consultant will follow his own approach in the implementation methodology, which is different from his colleague.

Alternatively, there is an implementation methodology built up by an experienced organization where information and data have been gathered from a range of experienced implementers, based on the best practices from a broad range of previous projects and experiences, across a range of business domains and client types. That organization is, of course, Microsoft, and the methodology is Microsoft Dynamics Sure Step.

Microsoft brought Sure Step to the Microsoft Dynamics market in 2007 and they have recently launched its online version. The common question from implementers is: why do we need a standard implementation methodology for ERP when we have our own?

At a high level, there are common phases of an ERP implementation project, but the depth and complexity of each phase depends on the nature of the project itself. The procedure to execute the project will depend on the consulting firm and its approach in project execution, as well was its style in managing customers. The phases are diagnostic, analysis, design, development, deployment, and operation. The key characteristics of the Microsoft Dynamics Sure Step methodology are as follows:

- It covers the main implementation project phases, activities, tasks, document templates, and output.

- It minimizes consultant effort to stop reinventing the documentation and templates.

- It not only covers the implementation phases (analysis, design, development, deployment, and operation), but also takes into consideration the sales and presales activities in the diagnostic phase.

- It is aligned with other Microsoft methodologies such as **Microsoft Delivery Methodology (SDM)**, **Microsoft Solution Selling Sales (MSSP)**, and **Microsoft Solution Framework (MSF)**. This gives it a variety of guidance built on Microsoft methodologies.

- It is designed especially for Microsoft Dynamics products (such as AX, NAV, SL, GP, and CRM).

- It complies with **Project Management Institute (PMI)** methodologies (scope management, time management, cost management, resource management, risk management, quality management, and procurement management).

- It includes a huge collection of templates and documents according to phase activity, and shows the integration between phases and activities.

- It contains implementation project types customization (Enterprise, Standard, Rapid, Agile, and Upgrade).

Exploring Microsoft Dynamics Lifecycle Services

Microsoft has announced the Lifecycle Services (LCS) tools to help partner and customer to be more engaged in the Microsoft Dynamics AX implementation project. LCS is a cloud-based solution that provides the required tools to let a customer collaborate with a partner and Microsoft in planning, managing, and operating the implementation project.

The Microsoft Dynamics LCS offers an assortment of services as follows:

- Business process modeling
- Infrastructure sizing
- Rapid configuration
- Customization analysis
- System diagnosis
- Issue search
- Upgrade analysis

Looking at Microsoft Dynamics AX user Interface

Microsoft Dynamics AX 2012 revealed significant changes in the user interface, making it more user friendly and easy to use for complex business transactions, in addition to the richness in accessing the application by the client whether via a tablet or mobile.

The Microsoft Dynamics AX application is considered as a single sign-in application, where the active directory is the base of logging in AX. The user logs in to Windows using the username and password chosen at the time of joining the domain on the active directory. In order to add a user to AX, they should be registered on the active directory first.

Rich client is the most commonly used interface accessed by users from their PC or laptop. The Microsoft Dynamics AX workspace is the main screen when starting the rich client.

The Microsoft Dynamics AX workspace is shown in the following screenshot:

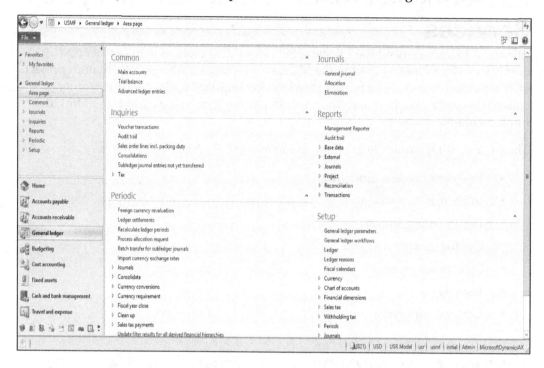

The main workspace is divided into the following sections:

- **The address bar**: The address bar or breadcrumb that provides access to Microsoft Dynamics AX companies and or modules is as follows:

The user could navigate to the company by pressing on the arrow icon as shown in the following screenshot:

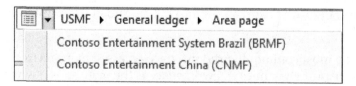

The user can navigate to the module by clicking on the arrow icon, as shown in the following screenshot:

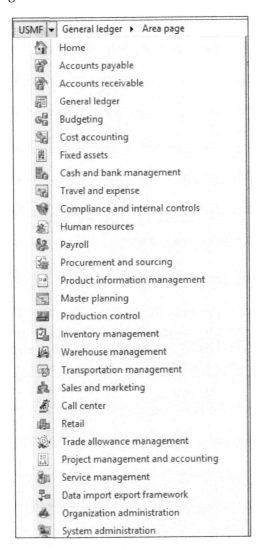

The user can navigate to the company modules' component by pressing on the arrow icon, as shown in the following screenshot:

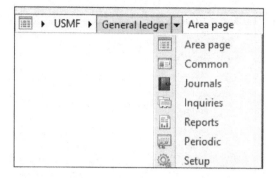

- **The jewel menu**: The second part of the Microsoft Dynamics AX workspace is the jewel menu that contains the basic AX commands **under the File menu**, as shown in the following screenshot:

Under **File**, there are commonly known commands such as **New**, **Open**, and **Save**, and other specific Microsoft Dynamics AX commands such as **Export to Microsoft Excel**, **Tools** (session date, calculator, and so on), and **View**, as shown in the following screenshot:

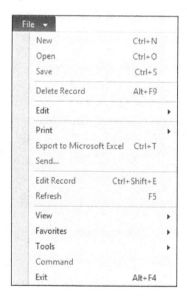

The jewel menu also contains the Help icon on the right-hand side, as shown in the following screenshot:

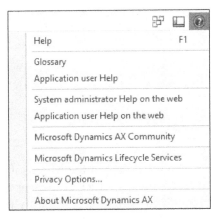

The jewel menu also contains the View icon on the right-hand side to modify the workspace setting, as shown in the following screenshot:

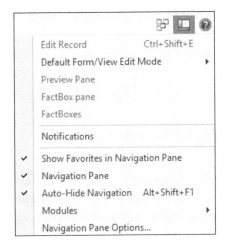

The jewel bar also contains the Windows icon on the right-hand side, to switch between open forms, as shown in the following screenshot:

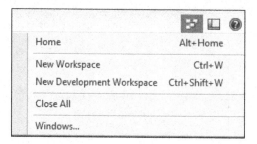

- **The Favorites menu**: The third part of the Microsoft Dynamics AX workspace is the **Favorites** menu, which is the upper part of the **Navigation Pane**. The **Favorites** menu contains the commonly used submenus, and it is personalized per user. Each user can add or arrange the favorites as per his/their needs. It is similar to the Windows explorer where a user can make a tree of folders and subfolders, as shown in the following screenshot:

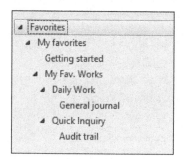

In order to add menus to **Favorites**, go to the content pane and navigate to **General Ledger | Journals**. Right-click on **Journals** and then select **Add to favorites**, as shown in the following screenshot:

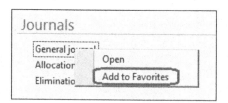

Then, move to the **Favorites** menu, right-click on **Favorites**, and select **Organize favorites**, as shown in the following screenshot:

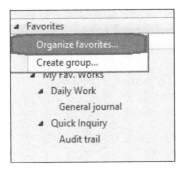

In the **Organize favorites** form, the user can manage their favorites and arrange the menu according to their needs by adding folders and subfolders, as shown in the following screenshot:

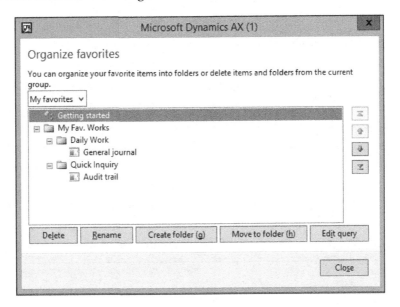

- **The Navigation Pane option**: The **Navigation Pane** option in Microsoft Dynamics AX is the workspace where the user can access the modules, forms, and list pages, as shown in the following screenshot:

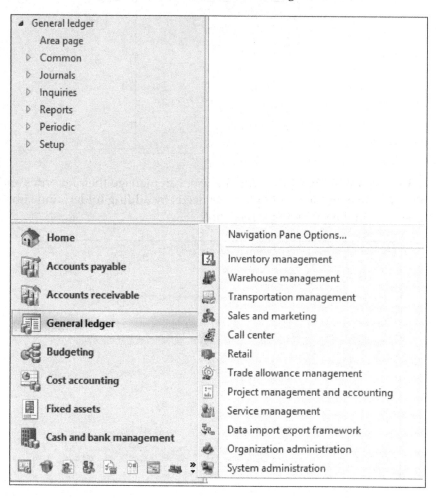

The Chevron icon shows the other modules. The user can arrange the order of modules by clicking on the **Navigation Pane Options…**. In the **Navigation pane options** window, use the up and down buttons to order the modules, and it is personalized per user, as shown in the following screenshot:

- **The Status bar option**: This is located at the bottom of the Microsoft Dynamics AX workspace. The **Status bar** option contains several types of information, as shown in the following screenshot:

- ○ The **Status bar** option has the following information:

  Document handling

  Help text

  Notifications

  Currency

Application object model

Application object layer

Current company

CapsLock status

NumLock status

Current user

Session date

Session time

Application object server name

Operation progress indicator

Database activity

°   The user can manage the information on **Status bar** from the user
    options, by navigating to **File | Tools | Options | Status bar**, as
    shown in the following screenshot:

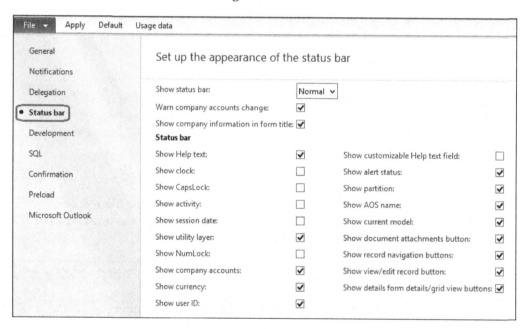

- **The content pane**: The center of the Microsoft Dynamics AX workspace is the content pane, where the user can access forms, list pages, reports, and setup. As shown in the following screenshot, the content pane contains the following main sections:
  - **Common**: This represents access to commonly used list pages for master data or transactions, for example, in accounts receivable, access to customer details and sales orders.
  - **Journals**: This represents access to module journals to create and post journal transactions.
  - **Inquiries**: This represents access to modules reporting in the form style.
  - **Reports**: This represents access to printable reports that can be shown on screen or printed in hard copy.
  - **Periodic**: This represents access to periodic jobs that are being run on a monthly or weekly basis.
  - **Setup**: This represents access to module setups and configuration.

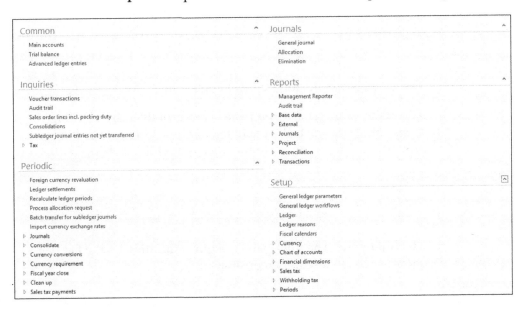

- • **The list page**: The list page, as shown in the following screenshot (all vendors), shows the vendor list. The user can create a new record from the list page by pressing *Ctrl + N*, editing an existing record, and/or posting daily transactions.

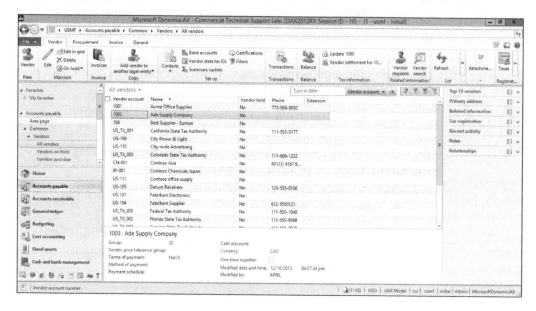

- ○ The list page has the following characteristics:

  The action pane: The action pane consists of the action buttons to execute a specific task or activity, as shown in the following screenshot. This is similar to the Microsoft Office ribbon.

  The filter pane: The filter pane is a quick filtration on the list page, as shown in the following screenshot:

The search can be executed from the search text, filter by selection, filter by grid, and advanced filter or sort.

Grid checkboxes: The grid checkboxes are used for multiple selections of records, as shown in the following screenshot:

	Vendor account	Name ▲	Vendor hold	Phone	Extension
☐	1001	Acme Office Supplies	No	773-998-8892	
☑	1003	Ade Supply Company	No		
	104	Best Supplier - Europe	No		
☑	US_TX_001	California State Tax Authority	No	111-555-0177	
	US-108	City Power & Light	No		
☑	US-110	City-wide Advertising	No		
	US_TX_003	Colorado State Tax Authority	No	111-666-1232	
☑	CN-001	Contoso Asia	No	80123) 4567 8...	
	JP-001	Contoso Chemicals Japan	No		
☐	US-111	Contoso office supply	No		
	US-105	Datum Receivers	No	123-555-0100	

- **The fact box**: The fact box is a new component that has been introduced in AX 2012 to display summarized information about the selected record, as shown in the following screenshot:

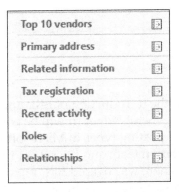

- **The preview pane**: This displays more detailed information about the selected record, as shown in the following screenshot:

1003 : Ade Supply Company				
Group:	20	Cash discount:		
Vendor price tolerance group:		Currency:	CAD	
Terms of payment:	Net30	One-time supplier:	☐	
Method of payment:		Modified date and time:	12/16/2013	04:07:34 pm
Payment schedule:		Modified by:	APRIL	

- **The fast tab**: This consists of a group of fields. The fast tab replaces the regular tabs on the form and also displays some summary fields, as shown in the following screenshot:

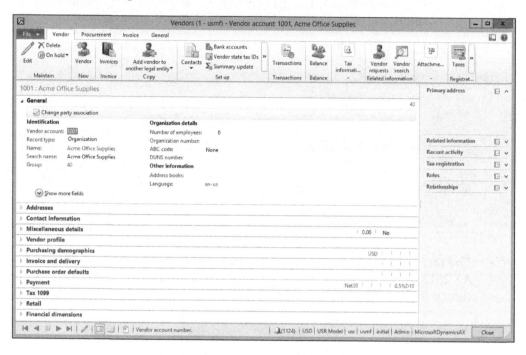

Summary

In this chapter, we discussed the introduction of ERP and its main characteristics of modules integration, with general ledger (it will be covered in detail in the next chapters), and then discussed posting types in Microsoft Dynamics AX. We also explored the ERP implementation team and the role of the application consultant in the implementation project. Then, we covered ERP reporting levels and needs, after which we moved on to Microsoft Dynamics Implementation Methodology Sure Step and LCS, and explored the interface of Microsoft Dynamics AX 2012.

In the next chapter, we will cover the general ledger, the types of main accounts, classifications, and control points. We will also explore the practices in the financial implementations of Microsoft Dynamics AX 2012.

2
Understanding the General Ledger

The **chart of accounts (COA)** is the backbone of **Enterprise Resource Planning (ERP)**. It is part of the financial module, which is the foundational module of ERP. It is a list of categorized ledger accounts (known as main accounts in Microsoft Dynamics AX 2012 R3) that is used by the organization to record all financial transactions, and it depends on the nature of the organization's business. The COA of manufacturing companies differs from trading companies, service companies, and so on. This chapter covers the following topics:

- Understanding the chart of accounts
- Classifying main accounts
- Controlling main accounts
- Understanding shared financial data
- Understanding financial management in action
- Opening balance
- Performing daily transactions
- Closing procedure

Understanding the chart of accounts

The classified skeleton of a main account is the responsibility of the controller from the customer side and the application consultant from the partner side, who bridges the application capabilities to the customers' requirements. This activity is designed in the analysis and design phases, and deployed in the deployment phase.

Main accounts are at the core of financial reporting and include the trial balance, balance sheet, income statement, working capital, and cash flow. The starting point in building COAs is identifying the financial reporting requirements to ensure that all classification levels and categories are captured in Microsoft Dynamics AX.

Classifying main accounts

The first classification of main accounts in Microsoft Dynamics AX is the type, which represents the nature of the ledger account, that is, is it a balance sheet account or a profit and loss account? The following figure shows an example of a balance sheet and an income statement that contains the profit and loss account:

Balance Sheet	Income Statement
Assets	Revenues
Fixed Assets	Sales Revenue
Fixed Assets	Sales Returns
Accumulated Depreciation	*Total Revenues*
Total Fixed Assets	Cost of Goods Sold
Current Assets	**Gross Profit**
Banks	**Operating Expenses**
Inventory	Manfacturing Expenses
Total Current Assets	Selling and marketing Expenses
Total Assets	Administration Expenses
Liabilities & Owner Equities	Depreciation Expenes
Current Liabilities	*Total Operating Expense*
Accounts Payable	Interest Income
Accruals	*Net Operating Profit*
Total Current Liabilities	**Net Income**
Long Term Liabilities	
Notes Payable	
Total Long Term Liability	
Owners' Equity	
Retained Earnings	
Total Owners' Equity	
Liabilities & Owner Equities	

Microsoft Dynamics AX classifies main account types into two main groups. The first group is **Transactional accounts**, where all financial transactions are recorded. The second group is **Reporting** accounts, which is used to report and classify caption totals, as shown in the following figure:

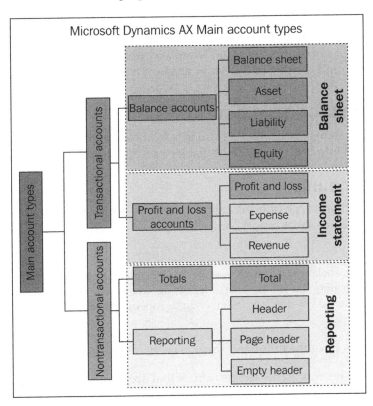

The transactional accounts that carry posted transactions on the application maintain a record of all the data related to the transaction. This includes the main account number, amount, transaction side (debit/credit), currency, transaction text, transaction type, in addition to original documents (that generate this entry), and who posted the transaction.

These classifications help at the reporting level and are considered the first classification layer for main accounts.

In order to view all the main account types, navigate to **General ledger | Setup | Chart of accounts | Chart of accounts**. You can double-click on **Main account** or click on **Edit**, go to the **General** fast tab, and then go to the **Main account type** combobox. Another option is to navigate to **General ledger | Common | Main accounts**. You can also double-click on **Main account** or click on **Edit**, go to the **General** fast tab, and then go to the **Main account type** combobox.

Using transactional accounts

Transactional accounts represent the primary classification of the main accounts. They are divided into two main groups: balance accounts, and profit and loss accounts.

Balance accounts

The first classification type of transactional accounts is balance accounts, which represent the balance sheet report components.

 The balance in a balance account is calculated from the account opening day till the date of reporting. In the year-end transaction, the closing voucher is transferred to the opening balance of the account.

Balance accounts have the following three classifications that represent their nature:

- **Assets**: This represents the resources that are owned by the organization and are used to carry out business activities such as producing a product
- **Liabilities**: This represents the claims against assets; for example, the obligations of borrowing money to acquire machines, or products
- **Equity**: This represents the claim on total assets; it is equal to total assets minus total liabilities

Profit and loss accounts

The second classification of transactional accounts is profit and loss accounts, which represents the **Income statement** report components.

> The balance of profit and loss accounts are reset to 0 each year. In the year-end transaction, the balances are rolled up in the retained earnings account.

Profit and loss accounts have two classifications that represent the nature of accounts: expense and revenue. The expense accounts represent the costs of assets that are consumed in the process of generating revenue; it is the actual or expected cash outflow. The revenue accounts represent the results from sales.

The following screenshot illustrates the main account type. To access this form, navigate to **General ledger | Common | Main accounts**. You can also double-click on **Main account** or click on **Edit** and then on the **General** fast tab.

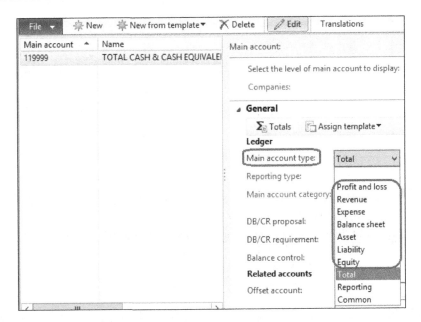

Using nontransactional accounts

Nontransactional accounts represent the financial reporting presentation, which is divided into two main types: totals and reporting. None of the transactions are allowed to be posted on these accounts.

Totals

Totals are used to sum up the caption or subcaption range of main accounts to give a quick overview of the account's balance; the following screenshot illustrates the setup of the total account type:

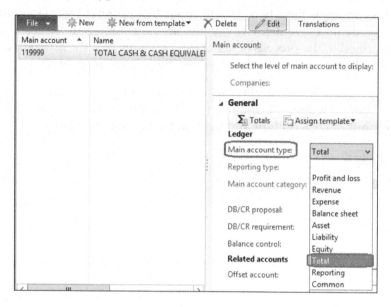

The total of accounts is managed through an account interval form in order to identify the range of total.

If there are subtotal accounts, they are neglected in the grand total. Do not worry – there are no duplications in the calculation of totals.

Reporting

The **Reporting** type dropdown is used to manage the presentation of financial reporting. The available options are **Header**, **Empty header**, and **Page header**, as shown in the following screenshot:

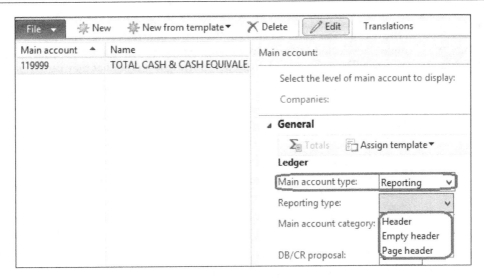

Main account categories

Main account categories represent a second level of classification and are used as a grouping layer for the main accounts. The main account category is used for reporting and in cubes for business intelligence.

 More than 50 ledger account categories are provided by default.

In order to view all the main account categories, navigate to **General ledger | Setup | Chart of accounts | Main account categories**. The following screenshot shows the **Main account category** screen:

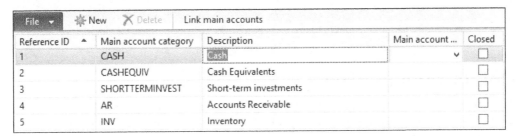

If the **Closed** checkbox is checked, that particular **Reference ID** value cannot be selected in the main account form. It is better to serialize the reference IDs in the logical order of reporting levels so that they can be used as a sorting identifier.

The following screenshot illustrates the main account; you can see the **Main account category** field under the **Ledger** fast tab:

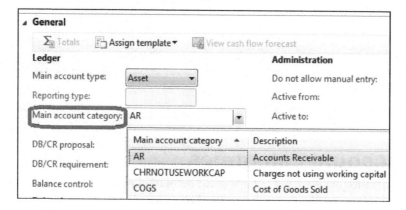

Controlling main accounts

As seen in the following figure, Microsoft Dynamics AX offers three main groups of controls over the main accounts. The first is specific to debit and credit controls, the second to account administration, and the third to posting validation.

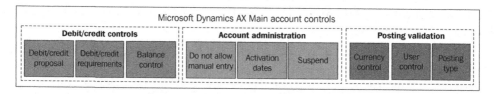

Debit/Credit controls

The **Debit/Credit controls** group is divided into three subgroups: the first is **Debit/Credit Proposal**, the second is **Debit/Credit requirements**, and the third is **Balance control**.

Debit/Credit Proposal

Every main account has a normal accounting side, be it debit or credit. The financial controller might prefer to have Microsoft Dynamics AX suggest to accountants the side of account (whether it is debit or credit) as a proposal and give the user the option to move to the other side according to the transaction.

For example, the customer account is proposed to be on the credit side. This is recommended for accountants with experience, as they can decide whether it is required to change the side of the account.

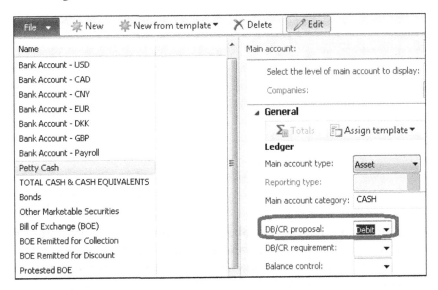

During the processing of a transaction, the cursor moves to the side that is configured in the debit/credit proposal (when the *Tab* key is pressed), as shown in the following screenshot. You can access it by navigating to **General ledger | Journals | General journal** and clicking on **Lines**.

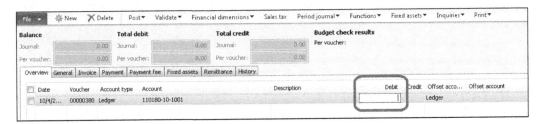

Debit/Credit Requirements

Every main account has a normal accounting balance, be it debit or credit, and this main account is debited or credited. The financial controller can prefer to get Microsoft Dynamics AX to control specific main accounts in order to prevent end users from shifting the entry side of the main account. For example, the rent account should always be debited against the bank account.

The following screenshot shows the debit/credit requirements of a main account:

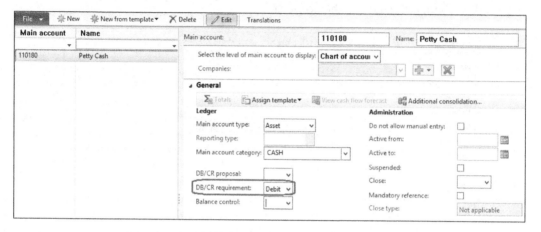

The main account configuration is **Debit**. The accountant attempts to enter transactions in the credit side, as you can see in the following screenshot. You can access it by navigating to **General ledger | Journals | General journal** and clicking on **Lines**, as shown in the following screenshot:

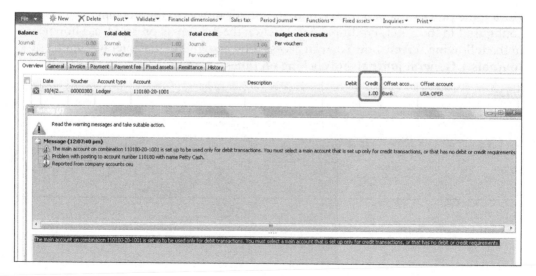

Balance Control

Every main account has a normal accounting side, be it debit or credit. If the balance contradicts this norm, it indicates a concern and should be outlined. The financial controller can have preferences to get Microsoft Dynamics AX to control a specific main account's balance in order to prevent any balance issues. For example, bank accounts should always be on the debit side. If they are on the credit side, this indicates an issue. As shown in the following screenshot, **Balance control** prevents this from happening:

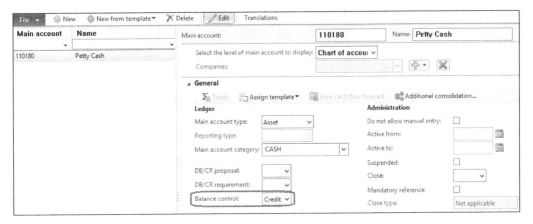

If the balance control is broken during the processing of a transaction, an **Infolog** window will pop up displaying the **A requirement for credit balance is selected for account #####, but this is violated by voucher #.##** message.

The main account's configuration in balance control is **Credit**. The current balance of the main account is credit -1,000. The current transaction credits the main account by -1,001.

While posting the entry, Microsoft Dynamics AX certifies the main account's balance control configuration and then calculates the current balance. The difference is shown in an **Infolog** window, as shown in the following screenshot. You can access it by navigating to **General ledger | Journals | General journal** and clicking on **Lines**.

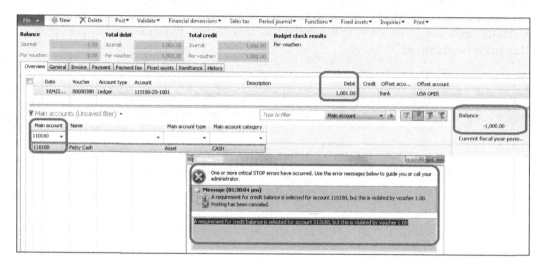

Using account administration

The main account administration is divided into three main groups. The first group is **Do not allow manual entry**, the second is **Activation dates**, and the third is **Accounts suspension**.

Do not allow manual entry

The integrity between the general ledger and subledger is an essential factor in ERP. It is characterized in the main accounts and subledgers. The subledger should guarantee that all posted transactions to the general ledger are from the submodules' end. Microsoft Dynamics AX controls the main accounts; this does not allow any direct transactions to be posted to the main account. This means that any transaction affecting a main account must be posted throughout the submodules posting the profile. This checkbox is **Do not allow manual entry**, which was known as **Locked in Journal** in Microsoft Dynamics AX 2009.

On the other hand, there are other accounts that does not need this control since it is not related to subledger posting profile, and it is okay to post transactions directly to these accounts.

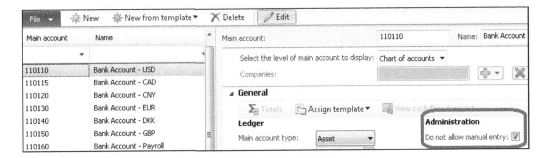

During the processing of a transaction, if an accountant wants to select a main account and this account is configured as **Do not allow manual entry**, an **Infolog** window will pop up that will display **Value (account ####) is not allowed for manual entry. Enter another value**. In other words, this means "select another account"; this is shown in the following screenshot:

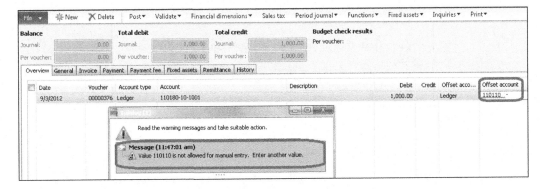

Activation date

The activation date is commonly used for newly created accounts (which will be active for operations at a future date) and in another scenario for main accounts (which can be deactivated after a specific period), as shown in the following screenshot:

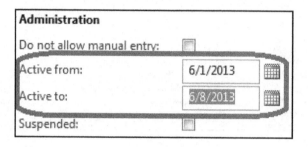

If an accountant wants to work with a main account, but it has not been a day since its activation, an **Infolog** window will pop up during the processing of a transaction that will display **Main account ###### is not active**, as shown in the following screenshot:

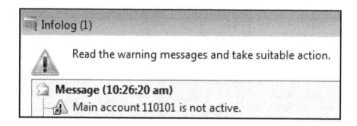

Suspending account

The suspending account is used in case there is an account that requires to be stopped from an operation, as it will not be used any more. As shown in the following screenshot, there is a control to suspend an account from operational posting:

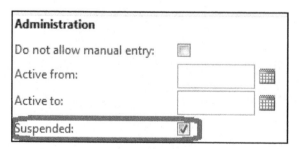

During the processing of a transaction, if an accountant selects a main account that is suspended, an **Infolog** window will pop up that will display **Main account ######** **is closed**, as shown in the following screenshot:

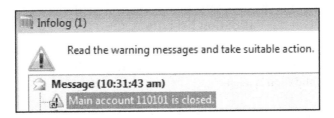

Using posting validation

Posting validation is divided into three main groups. The first group is currency control, the second is user control, and the third is posting type control.

Currency control

The financial controller can prefer to get Microsoft Dynamics AX to control specific currencies in order to stop transactions in other currencies in the main account.

For example, the controller requires the Egyptian bank main account to only accept transactions in Egyptian pounds (**EGP**) and prevents the transaction from posting if the transaction has a different currency, as shown in the following screenshot:

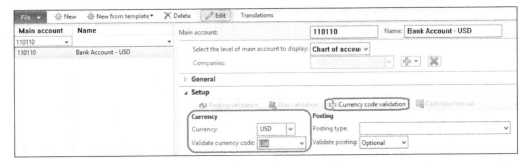

The **Currency code validation** options are as follows:

- **Optional**: This field is not authenticated at the time of posting. This is the default setting

- **To be filled in**: This field (provided by Microsoft Dynamics AX) checks whether the field is filled in for posting

- **Table**: This field (provided by Microsoft Dynamics AX) examines whether the field is completed for posting and that the value matches the value specified in the main account

- **List**: This field verifies that the field is filled in with one of the values that are defined on the **Validation list** button

> Currency code validation is only activated if the selected validation is a list.

During the processing of a transaction, if an accountant changes the currency, an **Infolog** window will pop up that will display **The currency must be EGP for account ######**, as shown in the following screenshot:

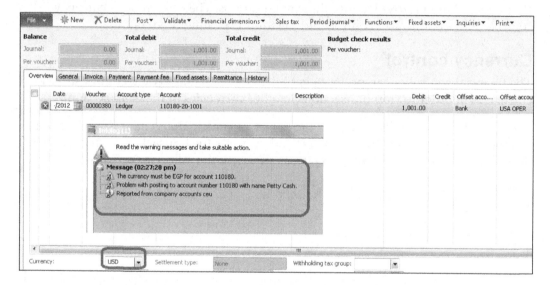

User control

Every main account might have a posting constraint per user. The financial controller can prefer to get Microsoft Dynamics AX to control specific accounts for certain end users who are permitted to post transactions on these main accounts, by navigating to **General ledger | Common | Main accounts**. You can also double-click on **Main account** or click on **Edit** and then go to the **Setup** fast tab.

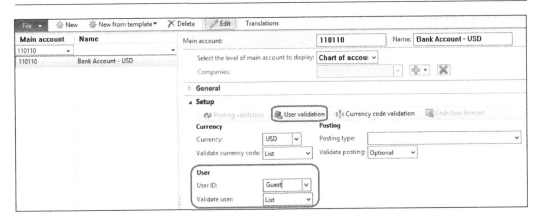

 User validation is only activated if the selected validation is a list.

During the processing of a transaction, if an unauthorized accountant tries to post a transaction on the main account, an **Infolog** window will pop up that will display **You are not authorized to use account #####**, as shown in the following screenshot:

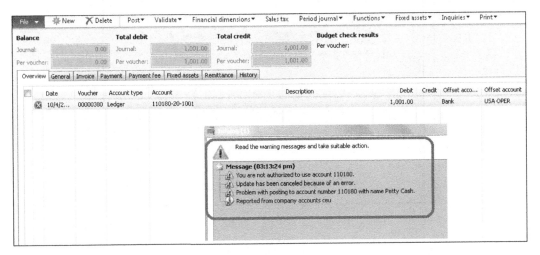

Posting type

The **Posting type** validation is a control that is used to stop posting on a specific type of transaction of the main account, as shown in the following screenshot:

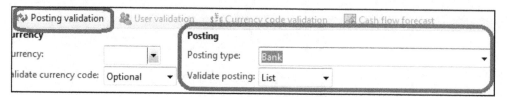

During the processing of a transaction, if a transaction breaks the posting type of the main account, an **Infolog** window will pop up that will display **The posting type for account ##### is not valid**, as shown in the following screenshot:

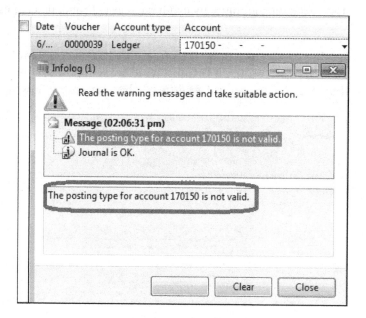

Understanding shared financial data

Microsoft Dynamics AX 2012 R3 introduced a new concept called shared financial data, which reduces the effort and time of deployment in a multiple-company environment and operational maintenance as well. A group of companies can share the same chart of accounts, currencies, and dimensions; this decreases the operation time. For example, a new main account will be available to all companies. The following figure explains the concept of shared financial data in detail:

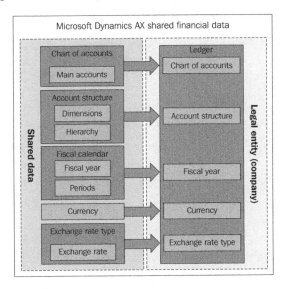

The financial data that will be shared between companies is as follows:

- **Chart of accounts**: This contains the main account
- **Account structure**: This contains the applicable dimensions of the main accounts
- **Fiscal year**: This contains the start date and end date of the fiscal year and the period's management
- **Currencies**: This represents the default currency and reporting currency
- **Exchange rate type**: This sets the monthly exchange rate for foreign currencies and the default budget exchange rate

To access the ledger window, navigate to **General ledger | Setup | Ledger**. The following screenshot shows the Microsoft Dynamics AX 2012 R3 ledger:

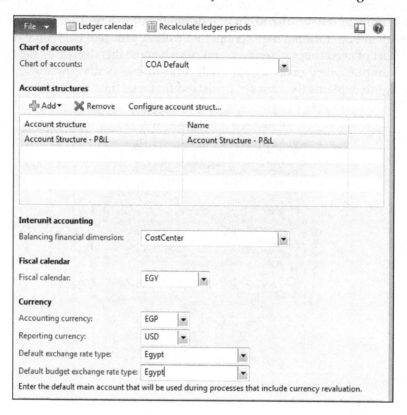

Exploring the sales tax mechanism

In this section, we will explore the sales tax mechanism in Microsoft Dynamics AX R3. The sales tax is registered on both the vendor/customer level and the item level to cope with international suppliers that reflect different tax rates for the same item. The system must recognize the same tax rate in the vendor/customer and item levels to process the transaction. The calculated reflection of the sales tax on the finance module is shown in the following figure:

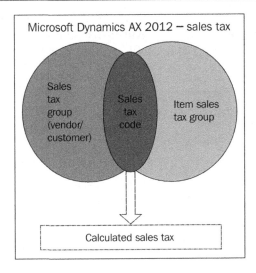

In order to define sales tax in Microsoft Dynamics AX 2012 R3, you have to create tax authority, period settlement, ledger posting group, sales tax code, sales tax group, and item sales tax group.

In order to create sales tax authority, navigate to **General Ledger | Setup | Sales tax | Sales tax authorities**. Link the tax authority with the vendor ID, as shown in the following screenshot:

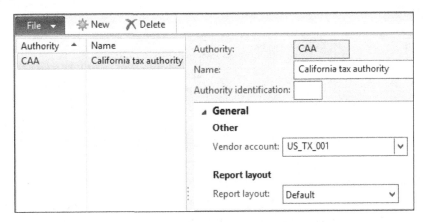

In order to create period settlement, navigate to **General Ledger | Setup | Sales tax | Sales tax settlement periods**. The **Authority** field is mandatory, and **Period interval** is the field with which the tax will be settled, as shown in the following screenshot:

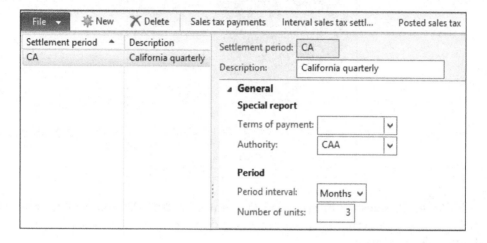

In order to create a sales tax posting group, navigate to **General Ledger | Setup | Sales tax | Ledger posting groups**. Identify the **Sales tax payable**, **Use tax payable**, and **Settlement account** fields, as shown in the following screenshot:

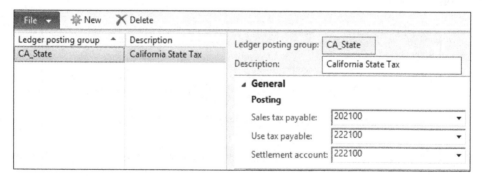

 The tax receivable will be available dynamically if the **Apply use US tax** checkbox is checked in the **General Ledger** parameters.

In order to create the sales tax code, navigate to **General Ledger | Setup | Sales tax | Sales tax codes**. In the **General** fast tab, assign the **Settlement period** and **Ledger posting group**. In the **Calculation** fast tab, assign the following parameters:

- **Origin**: This is the field that represents the origin from the which sales tax is calculated

- **Marginal base**: This represents the basis of tax limits

- **Calculation method**: This represents whether the sales tax is calculated for the entire amount or for an interval

These parameters are shown in the following screenshot:

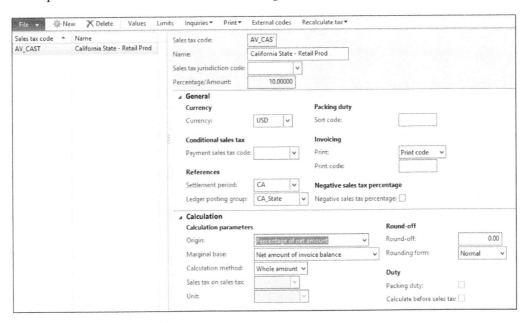

To identify the sales tax percentage, go to **Values**. Enter a value in the **Value** field, as shown in the following screenshot:

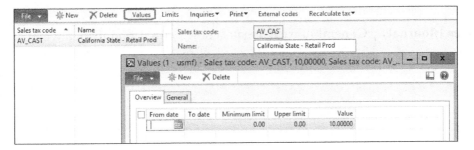

The sales tax can be changed based on the government regulation. To apply the changes in sales tax based on the government regulation, add a new line and enter the starting date to apply the new tax rate.

In order to create a sales tax group, navigate to **General Ledger | Setup | Sales tax | Sales tax group**. Under the **Setup** fast tab, add the **Sales tax code** value, as shown in the following screenshot:

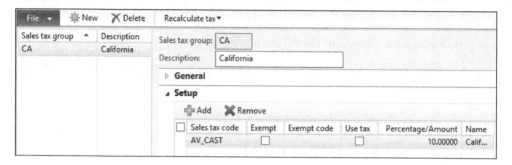

In order to create an item sales tax group, navigate to **General Ledger | Setup | Sales tax | Item sales tax group**. Under the **Setup** fast tab, click on **Add** and enter the **Sales tax code** value, as shown in the following screenshot:

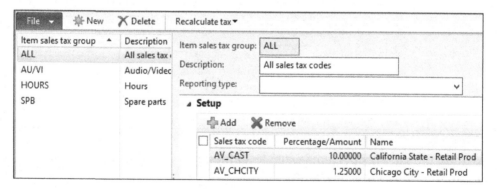

In order to apply the sales tax in a general ledger transaction, navigate to **General Ledger | Journals | General Journal**, create a new journal, and then move to lines.

In the voucher line, select the **Account type** value as **Vendor**, select the vendor ID, enter 1000 in the **Credit** side amount, and select the **Offset account** value. Then, select the **Sales tax group** and **Item sales tax group** fields; the system will calculate the sales tax amount, as shown in the following screenshot:

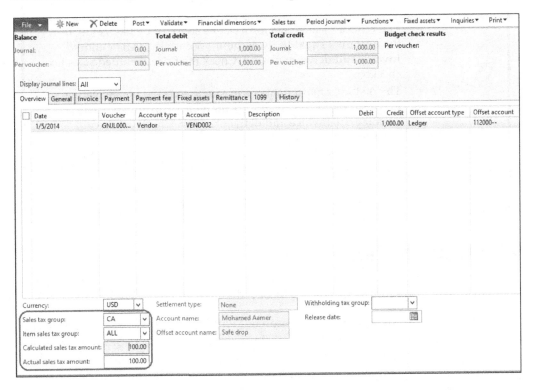

There is an effect on the price based on the sales tax rule, whether the price includes or excludes the sales tax can be defined as follows:

- **Price includes sales tax**: For a 10 percent sales tax and a $100 price, the system will allocate $90 to the undocumented liabilities account and $10 to the VAT account

- **Price excludes sales tax**: For a 10 percent sales tax and a $100 price, the system will allocate $100 to the undocumented liabilities account and $10 to the VAT account

Please note that price including sales tax rule is configured from the following paths:

- **General Ledger | Setup | General ledger parameters** and then go to the **Sales tax** tab. Check the **Amounts include sales tax** checkbox.
- The vendor master data form can be accessed by navigating to the **Accounts Payable | Common | Vendors | All vendors | Invoice and delivery** fast tab. Check the **Price included sales tax** checkbox.
- The customer master data form can be accessed by navigating to the **Accounts Receivable | Common | Customers | All customers | Invoice and deliver** fast tab. Check the **Price included sales tax** checkbox.
- On transaction journals, under the **Setup** tab, check the **Price included sales tax** checkbox.
- On the sales order and purchase order headers, in the **Setup** fast tab, check the **Price included sales tax** checkbox.

Withholding tax

The withholding tax is calculated and executed on the vendor payment process. The calculated reflection of the withholding tax on the finance module will be as follows:

- **Price includes sales tax**: For a 5 percent withholding tax, 10 percent sales tax, and a $100 price include the tax, $90 price exclude the tax, and this amount is the base of withholding tax ($90 * 5\%$). The system will allocate $4.5 to the withholding tax payable account, and $95.5 will be allocated to the payables account.

- **Price excludes sales tax**: For a 5 percent withholding tax, 10 percent sales tax, and a $100 price exclude the sales tax. This will be the base of the withholding tax calculation ($100 * 5\%$), and the amount including sales tax is $110. The system will allocate $5 to the withholding tax payable account and $105 will be allocated to the payables account.

The **Withholding tax** checkbox on the vendor master data form must be checked in order to let AX calculate the withholding tax during the payment process. In the vendor master data form, navigate to **Accounts Payable | Common | Vendors | All vendors | Invoice and delivery** fast tab and click on the **Calculate withholding tax** fast tab.

Understanding financial management in action

Here, we will understand the process of financial management through the opening balance and various daily transactions.

Opening balance

When a company migrates from a legacy ERP solution to Microsoft Dynamics AX, one of the important data migration tasks is creating opening balances in the new Dynamics AX system based on the closing balances of the previous closed period (often the fiscal year) from the legacy system.

In order to ensure the accuracy of your Dynamics AX's opening balances, it is important to take a systematic approach to the process of planning, designing, and executing the migration of data for trial balances and subledgers, as well as validation and reconciliation of these elements along with the general ledger, subledger, and financial dimensions. In this section, we will lay out the process and elements involved in creating new opening balances in Microsoft Dynamics AX from a legacy system.

Elements of opening balances are as follows:

- **Trial balance report**: This consists of data about balance accounts that move their balances from one year to another, and profit and loss accounts that represent the income statement results and do not move to another year.

- **Subledger**: This consists of data about fixed assets, banks, vendors, customers, and items. Subledgers are linked to the chart of accounts through the posting profile setup.

- **Validation and reconciliation**: This validates the balances between the subledgers (fixed assets, banks, vendors, customers, and items) and general ledger accounts which are known as trial balance accounts, taking into consideration the balance financial dimensions (business units, department, and purpose). The controllership and financial consultants should finalize and validate the design and deployment of financial dimensions or dimension rules.

Data integrity between the general ledger, subledger, and financial dimension is one of the main objectives of ERP. It must be considered from day 1 of the opening balances, as the opening balance transactions can affect daily transactions after going live.

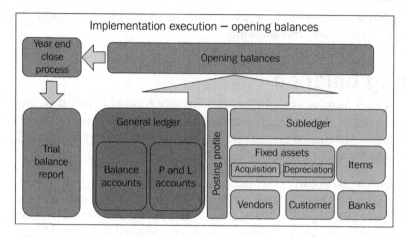

Best practices of uploading opening balances

After various attempts to upload opening balances to Microsoft Dynamics AX, the commonly followed approach is to separate the upload of ledger accounts (trial balance) and subledgers (vendors, customers, bank, inventory, and fixed assets). This is by using an error account in the subledger entries of the debit and credit sides only in order to balance the subledger:

- The Dr. Error account
- The Cr. Error account

This approach took a lot of time and effort in order to ensure that the general ledger's accounts and subledgers are reconciled and that the balance of error account is 0. Also, the opening balance methodology must be aligned with the financial controller.

Planning and designing

The master data and opening balance transaction upload is handled through **Data Import Export Framework (DIXF)**, which is newly introduced in Microsoft Dynamics AX 2012. This functionality helps consultants to gather the data that will be uploaded in Excel files, upload it to a staging table, validate the uploaded data, and then move it to the target tables.

The following steps should be followed in the planning and designing phases:

- Prepare and upload the master data into Microsoft Dynamics AX (chart of accounts, banks, fixed assets, financial dimensions, vendors, customers, and inventory items).

- Maintain a high level of coordination between the controllership and application financial consultants in the design phase, including the finalization of mapping between the old chart of accounts (legacy system) and the new one.

- The application financial consultants should ensure the setup of the required fields in the data-collection template that they will use in order to upload the opening balance.

- The accountant who will fill in the opening balance data collection sheet must understand the fields and how they will fill them in.

- Create a separate journal name under the general ledger journal and voucher number sequence for easier tracking.

- Create separate journal names under **Inventory Management** (the movement journal) and voucher number sequence for easier tracking.

- If adjustments are needed for the opening balance, use the same journal name and voucher number.

- The opening balances of the general ledger and subledger are uploaded together. Avoid separating the general ledger's upload and the subledger's upload as far as you can.

- The subledger's (vendors and customers) posting profiles should be assigned to the opening balance.

- Create the necessary fiscal periods for fixed assets acquisitions in old periods.

Execution

The opening balance will be executed in three waves: the acquisition and depreciation of fixed assets, items, and trial balance with subledger. The following are the methods we utilize to ensure correct execution:

- Wave one is fixed assets. The following are the methods to be used in wave one:

- Fixed assets acquisition will be executed through a fixed assets acquisition proposal. The acquisition for the assets will be in its actual date; this is to keep the system calculation away from manual intervention. The posting profile setup will generate the following entry:

  Dr. Fixed Assets Acquisition Accounts (Balance)

  Cr. Error Account

  If there are fixed assets that are acquired in a foreign currency, modify the acquisition entry with the currency's exchange rate.

- Fixed assets depreciation will be executed through a fixed assets depreciation proposal. The posting profile setup will generate the following entry:

  Dr. Error Account

  Cr. Accumulated Depreciation Accounts

- Wave two is inventory items. The following is the method to be used in wave two:

  - The inventory opening balance will be uploaded from the movement journal (the inventory subledger). The posting profile setup will generate the following entry:

    Dr. Inventory Accounts (Balance)

    Cr. Error Account

- Wave three is the trial balance with subledger. The following are the methods in wave three:

  - Identify the general ledger main account balances that are not affected by the subledger's posting profiles

  - General ledger accounts that are affected by subledgers will be broken down by their relevant subledgers (banks, vendors, and customers) and the accounts will be affected directly by the subledger's posting profile

  - Make sure that the assigned posting profile is the proper posting profile for each customer/vendor; this is for two reasons:

First, this will make sure that the customers' or vendors' opening balance hits the right account, whether it is an advances account or general payable/receivable account.

Second, this will ensure that the entries occurred during the settlement process (during the year's operations) will hit the right accounts.

- ○ Replace the fixed assets accounts with an error account in order to close the amount in the error account, which resulted from acquisition transactions
- ○ Replace the depreciation account with an error account in order to close the amount in the error account, which resulted from depreciation transactions
- ○ If there are balances in a foreign currency, upload the opening balance entry with the currency's exchange rate

Validation

Validation performs the following tasks:

- Closing vouchers to transfer all profit and loss balances to the retained earnings account
- Printing the trial balance report with the closing balance criteria

Performing daily transactions

This section covers the functionalities that help end users with their daily work, which facilitates the entry process and thereby saves time and effort.

As seen in the following figure, there are three main functionalities, **Account alias** (which is a new functionality delivered in Microsoft Dynamics AX 2012 R3), **Recurring entries**, and **Save voucher**:

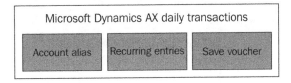

The account alias

The main account alias is a function that can be utilized for nonfinancial users who are not aware of the structure of a chart of accounts and the requirements to input data for a financial transaction. The main account aliases give the option to enter a predefined code for every combination of main accounts along with the financial dimensions. It is an alternative, manually selecting an individual dimension combination for every transaction. This is a usability function.

To access the account alias window, navigate to **General ledger | Setup | Chart of accounts | Ledger account alias**, as shown in the following screenshot:

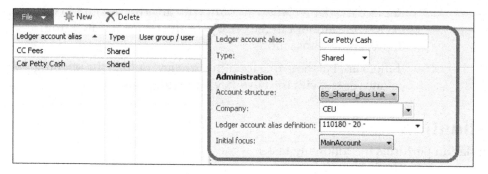

1. To access the general journal window, navigate to **General ledger | Journals | General journal | Lines**. In the **Account** column, enter the defined main account alias and click on the combobox; it filters to the entered alias and shows the account's structure as well.

2. Then, select the alias description and it is populated in the **Account** column with the account structure combination. The mouse cursor will be on a segment that has been specified in the **Initial focus** field in the setup form.

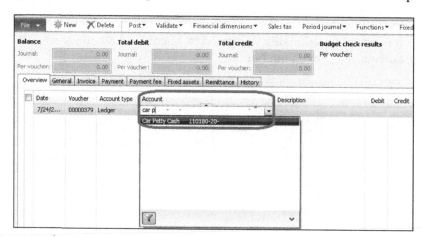

Recurring entries

Recurring entries are generally used for frequent transaction entries such as rentals and subscriptions. The accountant is able to create a periodic journal and generate an entry based on the transaction periods that are already set up.

In order to create a recurring entry (for example, for rent), you have to create a periodic journal name. For this, navigate to **General Ledger | Setup | Journals | Journal names** and create a journal name with the **Journal type** field as **Periodic**. The following screenshot shows **Periodic** in the **Journal type** field:

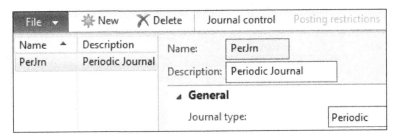

Then, as shown in the following screenshot, set the periodic journals for rent to be posted every month. For this, navigate to **General Ledger | Periodic | Journals | Post journals**; here, the periodic journal form opens up. Create a new journal entry by pressing *Ctrl + N*, and then click on **Lines**. In the lines form, enter the date, account type, account, debit or credit side, and offset account.

The **Unit** (whether days, months, years) and **Number of units** fields set the recurring times of the transaction. For the rent example, select **Vendor** in **Account type** and the vendor ID and enter the amount in the credit side. Set the suitable offset main account. The **Unit** field is **Monthly** and **Number of units** is **1**, which means it will recur every month, as shown in the following screenshot:

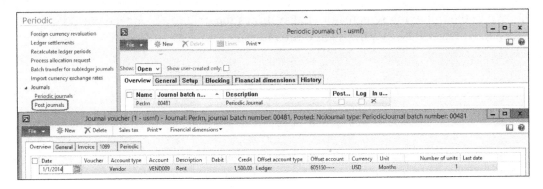

To execute a recurring transaction, navigate to **General Ledger | Journals | General journal** and create a new journal by pressing *Ctrl + N*. Then, click on **Lines**. In the journal voucher form, go to the **Periodic journal** menu and select **Retrieve journal**. In the open dialog box, enter **End date** as 1/31/2014 and select a periodic journal name, as shown in the following screenshot:

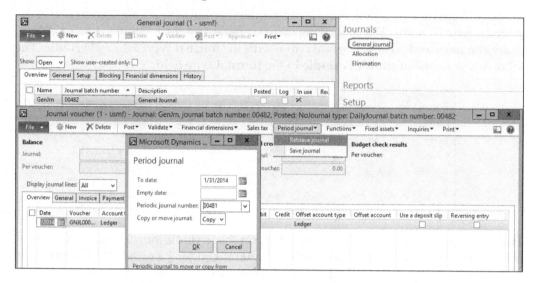

- **Copy**: The periodic transaction will be kept in the periodic journal, where it can be used in the future
- **Move**: The periodic transaction will be removed from the periodic journal

The result of this process retrieves the periodic transaction in the journal line, as shown in the following screenshot. It also shows the next usage for the period journal, which will be in **2/1/2014** in our example.

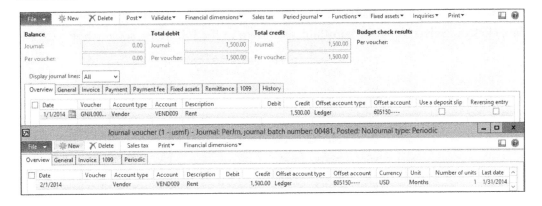

Saving a voucher

Saving a posted voucher and retrieving it in a new voucher is generally used for a long transaction entry.

Select a posted transaction to be saved. The options for saving are in percentages or amount.

To access the **Save voucher** window, navigate to **General ledger | Journals | General journal | Posted | Lines | Functions | Save voucher template**, as shown in the following screenshot:

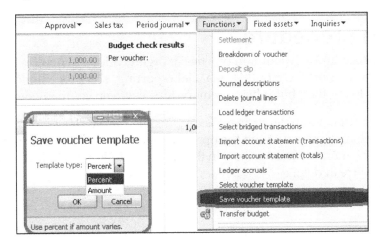

In order to create a new voucher in a newly created journal, click on **Functions** and then click on **Select voucher template**, as shown in the following screenshot:

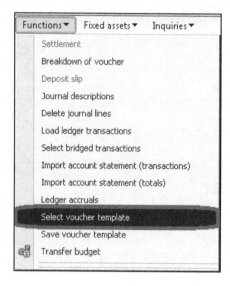

Microsoft Dynamics AX will show all the saved vouchers in headers and lines, displaying both sides of the transaction. A particular voucher will create a new unposted voucher.

Closing procedure

The closing procedure is a common practice at organizations to finalize the monthly transactions and report the monthly financial reporting. The procedure varies from one company to another, but it has common steps between company departments.

The finance controllership department is responsible for the closing procedure, where accountants follow up with the operations department to confirm that they have posted the monthly transactions in the ERP. The following figure explains the closing procedure in detail:

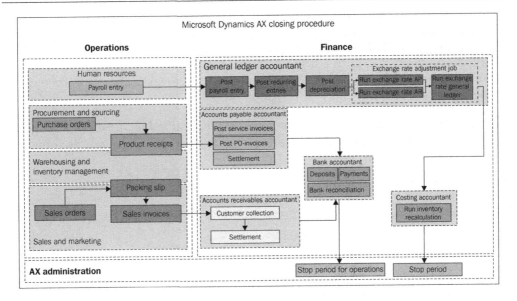

All the departments in a company are involved in the monthly closing process. The **Human resources** department calculates the payroll and generates the payroll entry to be validated and posted by the general ledger's accountant.

The **Procurement** department ensures that they have confirmed all purchase orders to be received at the warehouse and the warehouse keeper confirms receiving them as it affects the inventory quantities and values. On the other side, the accounts payable accountants match and post purchase order invoices as well as service invoices. They then execute payments of due invoices that are related to the closing month.

The **Sales** department verifies that they have confirmed all sales orders to be delivered to the customer and issue sales invoices accordingly, which generates the revenue and cost of goods sold. In the **Finance** department, the accounts receivable accountant posts the customers' collections and settlements.

During this time, the fiscal period is stopped for all operations to prevent any further operational entries in that month and only the financial team is allowed to post the financial adjustment entries.

The general ledger's accountant posts the recurring entries such as rental and accruals. So, first run the fixed assets depreciation and exchange rate adjustment for subledgers (accounts payable and accounts receivable) and then run the exchange rate adjustments for the general ledger.

The costing accountant runs the inventory recalculation to adjust the average cost of inventory items and adjusts the sold quantities by the proper cost. They stop the fiscal period after finalizing the inventory calculation.

The management of financial periods is an administrative task. There are three stages for the period status.

To access the **Period status** window, navigate to **General ledger | Setup | Ledger**, then click on the **Ledger calendar** button, and go to the **Periods** fast tab, as shown in the following screenshot:

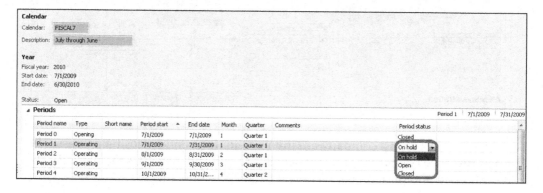

All transactions that are executed have the **Open** status in the **Period status** drop-down list.

After ensuring that all departments have entered and posted their transactions (relevant to the current month) as well as the financial post (the month-end adjustment transactions), the financial period status drop-down list is set to **Open** for a specific user group and modules.

In order to access the modules' access level path, navigate to **General ledger | Setup | Ledger**, then click on the **Ledger calendar** button, and go to the **Modules access level** fast tab.

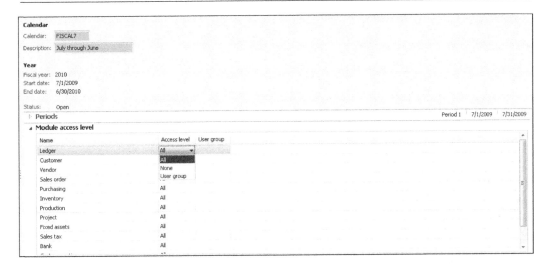

After dealing with the details of the financial department, make all the required adjustments for the current month. The financial **Period status** drop-down list is set to **On Hold** (formerly known as **Stopped** in Microsoft Dynamics AX 2009), which prevents any entry being posted in that period; but it can be reopened after that.

There is another possible scenario: changing **Period status** to **Closed**. However, this status cannot be reopened again.

Summary

In this chapter, we discussed the practices in the financial implementations of Microsoft Dynamics AX 2012. We focused on the general ledger, covering the types of main accounts, classifications, and control points. We also explained shared financial data, which is a new function introduced in Microsoft Dynamics AX 2012 R3. We also learned about opening balance best practices, daily transactions, and the monthly closing procedure.

In the next chapter, we will cover bank management basic configurations, controls, and integrations with other modules (general ledger, accounts payable, and accounts receivable), and we will also perform a bank reconciliation.

3
Understanding Cash and Bank Management

The cash and bank module is the place where a company's bank account, current, and deposit accounts are listed. In this module, a company can monitor and control their bank transactions. The financial controller and chief financial officer will be able to assess the cash position and bank reconciliation accuracy. This chapter covers the following topics:

- Understanding cash and bank integration
- Controlling cash and bank management
- Exploring cash and bank management in action
- Bank account reconciliation
- Bank facility – letter of guarantee

Understanding cash and bank integration

The modules' transactions represent the customer's deposits in the company's bank accounts, either by cash or by check, and also payments to vendors through cash or check. Bank reconciliation is an important procedure performed weekly or monthly (according to the number of transactions and the customers' business needs). This process should be performed once a month before the closing period to ensure that bank transactions (bank statements) are matched with book transactions, which are recorded in Microsoft Dynamics AX.

The following diagram shows the integration of cash and bank management:

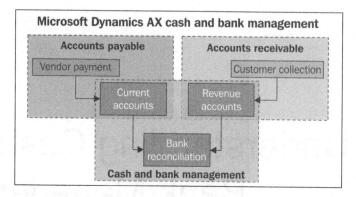

The cash and bank module is a shared module between the Accounts payable module and the Accounts receivable module (as seen in the preceding diagram), where the vendors' payments are executed by a check or cash that can be printed through Microsoft Dynamics AX. The customers' collections are deposited into the bank's account. The key factor here is the method of payment, which is assigned to a transaction level that may recall a specific bank account ID, require a check number, fire payment steps for the check process, and so on.

Controlling cash and bank management

Microsoft Dynamics AX offers five main controls over bank and cash management. It is one of the key objectives of ERP that it controls in order to make the most of having an ERP application in place. These control functionalities should be highlighted to the process owners to be utilized efficiently.

Microsoft Dynamics AX 2012 emphasizes control as well as new business functionalities. Some of these controls were newly introduced in Microsoft Dynamics AX 2012.

Some of the Microsoft Dynamics AX cash and bank controls are shown in the following diagram:

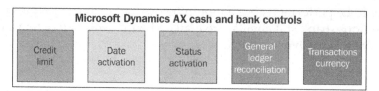

The controls shown in the preceding diagram are defined as follows:

- **Credit limit**: This allows for credit limit control on the bank account. This is a new feature introduced in the cash and bank management module.

- **Date activation**: This detects activation dates control. This is also a new feature in the cash and bank management module.

- **Status activation**: This detects the activation status on bank transactions. It's a new feature added in the cash and bank management module.

- **General ledger reconciliation**: This assigns one ledger account to more than one bank account.

- **Transaction currency**: This allows multiple currency transactions to be executed on the bank account.

Credit limit

The credit limit control stops posting transactions if it exceeds the credit limit that the bank can propose. To access the cash and bank credit limit tolerance window, navigate to **Cash and bank management | Setup | Cash and bank management parameters | General**. The following screenshot explains the credit limit tolerance control:

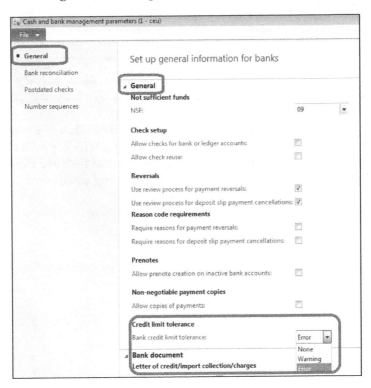

The **Credit limit tolerance** field must be activated under **Cash and bank management parameters**, where it gives a warning or an error, or it is deactivated. The credit limit amount is defined for every bank account under general information. The amount must be negative; if it is not, you will receive this message: **Credit limit must be in negative**, as you can see in the following screenshot. For cash and bank credit limit tolerance, navigate to **Cash and bank management | Common | Bank accounts**. Click on **Edit** or double-click to open the bank form under the **General** fast tab.

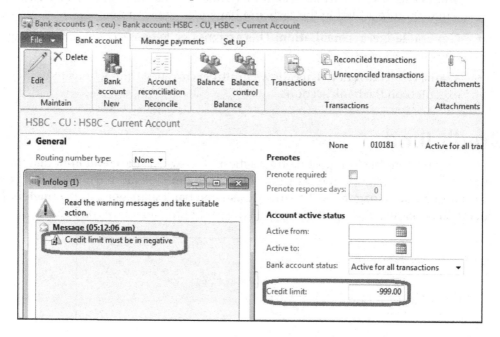

In the course of transaction processing, if an accountant validates or posts a credited amount that surpasses the bank's credit limit, an **Infolog** window will pop up showing a message that says, **You cannot post the journal because the bank's credit limit has been exceeded**, as shown in the following screenshot:

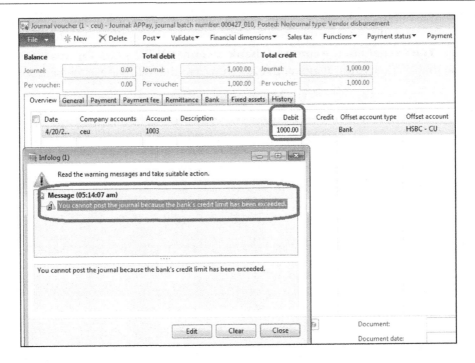

Date activation

Date activation of the bank account recognizes the activation range for every bank account. To access the cash and bank date activation window, navigate to **Cash and bank management | Common | Bank accounts**. Click on **Edit** or double-click to open the bank form under the **General** fast tab, as shown in the following screenshot:

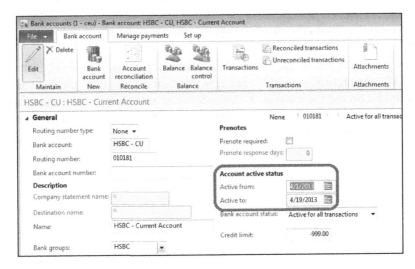

In the course of transaction processing, if an accountant posts or validates a transaction date that is not in the active date range, an **Infolog** window will pop up showing this message: **You cannot use the company bank account 'HSBC – CU' for this transaction because that bank account is not active**, as shown in the following screenshot:

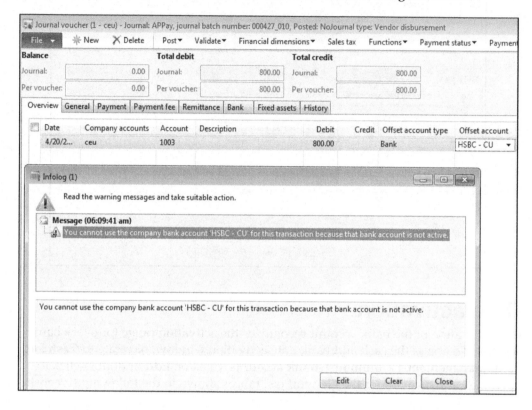

Status activation

As you can see in the following screenshot, status activation has three options: **Active for all transactions, Inactive for new transactions**, and **Inactive for all transactions**. To access the cash and bank status activation window, navigate to **Cash and bank management | Common | Bank accounts**. Click on **Edit** or double-click to open the bank form under the **General** fast tab.

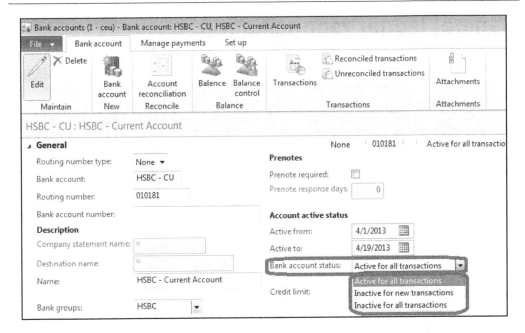

The three options of status activation are explained in detail as follows:

- **Active for all transactions**: This means that a bank account is active and available for all transactions.

- **Inactive for new transactions**: This means that no new transactions can be posted for a bank account. The existing transactions that have not been finalized yet, such as pending payments, will still take place as they were originally posted.

- **Inactive for all transactions**: This means no transactions, either new or existing, can be processed for a bank account.

General ledger reconciliation

The creation process of a new bank account must be assigned to a main account. Microsoft Dynamics AX 2012 gives a warning message to say that this account is already assigned to another bank's main account, and that should be considered during the reconciliation process with the general ledger's main accounts. As seen in the following screenshot, the warning message that appears is: **Main account ##### is already used by bank account USA OPER. If you associate multiple bank accounts with a main account, the General Ledger Bank Reconciliation report will contain information from multiple bank accounts.**

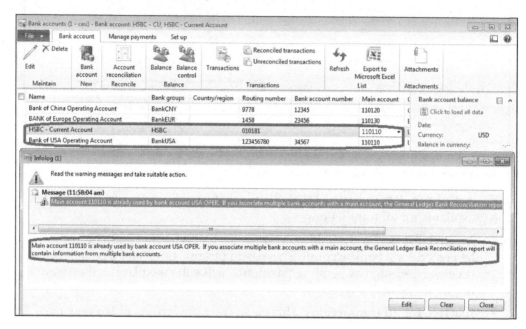

Transaction currency

The transaction currency for bank accounts could be one currency or multiple currencies; it is suggested to assign a single currency for every bank account. You have to navigate to the **Cash and bank management | Common | Bank accounts | Currency management** fast tab, as shown in the following screenshot:

In the course of transaction processing, if an accountant tries to post an entry in a bank account that does not permit multiple currencies, an **Infolog** window will pop up showing this message: **Currency EUR not allowed for account HSBC - CU**, as shown in the following screenshot:

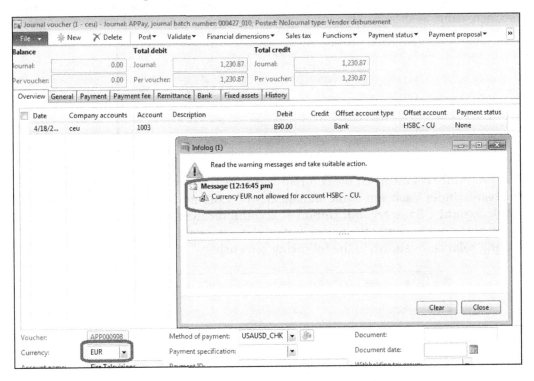

Exploring cash and bank management in action

The following section will explore cash and bank management in daily transactions. It will focus on bank account reconciliation, which is a key process to ensure that all recorded transactions match the bank statement; and the bank facility will focus on the letter of guarantee.

Bank account reconciliation

Bank account reconciliation is a validation process of the bank's account statement, and recorded transactions in the cash and bank management module through customer deposits and vendor payments.

There are two reconciliation mechanisms that you can apply for each bank account: the first one is the manual reconciliation mechanism, and the second one is newly introduced in Microsoft Dynamics AX 2012 R2, the automatic import of bank statements. You have to navigate to **Cash and bank management | Common | Bank accounts | Select bank account**. In the **Bank account** ribbon, click on **Account reconciliation**, as shown in the following screenshot:

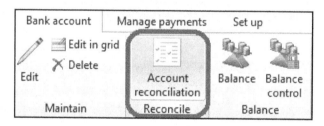

The procedure begins when the company receives the bank account statement from the bank. Under **Cash and bank management | Common | Bank accounts**, select **Bank account | Bank account ribbon | Account reconciliation**. In the account reconciliation form, enter the reconciliation date, statement number, and statement ending balance, as shown in the following screenshot:

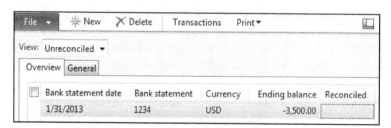

Under reconciliation transactions, only the booked transactions through Microsoft Dynamics AX modules are listed. If it matches the bank statement, mark it as **Cleared**, as you can see in the following screenshot:

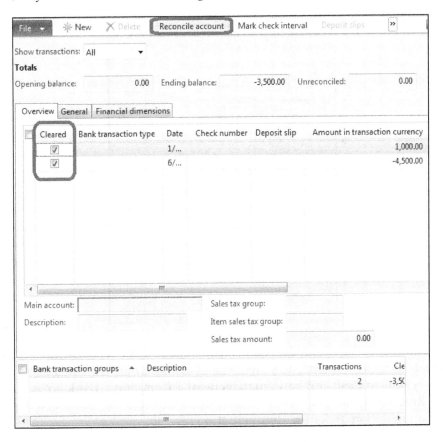

After marking all transactions, click on **Reconcile account** to confirm the reconciliation process. If the reconciliation is successful, an **Infolog** window will pop up displaying this message: **Account has been reconciled**. This is shown in the following screenshot:

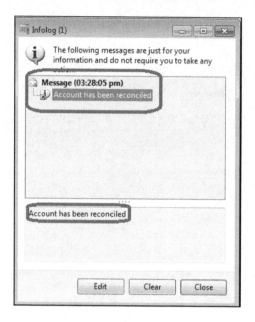

To automatically import bank statements, you must activate the **Advanced bank reconciliation** option. In order to activate the **Advanced bank reconciliation** option, navigate to **Cash and bank management | Common | Bank accounts | Edit | Reconciliation**. The following screenshot displays the **Advanced bank reconciliation** option under the **Reconciliation** fast tab:

As you can see in the following screenshot, the advanced bank reconciliation option cannot be turned off after activation:

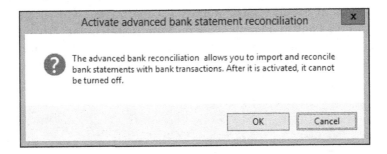

The following screenshot shows the **Generate Bank Documents** window:

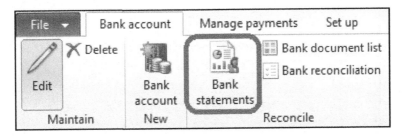

The manual process of importing bank statements starts by selecting **Bank account** and then by clicking on **Bank statements**, as you can see in the following screenshot. In order to go to the **Bank statements** section, navigate to **Cash and bank management | Common | Bank accounts**. Select a bank account, and then go to the **Bank account** ribbon and select **Bank statements**.

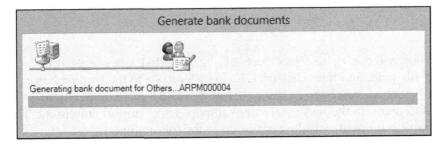

In the **Bank statement** screen, a journal line has been created with a status of **Open**. To import the bank statement, click on **Import statement**. To go to the **Bank statement** section, navigate to **Cash and bank management | Common | Bank statement**. The **Bank statement** screen is shown in the following screenshot:

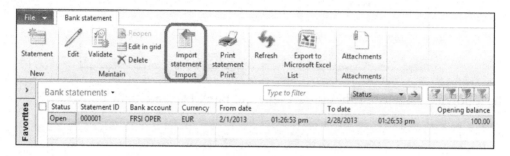

A dialog box will pop up to select the file to be imported. Choose a bank account, locate the file path, and then click on **OK**. In order to go to the **Import bank statements** section, you have to navigate to **Cash and bank management | Common | Bank statement**. In the **Bank statement** ribbon, select **Import statement**. The **Import bank statements** window is shown in the following screenshot:

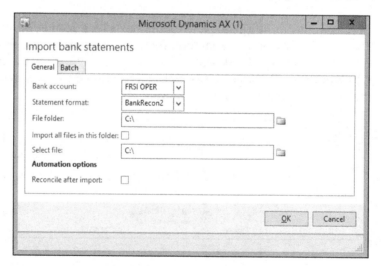

The **Bank statement** form contains the transaction lines of the imported bank transactions, in addition to the opening balance, ending balance, and net amount details. Click on **Validate** to validate the imported bank statement. If there is an error with the opening or ending balance, the validation process will stop. In order to edit the bank statement, you have to navigate to **Cash and bank management | Common | Bank statement | Edit**. The **Bank statement** screen is shown in the following screenshot:

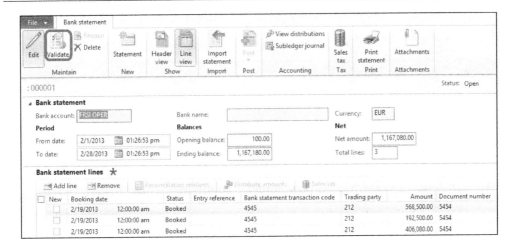

As you can see in the following screenshot, an **Infolog** window will pop up to confirm that the statement passes the validation process:

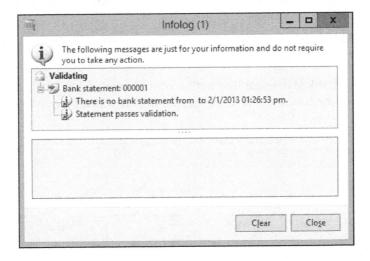

In order to match the bank transactions with the bank statement, go to the **Bank reconciliation** journal by navigating to **Cash and bank management | Journals | Bank reconciliation**, as shown in the following screenshot:

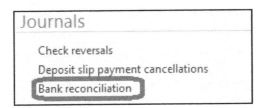

To create a new journal line, select **Bank account** and then click on **Lines**, as shown in the following screenshot:

The bank reconciliation worksheet contains the following fields:

- **Open statement lines**: This represents the imported transactions of the bank statement

- **Open bank documents**: This represents the bank transactions posted on Microsoft Dynamics AX

- **Matched statement lines**: This represents the matched line in the statement with posted transactions

- **Matched bank documents**: This represents the matched bank document in the statement with posted transactions

While checking a bank statement line with a posted transaction, click on **Match**. As you can see in the following screenshot, the matched lines move to the **Matched documents** tab:

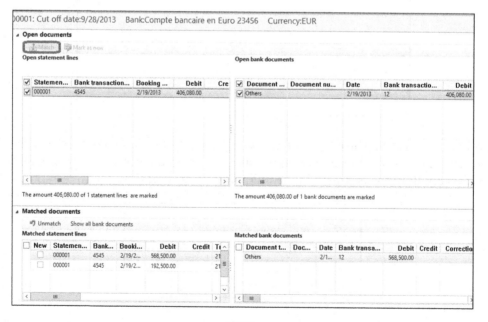

After matching all transactions against the bank statement, click on **Reconcile**, as shown in the following screenshot, in order to reconcile this statement and close it:

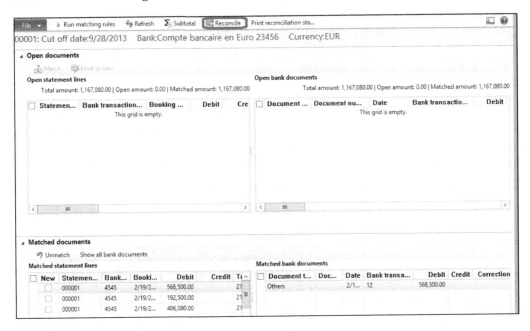

As you can see in the following screenshot, an **Infolog** window will pop up indicating that the reconciliation process is finished:

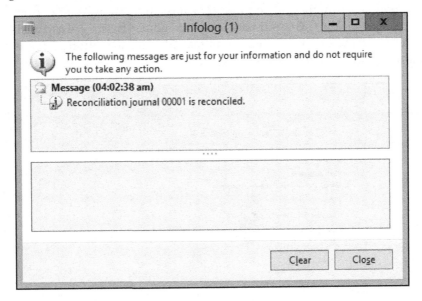

Bank facility – letter of guarantee

A letter of guarantee is an agreement by a bank (the guarantor) to pay a set amount of money to another person (the beneficiary) if the bank's customer (the principal) defaults on a payment or an obligation to the beneficiary. Letters of guarantee are not transferable, and apply only to the beneficiary named in the guarantee agreement. The principal can request an increase or decrease in the value of a letter of guarantee, subject to the terms of the agreement.

The following diagram illustrates the required configuration and setups in order to utilize the letter of guarantee function. The **Letter of Guarantee - LG** function configuration should be activated, in addition to the basic setups including **Bank documents posting profile**, **Bank facility agreements**, and **Bank facility**.

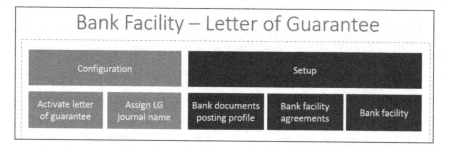

The first step in configuration is to activate the letter of guarantee checkbox on cash and bank management parameters, and assign the journal name that will be used to post the issuance commission and margin transaction. In order to perform this function, navigate to the **Cash and bank management | Setup | Cash and bank management parameter | Bank document** fast tab. The activation screen is shown in the following screenshot:

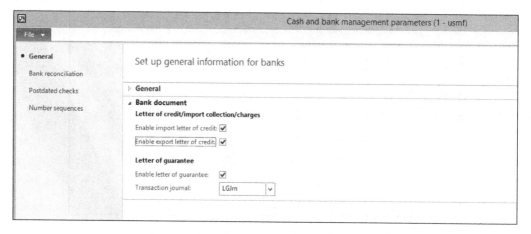

The journal name type is daily.

Create the bank facilities records by navigating to **Cash and bank management |
Setup | Bank documents | Bank facilities**. As shown in the following screenshot,
go to the **Facility groups** fast tab, create a new record by clicking on **New** or by
pressing *Ctrl + N*. Enter the **Facility group** code and the **Description** value.

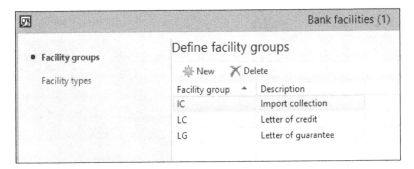

Then move to the **Facility types** fast tab, and create a new record by clicking on **New**
or by pressing *Ctrl + N*. Enter the **Facility type** code and the **Description** value, select
Facility group and **Facility nature** (whether it is **Letter of credit**, **Import collection**,
or **Letter of guarantee)**. The **Facility types** fast tab is shown in the following
screenshot:

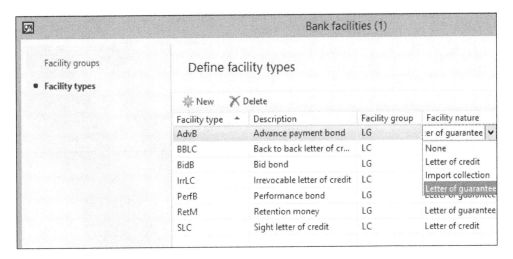

Create the bank facility agreements by navigating to **Cash and bank management | Setup | Bank documents | Bank facility agreements** on the **General** fast tab. Identify the start and end date of the facility agreement, in addition to the amount of facility limit and used amount. In the **Letter of guarantee** fast tab, identify the **Cash margin**, **Issuance commission**, **Extension commission**, **Increase value commission**, and **Decrease value commission**. The facility agreements are shown in the following screenshot:

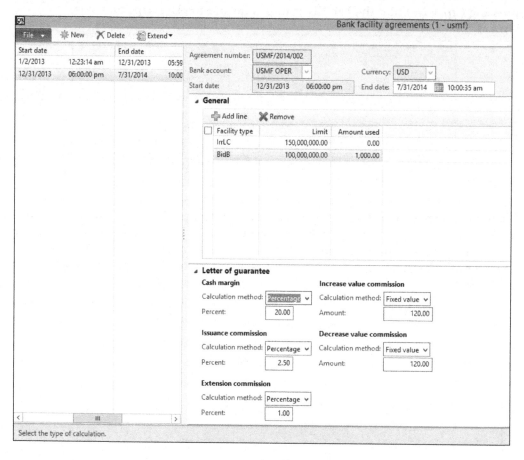

Create the bank documents posting profile by navigating to **Cash and bank management** | **Setup** | **Bank documents** | **Bank documents posting profile** where you can identify the accounts: **Settle account**, **Charges account**, **Margin account**, and **Liquidation account**. The posting profile could be distinguished by the bank facility type, facility group, and so on. The **Bank documents posting profile** window is shown in the following screenshot:

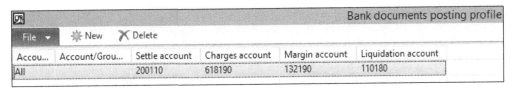

Accou...	Account/Grou...	Settle account	Charges account	Margin account	Liquidation account
All		200110	618190	132190	110180

The letter of guarantee is used in sales activities where the customer provides the guarantee to deliver goods or services against this guarantee. In the following section, we will explore a sales order transaction with the letter of guarantee.

Navigate to **Sales and marketing** | **Common** | **Sales orders** | **All sales orders**. The sales order menu is shown in the following screenshot:

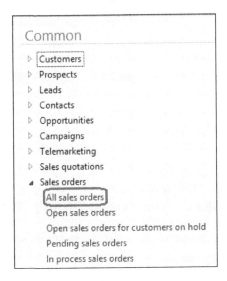

Create a new record by pressing *Ctrl + N*, select customer account, and then move to the **General** fast tab. In the **Bank document type** field, select **Letter of guarantee**. The sales order creation window is shown in the following screenshot:

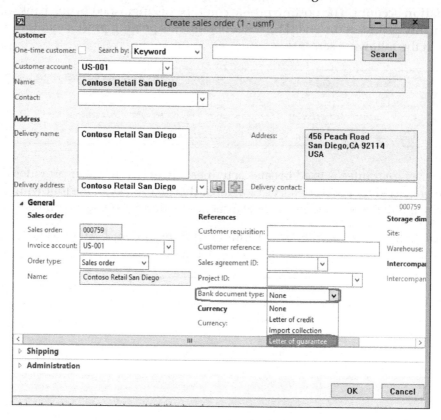

In the sales order form, select the item ID (such as sold, quantity, price, site, and warehouse) of the product. Then move to the **Manage** ribbon, and then select **Letter of guarantee**. The sales order form line is shown in the following screenshot:

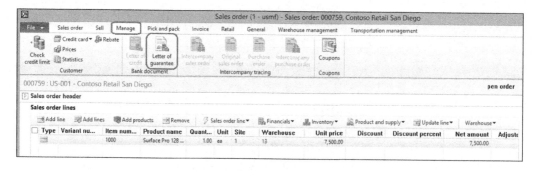

In the letter of guarantee form, click on **Request** to create a letter of guarantee request, select values for the **Type**, **Value**, and **Expiration date** fields. The letter of guarantee request is shown in the following screenshot:

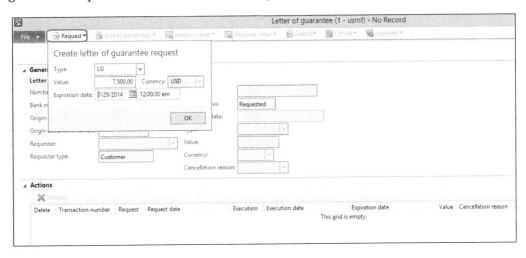

Then move to the letter of guarantee process. This process is executed from the cash and bank management module by navigating to **Cash and bank management | Common | Letters of guarantee**. The **Letters of guarantee** menu is shown in the following screenshot:

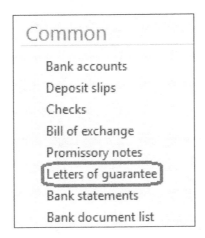

The first step in the letter of guarantee process is submitting the letter of guarantee to the bank. The current Status value is **Request**, and the Facility status value is **Requested**. The letter of guarantee, status, and other related information is shown in the following screenshot:

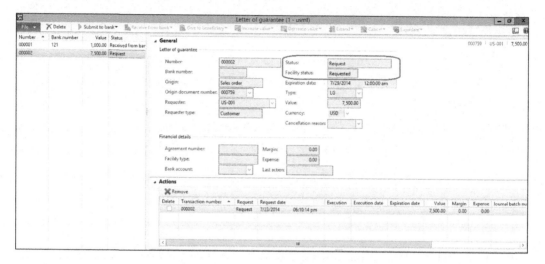

Click on **Submit to bank**, select the **Bank account** and **Facility type** values, and then click on **OK**. The submit to bank process is shown in the following screenshot:

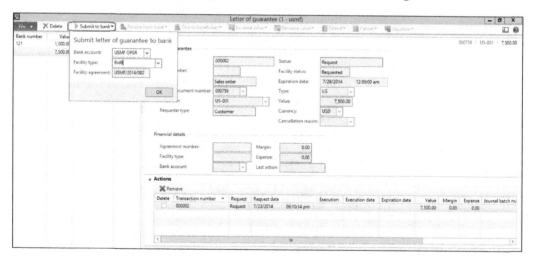

The **Status** field is updated to be **Submitted to bank**, and the **Facility status** field remains as **Requested**. The financial details are updated with the bank submission information. Status updates and updated submission information are shown in the following screenshot:

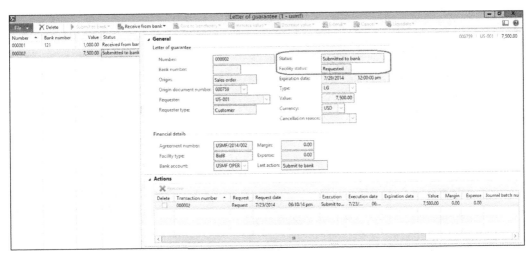

The company receives a confirmation from the bank and the system automatically calculates the **Margin** and **Expense**. A confirmation received from the bank function is shown in the following screenshot:

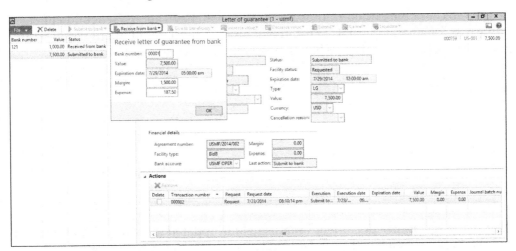

The system generates and posts a general journal transaction; the **Infolog** window pops up displaying the message indicating that the journal has been posted, as shown in following screenshot:

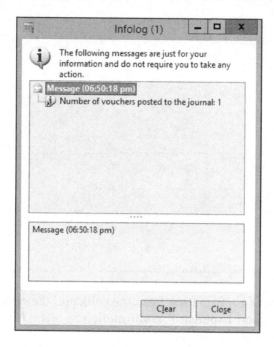

In order to check the posted transaction, you have to navigate to **General Ledger | Journals | General journal | Posted** and filter on the letter of guarantee journal name. The posted journals are shown in the following screenshot:

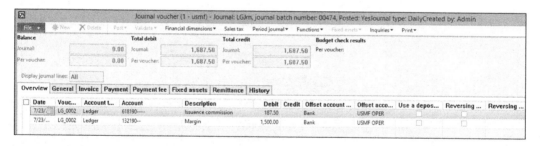

The letter of guarantee document's **Status** field is updated to be **Received from bank** and the **Facility status** field is updated to be **Open**. The letter of guarantee status update is shown in the following screenshot:

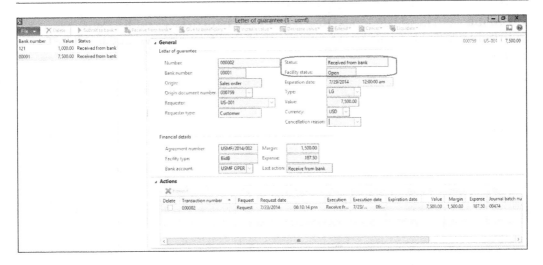

Then you should navigate back to **Sales and marketing | Common | Sales orders | All sales orders** and filter to the previously created sales order, and on the ribbon move to **Manage** and select **Letter of guarantee**, in order to request the letter of guarantee to the customer. The request of giving the letter of guarantee to the beneficiary is shown in the following screenshot:

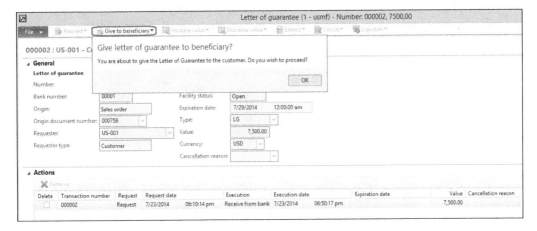

The **Status** field is updated to be **Request give to beneficiary** and the bank **Facility status** field remains as **Open**. The status update is shown in the following screenshot:

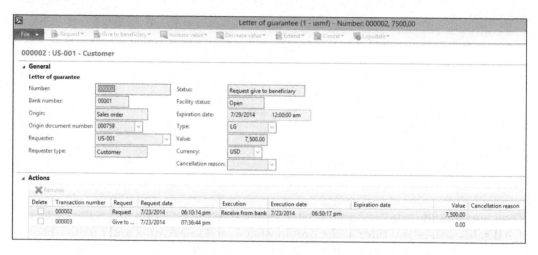

Then navigate to **Cash and bank management | Common | Letters of guarantee** to give the letter of guarantee to the beneficiary. The following screenshot shows the action of giving the letter of guarantee to the beneficiary:

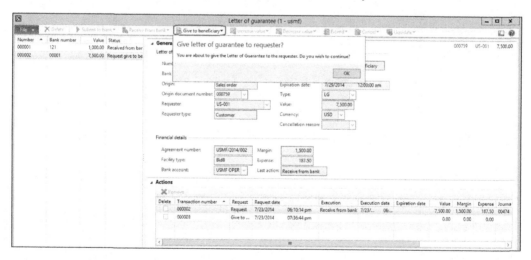

The **Status** field is updated to be **Given to beneficiary** and the **Facility status** field remains as **Open**. The letter of guarantee is shown in the following screenshot:

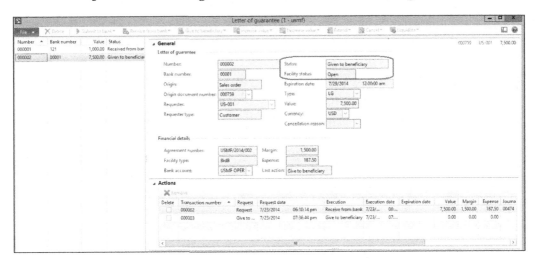

There are other options that could be performed after this stage; they are as follows:

- Increase or decrease the letter of guarantee
- Cancel or extend it
- Liquidate the letter of guarantee

Summary

This chapter covers the integration of the cash and bank modules with Accounts payable, Accounts receivable, and the general ledger. We discussed the controls offered by Microsoft Dynamics AX 2012. We also explored the bank reconciliation transactions that are executed at the end of each month. Then we explored the letter of guarantee as the bank facility option.

In the next chapter, we will cover accounts payable integration with another module, vendors' master data, and controls. We will then move to accounts payable transactions, invoicing, payment, and settlement.

4
Understanding Accounts Payable

The accounts payable cycles are vendor invoicing and payment. These business processes manage and control the execution of vendor expenditure processes. These processes are based on procurement, purchasing, and product reception cycles in the procurement and sourcing processes. This cycle is known as the procure to pay cycle. This chapter covers the following topics:

- Understanding accounts payable integration with other modules
- Exploring vendor master data characteristics
- Exploring accounts payable controls
- Exploring accounts payable transactions

Understanding accounts payable integration with other modules

The Accounts payable module manages and controls vendor transactions from the accounting point of view, where it records vendor master information and the basic transactions related to vendor invoicing, payment, and settlement. The accounts payable function is integrated with other business functions.

The first integration point with the procurement and sourcing business functions is procuring goods and services to the company, the second integration is invoicing the purchase order based on the received goods in the warehousing, and the third integration with cash and bank management business functions is performing vendor payment and settlement against invoices. The full cycle of procure to pay is shown in the following diagram:

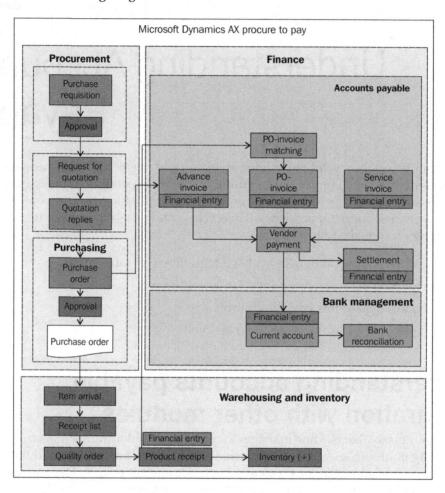

The normal practice of enterprise organizations is that no purchase orders are created directly. This can lead to creating purchase orders that are not needed and exposing the company to uncontrolled expenditures. This business process must be controlled, as it is the source point of company expenditure. On the other hand, it can significantly impact the inventory cost, which will be reflected in the cost of production for a manufacturing environment along with the cost of sales, and this affects the company's profitability accordingly.

The purchasing process of items typically goes through specific internal procedures to replenish items known as finished goods for a distribution environment/raw materials for a manufacturing environment from the procurement department. The procurement process begins by either automatic planned order from operations for specific items based on sales consumption against on-hand inventory, or entering the purchase requisition manually.

The purchase requisition goes through a workflow approval cycle that gives the necessary control to operations management to examine the requested quantities and might require top management approval according to the organization's internal policies. In some projects or business scenarios, the purchase requisition cycle is not utilized; in such cases, a sole vendor supplies specific materials and the workflow can be utilized on the purchase order itself through the change management functionality that was newly introduced in Microsoft Dynamics AX 2012.

The approved purchase requisition is passed to the procurement agent (buyer) to execute the request for the quotation process, where it records the vendors who will potentially supply the required items. A request for a quotation is then sent to them. When the vendor sends back their replies, the procurement agent (buyer) records their replies and identifies the awarded vendor who will supply the required items. The approved purchase requisition can then be transformed into a purchase order if the item is supplied from a sole vendor, which is defined in the workflow configuration. The purchase order can then go through the approval workflow cycle and be confirmed.

The following are the purchase order types:

- **Purchase order**: This is a commitment document sent to a vendor to supply the required goods/services.
- **Journal**: This is a draft/template document that does not accept any further transactions, nor does it affect inventory or finance.
- **Returned order**: This is a credit note document used to reverse a purchase order invoice.
- **Purchase agreement**: This is a commitment document that is sent to a vendor to supply goods/services over specific time periods and prices. This is a new function introduced in AX 2012, and it replaces blanket order in AX 2009.

The following are the purchase order statuses:

- **Open Order**: This indicates that the purchase order has either been newly created, not totally received, or not totally invoiced
- **Received**: This indicates that the purchase order is fully received

- **Invoiced**: This indicates that the purchase order is fully invoiced
- **Canceled**: This indicates that the ordered quantities in the purchase order have been totally canceled

The following are the purchase order approval statuses:

- **Draft**: This indicates that the purchase order is a draft that has not been submitted for approval in the purchase order workflow.
- **In review**: This indicates that the purchase order was submitted for approval in the purchase order workflow and the approval is pending.
- **Rejected**: This indicates that the purchase order was rejected during the approval process.
- **Approved**: This indicates that the purchase order is approved.
- **Confirmed**: This indicates that the purchase order is confirmed; a purchase order cannot be confirmed until it has been approved.
- **Finalized**: This indicates that the purchase order is made final. It is financially closed and can no longer be changed.

The following are the purchase order document statuses:

- **None**: This indicates that the purchase order is created and no further documents have been posted
- **Purchase Order**: This indicates that the purchase order has been confirmed
- **Receipt List**: This indicates that the receipt list document has been posted on the purchase order
- **Product Receipt**: This indicates that the product receipt document has been posted on the purchase order
- **Invoice**: This indicates that the purchase order invoice has been posted

The product reception process occurred in two steps. The preliminary reception (receipt list) assigns inventory dimensions such as serial number and batch number, in addition to the quality inspection if required. The product receipt increases the physical quantities in the inventory and reduces the quantity remaining in the purchase order.

 The product receipt transactions do not reflect any transactions on the vendor.

The vendor invoice is the document that represents the company's liability to vendors who deliver goods or services to the company. Afterwards, the payment process is executed based on the vendor invoices. The normal practice in enterprise organizations is that the vendor payments will have two different scenarios: payment after receiving the goods/service invoice or advance payment before rendering any reception process. The advanced payment can be assigned to a specific purchase order. Each payment transaction is settled against a vendor invoice. This affects company liabilities and projection of future vendor payments. The payment transactions are executed by several methods of payments; the most commonly used method is from bank accounts. The following diagram shows the document integration between invoices, payment, and settlement:

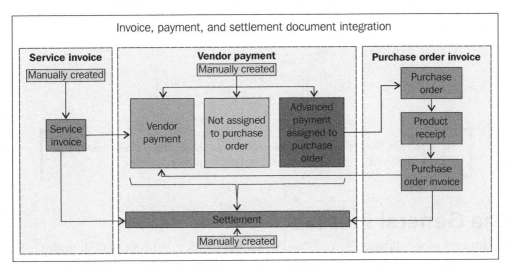

There are service and purchase order invoices, the payments transaction that can be an advance payment that is assigned to a particular purchase order or not related to a purchase order, and the settlement transactions that settle the payments against invoices.

Each transaction is represented in a document type in Microsoft Dynamics AX, with the document that contains the details of the transaction. The transaction data, irrespective of whether it is inherited from the master data, entered manually, and/or automatically inherited from another transaction, is linked to a specific reference. The integration between invoice and payment transaction documents gives visibility to trace the original purchase order and the reception document, which is related to the invoice, together with who approves the invoice and payment.

Exploring vendor master data characteristics

The vendor record has essential information that directly affects accounts payable transactions. In section, we will cover the basic information that should be considered when creating a new vendor record.

In order to create a new vendor record, the user should navigate to **Accounts Payable | Common | Vendors | All vendors**, as shown in the following screenshot:

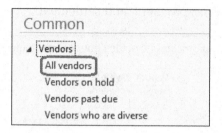

 On the vendor list page, press *Ctrl + N* to create a new vendor record, or through the ribbon, click on **New vendor**.

The General fast tab

As shown in the following screenshot, when the vendor form is opened, under the **General** fast tab, the mandatory fields are **Vendor account** and **Group**:

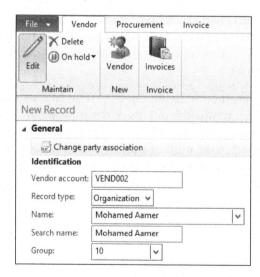

Vendor account can be assigned manually or automatically through the number sequence.

Group is a mandatory field that represents the vendor group that this particular vendor belongs to, and this is considered as the integration point between accounts payable and general ledger through the posting profile; however, the posting profile can be on the level of the vendor code. The vendor grouping is a joint effort between the procurement department and the financial department, as the procurement perspective is grouping the vendor from the operational point of view and reporting. On the other hand, the financial grouping as per the relevant account will get the financial posting when the operational action occurs.

The Purchasing demographics fast tab

In the **Purchasing demographics** fast tab shown in the following screenshot, the **Currency** field is mandatory. This represents the default currency for this particular vendor transaction; however, it can be changed at the transaction level as per the business case.

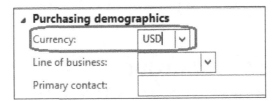

Invoice and delivery fast tab

Switching to the **Invoice and delivery** fast tab in this section, we will cover three field groups: **Invoice**, **Sales tax**, and **Withholding tax**.

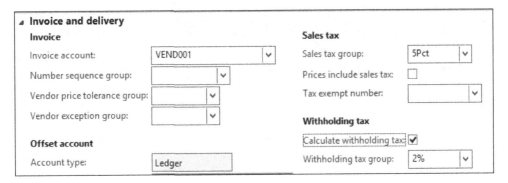

The Invoice field group

In the **Invoice** field group, the **Invoice account** field represents the account used in the invoicing process (the default invoice account is the vendor code), but Microsoft Dynamics AX gives flexibility to point invoice posting to another vendor. Assuming that there are two different vendors supplying goods, the invoice will be issued to one of the two vendors.

The relation between vendor code and invoice account, where the vendor invoice can be linked to one vendor code or multiple vendor codes, is shown in the following diagram:

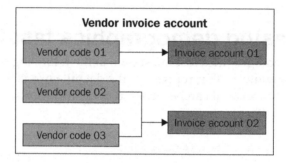

The Sales tax field group

The **Sales tax** field group represents the tax treatment that will be applied to this vendor. It can be the sales tax, prices including or excluding sales tax, and the tax exempt number if there is any. An explanation of each field of the **Sales tax** field group is as follows:

- **Sales tax group**: This field represents the sales tax group assigned to this particular vendor, and this record will be the default value for all transactions that will be inherited from the vendor master data

- **Price include sales tax**: This field indicates that the invoice amounts should include or exclude sales tax

- **Tax exempt number**: This field is used for reporting and statistical extractions

> Sales tax group can be set as the default at the vendor group level; just navigate to **Accounts Payable | Setup | Vendors | Vendor group**. Also, it can be overridden by the user on the vendor form.
>
> Setting sales tax at the vendor group level will cascade down to newly created vendors in this group. This ensures that the sales tax will be filled in automatically. On the other hand, it can be overridden on the vendor form or at the transaction level for exceptional cases. It is recommended not to leave the overwrite permission with the end users to avoid issues in the posted sales tax.

The Withholding tax field group

The **Withholding tax** field is activated at the vendor level by marking the **Calculate withholding tax** field, and this will activate the withholding tax code field to assign the withholding tax code that will be applied during the payment process.

Let's switch to the **Purchase order default** fast tab. In this section, we will explore the **Discount** field group.

The Discount field group

The **Discount** field group represents the discount and pricing options that can be applied on this particular vendor. As shown in the following screenshot, the **Discount** field group consists of discount and pricing groups that this vendor belongs to:

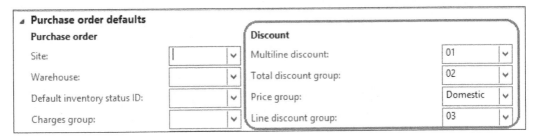

Vendor price/discount groups

The **Vendor price/discount groups** consist of the four pricing groups shown in the following diagram:

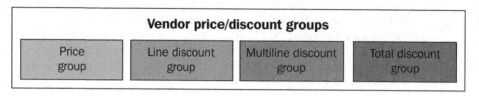

From the preceding diagram, we can see:

- **Price group**: This represents the vendor's price group used for price proposal upon purchase; this price group is attached to the vendor master

- **Line discount group**: This represents the purchase line discount used for purchase; this is attached to the vendor master

- **Multi line discount group**: This represents the multi-line discount group used to control discounts across several purchase lines; this is attached to the vendor master

- **Total discount group**: This represents the total discount that attaches the vendor master data to a total discount group

In order to create vendor price/discount groups, you need to navigate to **Inventory management | Setup | Price/discount | Vendor price/discount groups**; this is shown in the following screenshot:

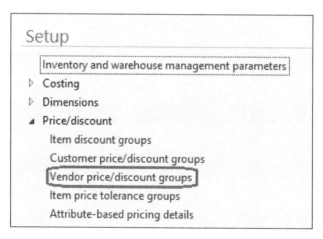

The **Vendor price/discount groups** form shows the **Price/discount** options and helps create groups for each **Price/discount** option, as shown in the following screenshot:

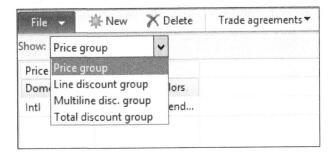

 The **Price/discount** option must be activated by navigating to **Procurement and sourcing** | **Setup** | **Price/discount** | **Activate price/discount**.

In the **Domestic** value created for the price group, navigate to **Trade agreements** | **Create trade agreements**, as shown in the following screenshot:

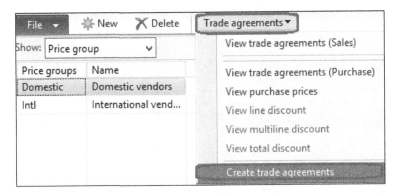

The trade agreement journal will pop up; create a new journal by pressing *Ctrl + N*, select the journal name, and then click on **Lines**. The prices defined in the trade agreement represents a combination between vendor and item; this combination has flexibility with the following options:

- **All**: Any transaction occurring for any vendor will inherit the price that is assigned to all vendors

- **Group**: Any transaction for a particular vendor price group inherits the price that is assigned to the price group

- **Table**: Any transaction that occurs for a vendor will inherit the price that is assigned to this particular vendor

As shown in the following screenshot, select **Price (purch.)**. Now, select **Account code** as **Table** to make this price correspond to a particular vendor; in **Item relation**, select **Table** to make this price correspond to a particular item when it is purchased from the mentioned vendor and from a specific warehouse.

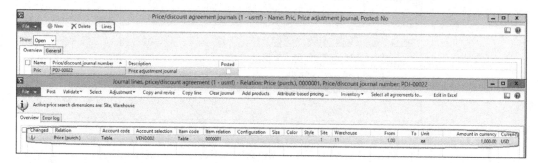

As shown in the following screenshot, the reflection of this setup is to recall the purchase price on the purchase line automatically from the posted trade agreements journal:

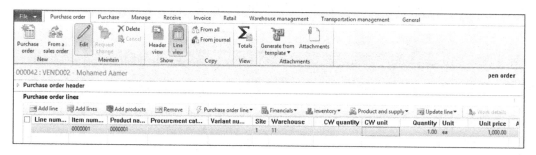

The Payment fast tab

In the **Payment** fast tab, under the **Payment** field group, the information needed for vendor payment arrangements is shown (see the following screenshot). The available fields are **Terms of payment**, **Method of payment**, **Payment type**, **Payment specification**, and **Cash discount**.

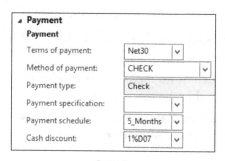

Terms of payment

The **Terms of payment** field represents the calculated due date to pay the vendor. The terms of payment creation form is shown in the following screenshot. In order to access this form, navigate to **Accounts Payable | Setup | Payment | Terms of payment**.

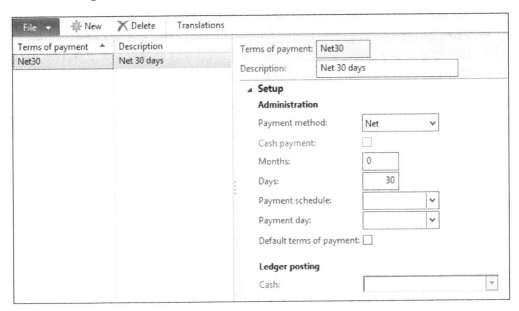

Identify the due date base in the **Payment method** combobox that contains six options. Assume that the vendor invoice is posted on January 1, 2014 and the number of days is 20; the due date will be changed based on the selected payment method option, as shown in the following diagram:

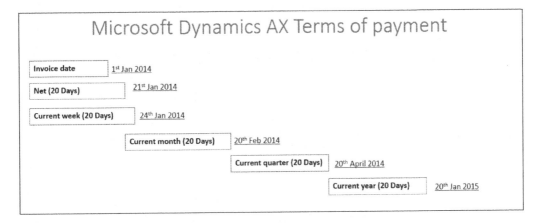

From the preceding diagram, we can see:

- **Net**: The due date will be calculated from the invoice posting (1st Jan + 20 days), which is **21st Jan 2014**

- **Current week**: The due date will be calculated from the end of the week that the invoice was posted in (4th Jan + 20 days), that is, **24th Jan 2014**

- **Current month**: The due date will be calculated from the end of the month that the invoice was posted in (31st Jan + 20 days), in this case **20th Feb 2014**

- **Current quarter**: The due date will be calculated from the end of the quarter that the invoice was posted in (31st March + 20 days), which in this case is **20th April 2014**

- **Current year**: The due date will be calculated from the end of the year that the invoice was posted in (31st December + 20 days); here it will be **20th Jan 2015**

- **Cash on delivery (COD)**: This represents the cash payment upon delivery; with this option, a ledger account must be specified that will be used while posting a purchase order invoice

Method of payment

A payment method refers to the way the vendor is paid whether by check, bank transfer, or cash. In order to access the method of payment form, navigate to **Accounts Payable | Setup | Payment | Method of payment**, as shown in the following screenshot. Setting the required controls will be applied on the transaction if it is using this particular method of payment, in addition to the file formats of checked printouts.

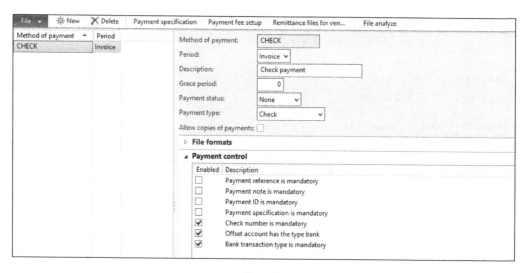

Payment schedule

The **Payment schedule** field represents the installment that will be used after invoicing. In order to access the payment schedule form, navigate to **Accounts Payable | Setup | Payment | Payment schedule**. This is shown in the following screenshot; our main aim is to identify the type of installment, that is, whether it is over a fixed number of months or has a fixed amount:

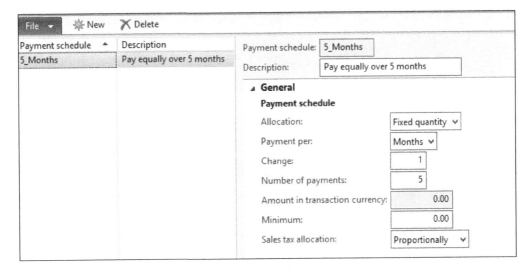

Assume that the purchase order invoice is posted on January 1, 2014, its amount is 5000 USD, and it is assigned a payment schedule of 5 months, with the terms of payment set as net 30 days. Navigate to **Accounts Payable | Common | Purchase orders | All purchase orders**; then, on the purchase order form, navigate to **Header view | Price and discount** and assign the payment schedule.

In order to check payment installment dates, in the ribbon, navigate to **Invoice |
Bill | Payment schedule**. The payment schedule form will pop up. Then, go to the
Payment lines tab; the following screenshot shows the payment schedules where
the payment is divided into five installments for five months:

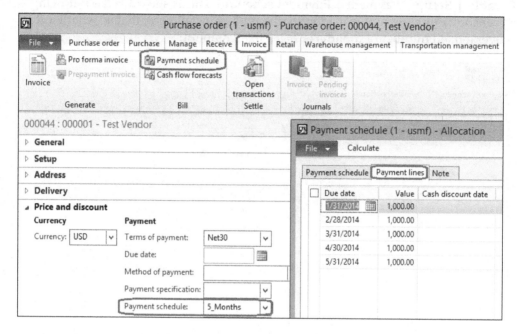

Cash discount

The **Cash discount** field represents the discount that will be applied during the
vendor payment if it is paid before the due date; it has the flexibility to assign the
next cash discount. In order to create the cash discount record, navigate to **Accounts
Payable | Setup | Payment | Cash discount**, as shown in the following screenshot.
The **Setup** fast tab identifies the discount percentage, number of months, and
number of days. It is important to assign the main account for the vendor discount
in order to apply the discounted amount to a particular main account.

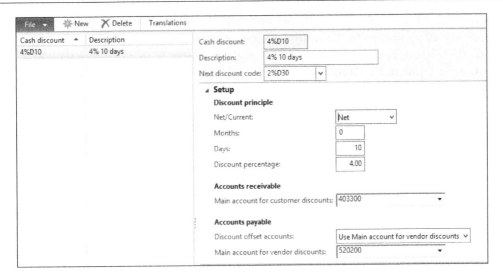

Assuming that an invoice has been posted on January 1, the cash discount is **4%** if the invoice is paid within **10** days and the terms of payment is net 20 days.

As shown in the following screenshot of the vendor invoice journal, the cash discount date is January 11 and its amount is -40:

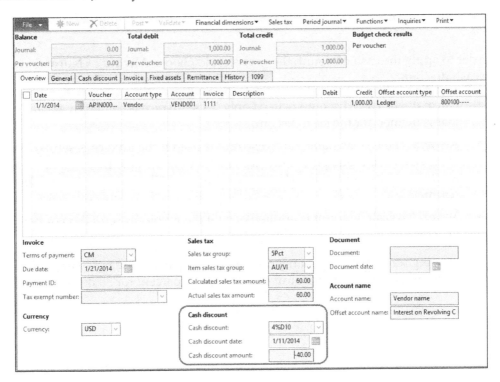

When we go to create a payment transaction and settle it against the posted invoice on January 10, as shown in the following screenshot, the payment amount is 1020 (1060 - 40 = 1020). To access the payment amount, navigate to **Accounts Payable | Common | Journal | Payments | Payment journal | Lines | Functions | Settlement**.

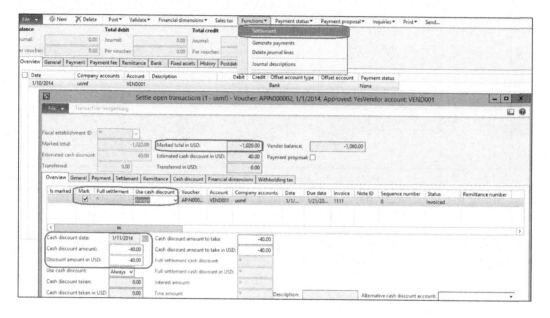

In order to apply the cash discount, the user should choose **Always** or **Normal** under **Use cash discount**:

- **Normal**: The cash discount is used only if the invoice is settled by the date that is defined for the cash discount.

- **Always**: The last available cash discount is used if the invoice is settled after the cash discount date. If the invoice is settled by the date that is defined for the cash discount, the cash discount amount is the same as if you select **Normal**.

- **Never**: No cash discount is applied even if the invoice is settled on or before the discount date.

In the following screenshot, we changed the payment day to January 19 and the cash discount goes to the next cash discount code, that is, 2 percent for 30 days:

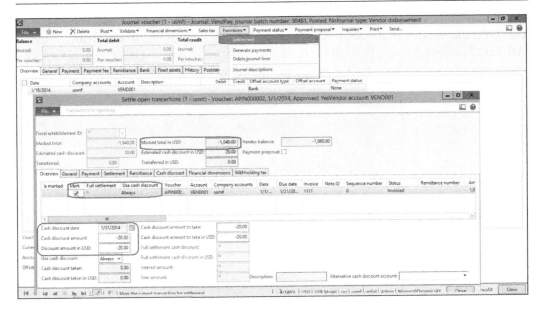

In this section, we explored vendor master data, purchasing demographics, and vendor sales tax treatment, in addition to withholding tax. Then, we explored the price and discount options, in addition to alternatives of payments, terms of payment, and methods of payment.

Exploring accounts payable controls

The accounts payable controls are an essential task to be discussed during the analysis and design phases and assessed in the operation phase for enhancements. Microsoft Dynamics AX 2012 R3 addresses the required procedures for accounts payable controls. It is significant to the business in order to control the execution of accounts payable processes, as it directly affects the company's liabilities; this is why it should be controlled and monitored. In the upcoming sections, we will explore the vendor hold activities, invoicing controls, and posting profiles.

Vendor hold activities

In daily business operations in accounts payable, the accounting manager might need to stop transactions on a specific vendor; the on hold function for vendors in Microsoft Dynamics AX 2012 R3 is located at the vendor level. To access this function, navigate to **Accounts Payable | Common | Vendors | All vendors | Maintain**. In the ribbon, click on **On hold**.

As shown in the following screenshot, the **On hold** function has several options based on the vendor transaction type, that is, **Invoice**, **Payment**, **Requisition**, **Never**, **All**, and **No**, which is the default value. These options can be used to control vendors from executing particular transactions, or to stop a vendor altogether.

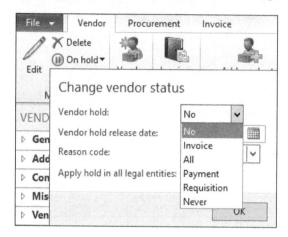

The **On hold** options for the vendor transaction types are as follows:

- **No**: This represents that the vendor is allowed for all transaction types, but if the vendor is inactive, it will be set on hold automatically when running the vendor inactivity job
- **Invoice**: This represents that the vendor is prevented from executing invoice transactions only
- **All**: This represents that the vendor is prevented from executing any transaction
- **Payment**: This represents that the vendor is prevented from executing payment transactions only
- **Requisition**: This represents that the vendor is prevented from executing purchase requisition transactions only
- **Never**: This represents that the vendor is allowed for all transaction types, but the vendor will be excluded when running the vendor inactivity job and will not set on hold automatically

To automatically put a vendor who was recently inactive, the **On hold** function automatically runs the **Vendor inactivation** job by navigating to **Procurement and sourcing | Periodic | Vendors | Vendor inactivation**.

As shown in the following screenshot, when we set the **On hold** value as **All** for example, the system shows an **Infolog** window to indicate that the vendor has been set on hold:

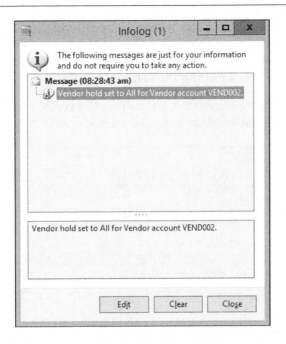

If an end user tries to select a vendor with the **On hold** status as **All**, the system will prevent creating any transaction if the vendor status is on hold, as shown in the following screenshot, where the user tried to create a purchase order:

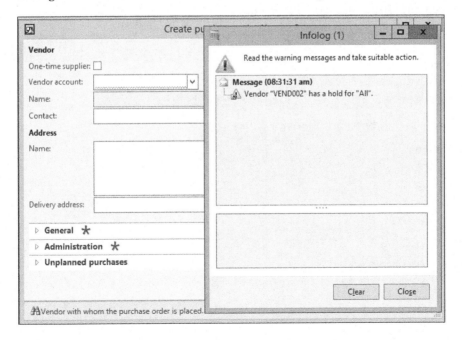

There are other options for **On hold**, where the accounting manager can plan the future release date of the vendor from the **On hold** status for a particular transaction. In the **On hold** selection, set the **Vendor hold release date** field; this will be considered as the last day of putting the vendor on hold.

As shown in the following screenshot, we will set the vendor on hold for a particular transaction and set the release date; here, the release date is August 30, 2014:

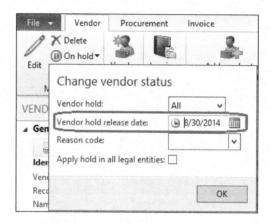

If a user tries to create a transaction for this vendor on August 29, the system will prevent the transaction from being created, and as shown in the following screenshot, an error message will pop up:

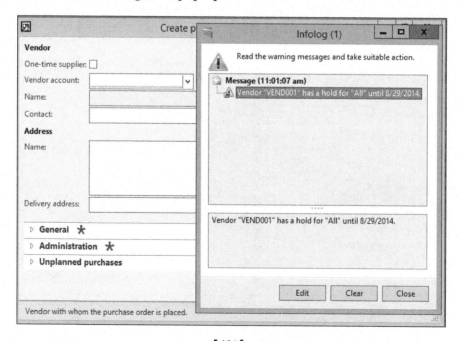

The vendor hold release date is based on the computer (machine) date.

Invoice matching controls

There are several options for invoice matching controls in Microsoft Dynamics AX 2012 R3; in the following section, we will explore the invoicing matching policies and options. The following diagram illustrates the invoice matching options:

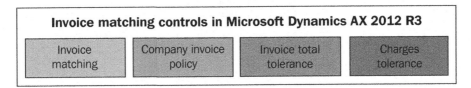

Invoice matching

The vendor invoice matching process is a control point that is concerned with the invoices received from the vendors before recording the invoice as a liability on the company. There are two types of invoice matching, and they are as follows:

- **Three-way matching**: This is normally used with inventory items, where three documents are compared: the vendor invoice against the purchase order document and the product receipt document.

- **Two-way matching**: This is normally used with service items, where two documents are compared: the vendor invoice against the purchase order. This requires manual approval to pass these transactions.

The following diagram illustrates vendor invoice matching:

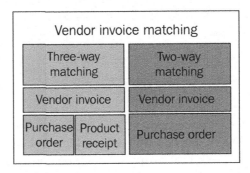

The basic document in three-way matching is **Vendor Invoice**, where it compares the price and quantities in the vendor invoice document against the price in the purchase order, which was already agreed upon, and the actual received quantities in the reception process. This is important for processing payments only to vendors on the agreed prices and the actual delivered quantities in the warehouses.

The following diagram illustrates the three-way matching concept:

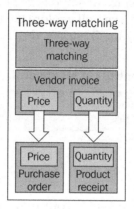

The basic document in two-way matching is also **Vendor Invoice**, where it compares the price of the vendor invoice against the price in the purchase order; as this is for inventory items, there is no need to compare quantities. It is a new feature delivered in AX 2012 where we differentiate the matching process of inventory and noninventory items. The following diagram illustrates the two-way matching concept:

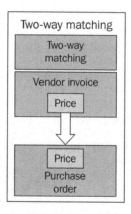

There are numerous layers of vendor invoice matching in Microsoft Dynamics AX 2012 R3 that give you the flexibility to apply matching controls, of which all are required in real-life business. The invoice matching control must be activated on the legal entity level:

- The first layer is the company layer where we identify a matching policy (whether it is two-way, three-way, or not required); this policy will be cascaded down to all vendors and items on this particular legal entity. The acceptable price tolerance is the base of comparison between the vendor invoice and the purchase order price. The price tolerances can be for all vendors and items, or for a specific vendor or item, and finally for a specific combination of vendors and items. On this layer, we configure the matching policy for total invoice tolerance and charge tolerance.

- The second layer matches the policy level, where we identify the exceptions from the company-wide configuration; this exception can be applied on the matching policy for a specific vendor, an item, or a combination of vendors and items, where we can modify the default company-wide parameters. If the company's matching policy is three-way matching for all vendors, and the controller decided to exclude the service vendors from this policy and apply two-way matching on these services vendors, then the controller could exclude the trusted vendors from the matching policy at all. The exception could be done on the invoice total level, or miscellaneous charge code level.

- The third layer is vendor invoice policies where configuring a precise combination on a purchase order header or purchase order line has to be approved before posting. This can be applied for risky purchases where the purchase amount exceeds a certain amount.

The following diagram illustrates the vendor invoice matching layers in Microsoft Dynamics AX 2012 R3:

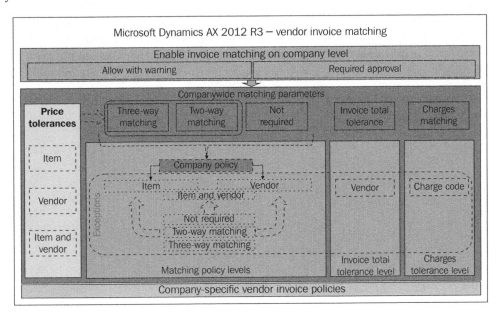

[In order to activate the invoice matching validation on Microsoft Dynamics AX 2012 R3, navigate to **Accounts Payable** | **Setup** | **Accounts payable parameters** | **Invoice validation**.]

As shown in the following screenshot of the Accounts payable parameters, mark the **Enable invoice matching validation** checkbox and set the procedure that will be applied if there are matching discrepancies, that is, whether it should be **Allow with warning** or **Require approval**. The first option allows posting a transaction with a matching discrepancy, and the second option prevents from posting an invoice transaction with a matching discrepancy.

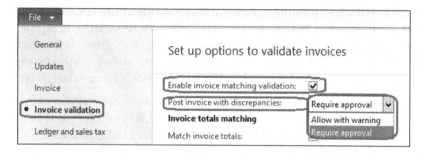

In the **Price and quantity matching** field group, set whether or not the company-wide matching policy is required, and if it is, whether it is two-way matching or three-way matching. Identify the matching policy override, that is, whether it is **Higher than company policy** or **Lower than company policy**. Set the **Display unit price match icon** field as **If greater than tolerance** or **If greater than or less than company policy**. Set the **Match price totals** field as **None, Percentage, Amount**, or **Percentage and price**.

This is a company-wide configuration on a legal-entity level. This can be overridden by the matching policy.

The following screenshot shows the **Price and quantity matching** field group:

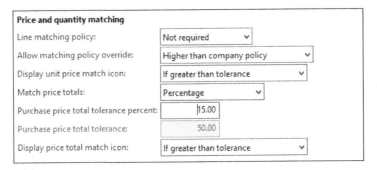

Price tolerance

The path to access the price tolerance is shown in the following screenshot; go to
Accounts Payable | Setup | Invoice matching | Price tolerances.

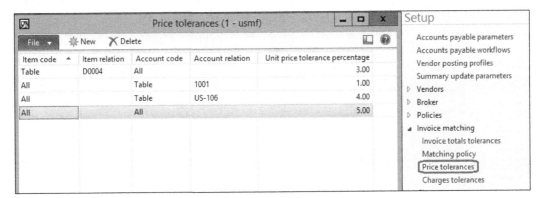

In the **Price tolerances** form, set the acceptable unit price tolerance percentage; this
indicates the relation between the vendor and supplied items. It is flexible because
we can set a different price tolerance for each vendor or each item. Otherwise, it can
be set to a combination of vendors and items. Remember that **Group** dominates over
All, and **Table** dominates over **Group** and **All**.

In order to configure the exceptions on the matching-policy level, that is, whether it is on vendors, items, or a combination of a vendor and an item, navigate to **Accounts Payable | Setup | Invoice matching | Matching policy**. As shown in the following screenshot of **Matching policy**, this illustrates the company-wide configuration of the line matching policy. In the **Matching policy level** combobox, select **Vendor, Item**, or **Item and vendor**. Assign the line matching policy for each vendor, item, or item and vendor, where we will be able to keep the default company-wide parameters as **Company policy**. Otherwise, assign a different matching policy according to organization needs (whether it should be two-way matching, three-way matching, or not required at all).

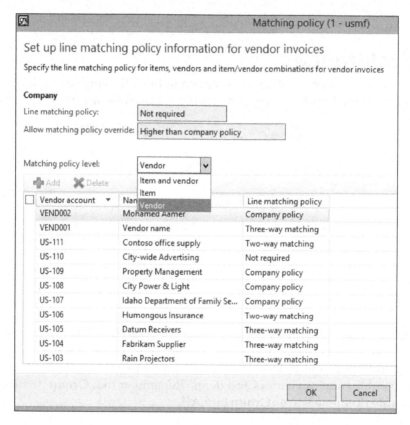

The following screenshot displays the execution of a purchase order invoice with difference in price and quantity with three-way matching that has a line matching policy assigned.

There is a prerequisite for this scenario; create a purchase order by navigating to **Accounts Payable | Common | Purchase order | All purchase orders**. Now, create a new order and select vendor ID.

Create a purchase line and then add the required fields: item ID, site, warehouse, quantity 1, and price, which in this case is 1000 USD. Then, post the product receipt by navigating to **Receive | Product Receipt**; enter the product receipt number and click on **OK**. As shown in the following screenshot, which shows the purchase order's **Line** fast tab, expand **Line details | Setup | Matching policy**:

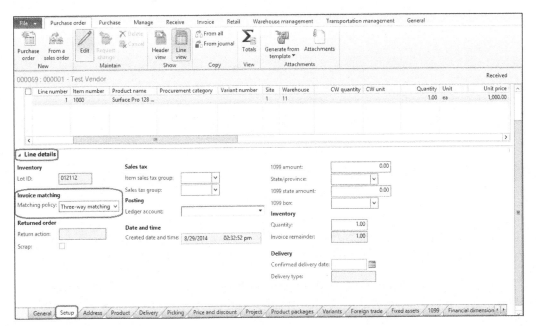

 Matching policy automatically inherits from a configured matching policy and can be changed on the purchase order line. It works in one direction from lowest to highest if the change is from the not required matching policy to two-way or three-way matching policy, but not vice versa.

Go to the **Invoice** ribbon and enter the invoice number assuming that the invoice has a difference in price, which is 1050.01 USD; the price tolerance is 5 percent, which means 1050.00 USD, so the invoice price is greater than the acceptable tolerance by 0.01 USD. Also, quantity difference from the product receipt is by 2 pieces. The following screenshot shows the purchase order invoice with matching variance with quantity and price. In order to check the details of variance, go to the **Review** ribbon and select **Matching details**.

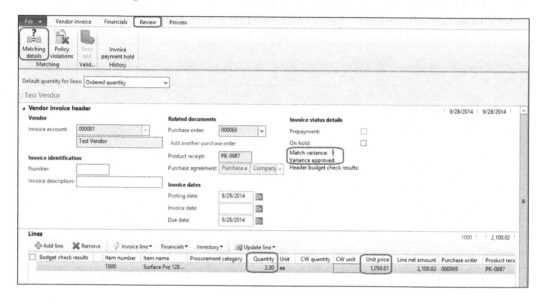

The preceding screenshot depicts the invoice matching details form. The header shows the exclamation mark, which indicates that there are differences in quantity and price.

In the details level, the comparison between the purchase order and invoice prices is shown. This is in addition to the comparison between the product receipt quantity and vendor invoice quantity.

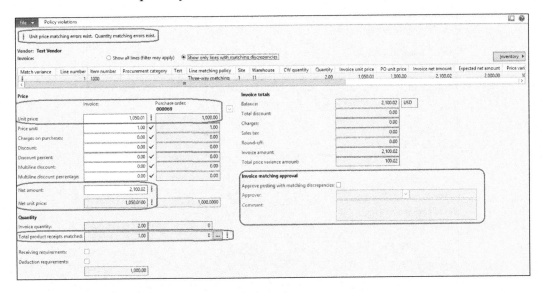

The invoice control can be extended to check the total purchase order amount, in addition to the total invoice amount.

In the following example, the total purchase order amount of a purchase order has two-way matching, where we compare the purchase order invoice price against the purchase order price. The purchase order price is 1000 USD and the purchase order invoice price is also 1000 USD. During the matching process, the user adds an additional piece of data (for example, change quantity to be 2) and the purchase price is with the acceptable tolerance, so the purchase order total amount is 2000 USD. The configured acceptable tolerance for the purchase price total is 15 percent, which means 1150 USD.

The invoice matching form indicates **Unmatched purchase order total**, as shown in the following screenshot:

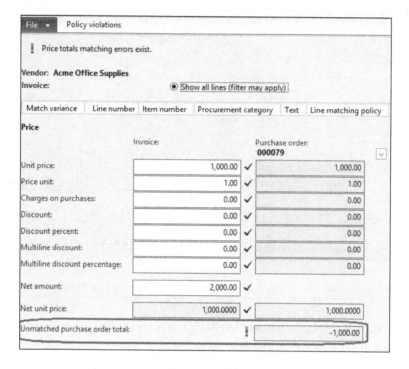

In the preceding example, assume that the invoice quantities are equal to the purchase order quantity, but we're adding additional service items on the vendor invoice by 100.01 USD. The invoice matching form indicates the **Invoice amount** discrepancy, as shown in the following screenshot:

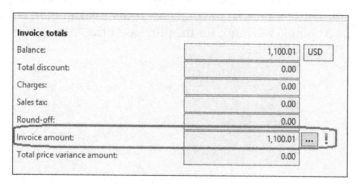

In the following screenshot, the **Invoice totals** matching details is illustrated, showing the invoice total tolerance percentage, actual invoice total, expected invoice totals, and variance percentage:

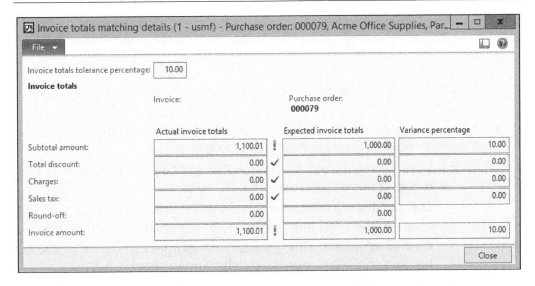

In the preceding example, assume that the purchase order line has assigned charges with 100 USD, and the invoice quantities are equal to purchase order quantity, but the purchase order invoice lines charges have been modified to 125.01 USD and the acceptable charges tolerance is 25 percent.

The selected charges should be added to the vendor invoice, which only has **Customer/ Vendor** on the credit side. In order to create a charges code, navigate to **Accounts Payable | Setup | Charges | Charges code**. As shown in the following screenshot, the charges form illustrates the setup for the charges, and it is important to let Microsoft Dynamics AX consider the charges during the invoice-matching process; for this, the **Compare purchase order and invoice value** checkbox must be checked:

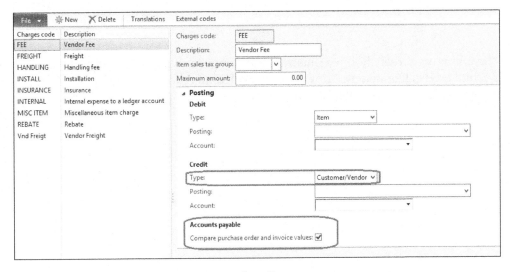

In the preceding screenshot:

- **Debit**: This represents the debit side, which will be affected by the added charges.
- **Credit**: This represents the credit side, which will be affected by the added charges.
- **Type**: This represents the different types, which are **Item**, **Ledger**, and/or **Customer/vendor**. They are explained as follows:
    - ° **Item**: This represents the charges that will be posted on the item; this is only applicable for the debit side
    - ° **Ledger**: This represents the charges that will be posted on a particular ledger account and must have a posting type and account number
    - ° **Customer/Vendor**: This represents the charges that will be posted on the customer/vendor on the purchase order or sales order

As shown in the following screenshot, the invoice matching form indicates a discrepancy in the compared charge:

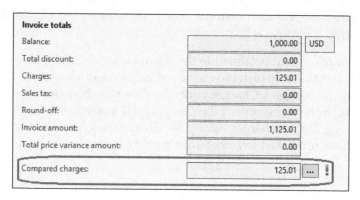

In the following screenshot, we illustrate the compare charges values, and show the actual total calculated amount, expected calculated amount, variance amount, variance percentage, and tolerance percentage:

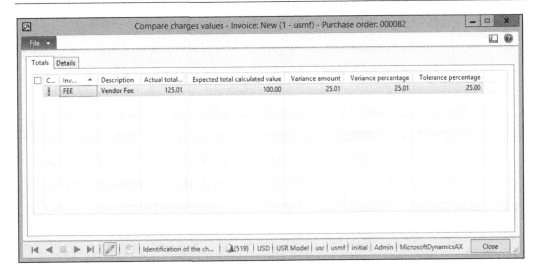

The invoice number

The invoice document represents the vendor invoice recording in company accounts (liability). The invoice has a reference number (invoice number) based on the vendor serial number and the accounts payable accountant records the invoice number, which can be used in the reconciliation process with the vendor; it is used in the payment process as well. In Microsoft Dynamics AX 2012 R3, the invoice number is a mandatory field and can be controlled to be a unique value. This uniqueness is considered per vendor and can be within the fiscal year. In order to access the invoice number control, navigate to **Accounts Payable | Setup | Accounts payable parameters | Invoice** and go to the **Check the invoice number used** section.

The following screenshot illustrates the available options of the invoice number control:

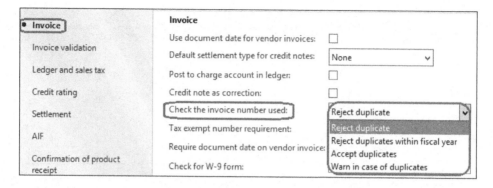

The **Check the invoice number used** field has the following options:

- **Reject duplicate**: This option will forbid using the same invoice number from the same vendor. For example, if vendor A has the invoice number INV-001, this value cannot be used with the same vendor, but can be used with vendor B.

- **Reject duplicates within fiscal year**: This is the same as the previous option, in addition to the validation that will be executed during the fiscal year.

- **Accept duplicates**: This option accepts duplicates.

- **Warn in case of duplicates**: This option gives a warning message if the value has been used before.

The Posting profile

The posting profile represents the integration point between the general ledger and subledger, and it generates the financial entries automatically according to the posting profile's setup. The Accounts payable posting profiles are assigned to the module parameters; navigate to **Accounts Payable | Setup | Accounts payable parameters | Ledger and sales tax**, and go through the following process:

- In the **Posting** fast tab, assign the posting profile for general accounts payable transactions; in other words, this represents the accounts payable account

- In the **Prepayment journal voucher** fast tab, assign the posting profile for advance payment transactions; in other words, this represents the advances from the vendor account

- In the **Prepayment** fast tab, assign the posting profile for prepayment invoices

These options can be seen in the following screenshot:

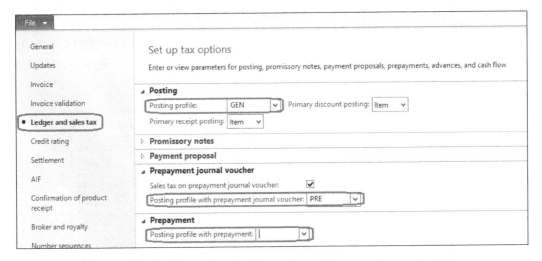

Exploring accounts payable transactions

This section will explore the transactions of the Accounts payable module; transactions are divided into two main categories, invoicing and payment:

- **Invoicing**: This is divided into purchase-order-related invoices and nonpurchase-order-related invoices:

    ○ **The purchase-order-related invoices**: These invoices represent the invoices that are normally attached to a purchase order(s). Invoices related to a purchase order can be the final invoice of the purchase order, which is received after delivering the goods, or the prepayment invoice, which is recorded before delivering the goods. The attached prepayment invoice to a particular purchase order is a new functionality released in Microsoft Dynamics AX 2012.

    ○ **The nonpurchase-order-related invoices**: These invoices represent the vendor liabilities for services rendered to the company; there are two types of recording service invoices. The first is noninventory invoices, which are related to nonstockable items and are commonly used by the company departments to record their expenses. The other type is the invoice journal for services, which is posted directly to the expense account; it is commonly used by accountants.

- **Payment**: The second category is the vendor payment. There are two types. The first is a prepayment transaction, which is considered as vendor advances. This can be assigned to a particular purchase order, or need not be assigned to a purchase order. The second type is the vendor payment, which is settled against the vendor invoice.

The categories are summed up in the following diagram:

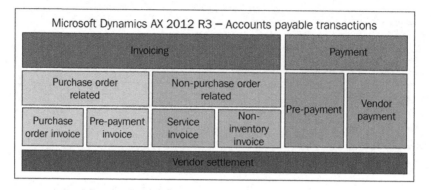

The purchase order invoice

The purchase order invoice document can be posted from two different forms; the first form is the purchase order form, and the second form is the vendor open invoices.

Open the vendor invoices form. This is a new function in Microsoft Dynamics AX 2012. This form is used also for nonpurchase order invoices.

In order to post a purchase order invoice from the purchase order form, navigate to **Accounts Payable** | **Common** | **Purchase orders** | **All purchase orders** after choosing the required purchase order, then go to the **Invoice** ribbon and navigate to **Generate** | **Invoice**. The following screenshot illustrates the **Purchase order invoice** menu:

In the vendor invoice form, the purchase order and product receipts are retrieved automatically; then, enter the invoice number and description. Click on **Post** to generate the invoice transaction. The following screenshot shows the vendor invoice form:

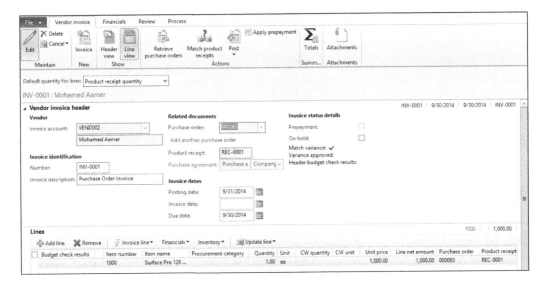

 The vendor invoice form is the nonpurchase order invoice when accessed from **Accounts Payable** | **Common** | **Vendor invoices** | **Open vendor invoices**. Also, it is a shared form.

The relation between the vendor invoice, product receipt, and purchase order is that the purchase order has more than one product receipt and the invoice can cover one purchase order with more than one product receipt. In some business cases, the vendor invoices cover receptions that occur on more than one purchase order.

The following diagram illustrates the relation between the purchase order, product receipt, and invoice:

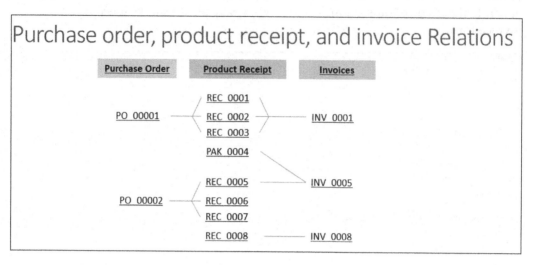

This business scenario can be managed on Microsoft Dynamics AX 2012 R3 in several ways. The following section illustrates the most common functionalities to post an invoice that covers more than one product receipt or purchase order.

Navigate to **Account Payable | Periodic | Maintain vendor invoices** on the vendor invoice form under the **Vendor invoice** ribbon; there are two options there, whether to retrieve the product receipts or the purchase order, as shown in the following screenshot:

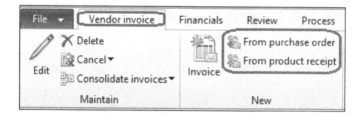

The first option, **From purchase order**, opens the filtration query, as shown in the following screenshot. The user can retrieve information based on values on the query; this can be a product receipt, vendor ID, and so on.

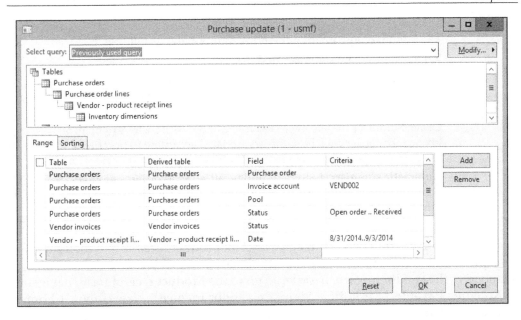

As shown in the following screenshot, two lines have been retrieved according to the entered query, that is, two purchase orders with two different product receipts. This represents two different invoices for each line.

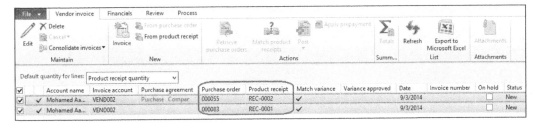

In order to consolidate the two invoices in one invoice document, go to the **Maintain** ribbon and select **Consolidate invoice**. Now, select **Consolidate invoices**. The following screenshot illustrates the consolidate option:

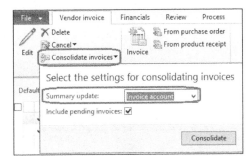

The **Summary update** dropdown has four options, as follows:

None: There are no summary updates.

Invoice account: Summary update all selected orders according to the criteria set in the **Accounts payable parameters** or **Summary update parameters** form.

Order: Summary update a selected range of orders into, for example, one invoice. The orders will be summary updated according to the criteria set in the **Accounts payable parameters** or **Summary update parameters** form.

Automatic summary: Summary update all selected orders automatically according to the criteria set in the **Accounts payable parameters** or **Summary update parameters** form.

The second option, **From product receipt**, lists all product receipts and their lines. As represented in the following screenshot, the marked product receipts will be included in the vendor invoice. In order to go to the **Product receipt** form, navigate to **Accounts Payable | Periodic | Maintain vendor invoice | New ribbon | From product receipt**.

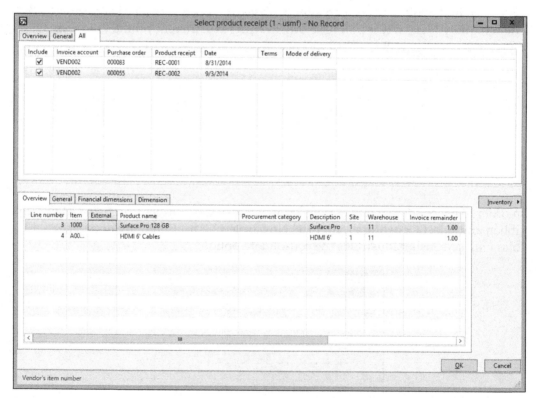

There is another functionality that can be used to post one vendor invoice for multiple purchase orders or product receipts. Navigate to **Accounts Payable | Common | Vendor Invoices | Open vendor invoices**, create a new record, and enter the invoice number and description. Then, go to **Retrieve purchase orders** under the ribbon.

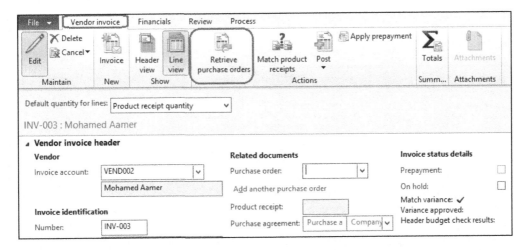

As shown in the following screenshot, a list of purchase orders with their product receipts is shown in this form. The user can mark which product receipts will be included in the invoice.

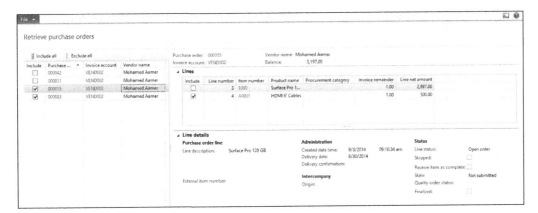

 This invoice is already consolidated into one invoice.

The following screenshot shows that the invoice-related documents are multiple and are on the lines of the relation between the purchase order and product receipt:

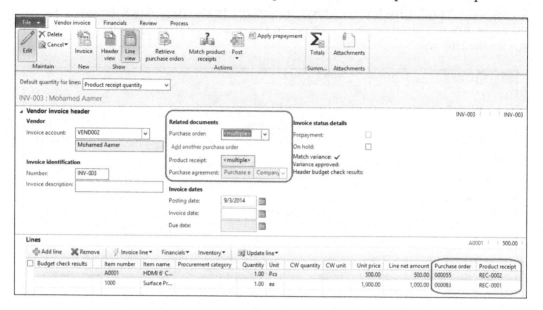

In order to inquire about the vendor balance, navigate to **Accounts Payable | Common | Vendors | All Vendors** and click on the **Balance** ribbon. As shown in the following screenshot, the balance form shows the current vendor balance:

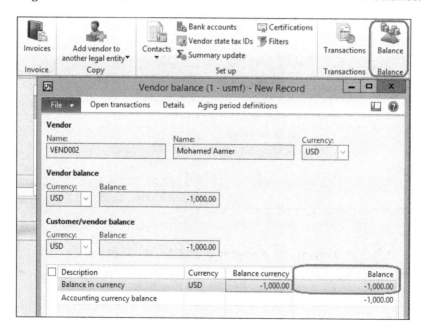

The purchase order invoice automatically generates the liability financial entry based on the vendor posting and inventory posting profiles. The inventory posting profile must be carefully structured during the design phase where the controller should understand the mechanism of invoice posting well.

The generated invoice entry is divided into four lines; two entries represent the produce receipt entry reversal, and the other two entries represent the vendor liability entry:

- The financial entry of a product receipt is enhanced in Microsoft Dynamics AX 2012 R3 to be a two-liner entry as follows:
    - ° Dr. Product receipt account
    - ° Cr. Vendor accrual account

- The other two entries represent the vendor liability as follows:
    - ° Dr. Vendor accrual account
    - ° Cr. Product receipt account
    - ° Dr. Purchase inventory receipt
    - ° Cr. Vendor balance

 The inventory posting profile access path is **Inventory Management | Setup | Posting | Posting | Purchase order**.

The prepayment invoice

The prepayment invoice function is not covered in the previous versions of Microsoft Dynamics AX. The vendor prepayment function gives a company's controller the ability to minimize the risk by applying the segregation of duties between company departments and control prepayment process, where accounts payable does not perform the prepayment transaction without assigning the prepayment linked to the purchase order and harmonizing the business process between procurement and accounts payable. Assume that the company has agreed with a vendor to supply goods to the company and the vendor has a condition to receive a prepayment before executing the goods delivery, and this is a normal practice in the daily business.

The vendor prepayment cycle is executed among the procurement agent, accounts payable, and bank accountants. The following diagram illustrates the business process of the prepayment:

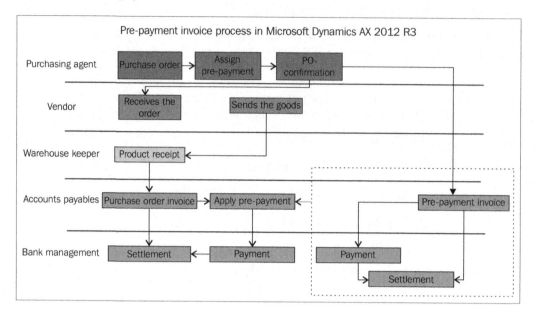

From the preceding diagram, we can see that:

- The procurement agent creates a purchase order
- The procurement agent assigns the prepayment to a purchase order as per the agreement with the vendor; here, the prepayment is a fixed amount or a percentage from the total purchases of the PO
- The procurement agent confirms the purchase order
- The vendor issues a prepayment invoice
- The Accounts payable accountant posts the prepayment invoice, and the prepayment invoice amount is inherited from the previous prepayment assignment
- Bank accountants have open invoices that need to be paid and settled against the payment
- After the warehouse keeper receives the goods in the warehouse, the vendor sends the final invoice
- The accounts payable accountant applies the prepayment to the final invoice and posts the PO invoice. If the AP accountant does not apply the prepayment invoice to the PO invoice, they can apply it later on

- The bank accountant opens the invoice with a vendor residual balance that needs to be paid and settled against the payment

In order to assign a prepayment invoice on a created purchase order, navigate to **Accounts Payable | Common | Purchase orders | All purchase orders**. Navigate to **Purchase | Prepayment**, as shown in the following screenshot:

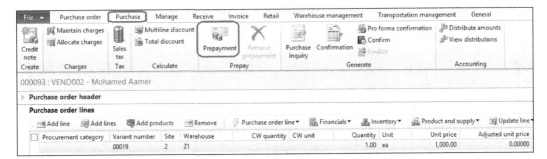

The prepayment form will pop up as shown in the following screenshot; enter the prepayment description, select whether the prepayment will be **Fixed** or **Percentage** from the purchase cost, and select the procurement category:

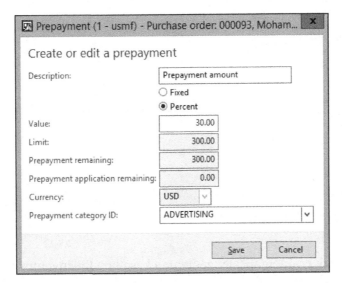

 The purchase order must be confirmed in order to generate the prepayment.

As shown in the following screenshot, navigate to **Invoice** and select **Prepayment invoice** in the purchase order form:

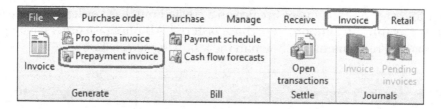

 The prepayment account must be selected in the inventory posting profile under the **Purchase order** tab.

Navigate to **Inventory and Management | Setup | Posting | Purchase order**.

Then, post the prepayment invoice from the vendor invoice form, as shown in the following screenshot, and enter the invoice number and description:

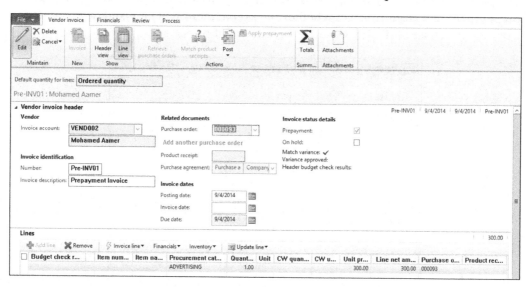

The financial entry is automatically generated based on the inventory posting profile as follows:

- Dr. Prepayment

- Cr. Vendor balance

At this point, there is a liability on this particular vendor with the prepayment amount, and this liability appears in the open transactions, which are not settled yet. This form is **Settle open transactions**; in order to access this form, navigate to **Accounts Payable | Common | Vendors | All vendors**, select a particular vendor, then go to the **Invoice** ribbon and select **Settle open transactions**, as shown in the following screenshot:

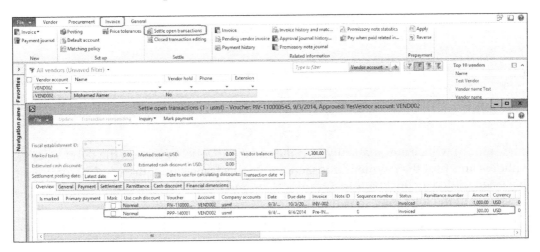

The prepayment invoice is ready to be paid; in order to perform a vendor payment transaction, navigate to **Accounts Payable | Journals | Payments | Payment journals**, create a new journal number, and then go to **Lines**. Select the vendor code and then go to **Functions | Settlement**. The following screenshot illustrates the journal and its line along with the settlement access path:

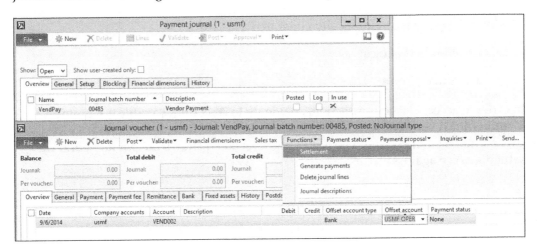

As shown in the following screenshot, in the **Settle open transactions** form, mark the invoice that will be paid and close the form:

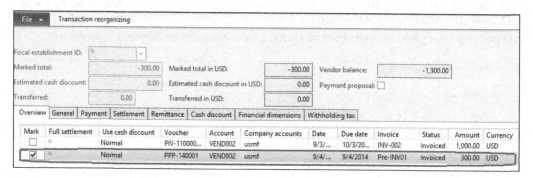

The amount will be automatically populated on the voucher line on the debit side; validate and post the payment transactions. In this transaction, the vendor invoice has been settled against payment transactions and moved to closed transactions, as shown in the following screenshot:

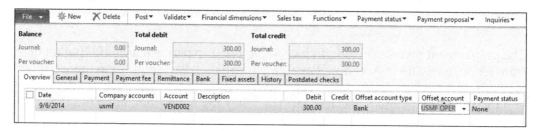

The financial entry is automatically generated as follows:

- Dr. Vendor balance

- Cr. Bank account

In order to access closed transactions, navigate to **Accounts Payable | Common | Vendors | All vendors**; select a particular vendor and then navigate to **Invoice | Closed transaction editing**. The following screenshot shows the payment and the settled invoice against it:

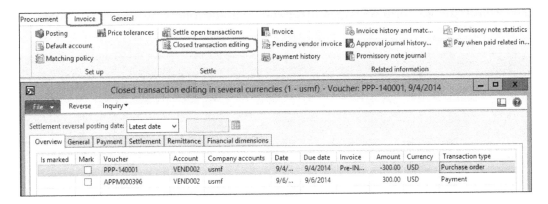

> The settled transactions can be reversed from the closed transactions editing form.

Then, post the purchase order invoice and consider the prepayment amount by applying the prepayment on the final vendor invoice in order to get the realistic vendor liability; there are two scenarios here: apply the prepayment before a post-purchase order invoice or after posting the vendor invoice.

> The prepayment has a transaction type as payment.

The following screenshot illustrates the prepayment application process before posting the purchase order invoice; navigate to **Accounts Payable | Common | Purchase Orders | All purchase orders**, select the purchase order that needs to be invoiced, go to the **Invoice** ribbon, and select **Invoice**:

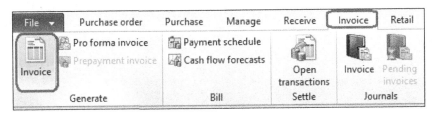

The vendor invoice form will open up as shown in the following screenshot; enter the invoice number and invoice description. To do this, go to **Apply prepayment**.

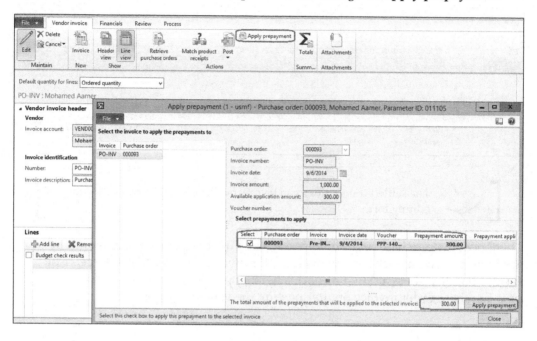

The applied prepayment amount appears in the invoice line with a negative sign; this will lead to the net invoice amount (*total invoice amount - prepayment amount*). As shown in the following screenshot, the total invoice (1000) minus the prepayment amount (300) equals 700, so the net invoice amount is 700:

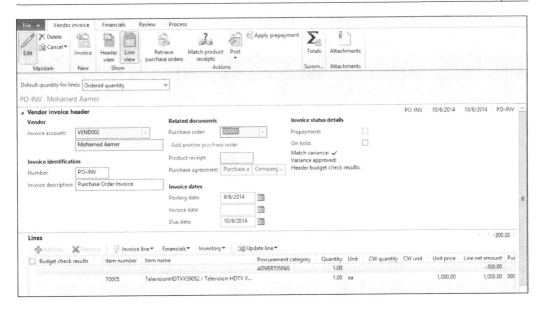

The invoice financial entry for a purchase order invoice that has a prepayment applied is generated; the entry consists of four lines; two lines for the prepayment application and the other two lines for the liability entry, as follows:

- Dr. Vendor balance (the prepayment amount)

- Cr. Prepayment (the prepayment amount)

- Dr. Purchase inventory receipt (the total purchase order amount)

- Cr. Vendor balance (the total purchase order amount)

The nonpurchase order invoices can be service invoices recorded by the accounting team recording the invoice through **Invoice Journal**, or the invoices recorded by the concerned departments, where each department will record their expenses invoices through the new vendor invoice form that has been newly introduced in Microsoft Dynamics AX 2012.

The invoice journal is accessed by navigating to **Accounts Payable | Journals | Invoices | Invoice journal**, as shown in the following screenshot. We can see the invoice journal lines; select the vendor ID and enter the invoice number, the amount in the credit side, and the ledger offset account. The posted **Invoice journal** generates a vendor liability and ledger entry as well.

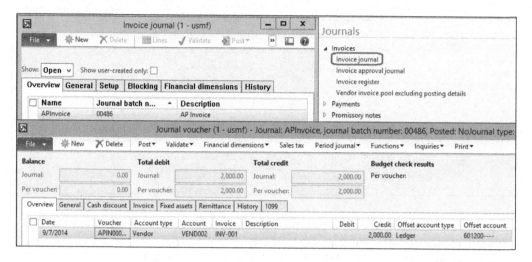

 The invoice journal can go through a process of recording through **Invoice register** and then **Invoice approval journal**.

The noninventory invoices are mainly used with nonstocked items, where each service item is represented as a specific expense type. This concept is more familiar for departments rather than selecting ledger accounts, as the concerned department that entered the expense invoice does not have experience in accounting, and descriptive expense service items are more familiar with data entry.

In order to access the **Open vendor invoice** form, navigate to **Accounts Payable |
Vendor invoices | Open vendor invoices**.

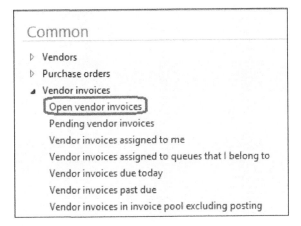

In order to create a new invoice record, navigate to the **Invoice** ribbon and select
Vendor invoice, as shown in the following screenshot:

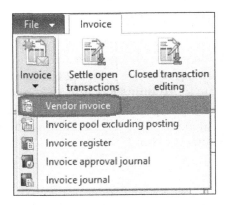

In the vendor invoice form, select the vendor ID and enter the invoice number, description, item number, and then the amount, as shown in the following screenshot:

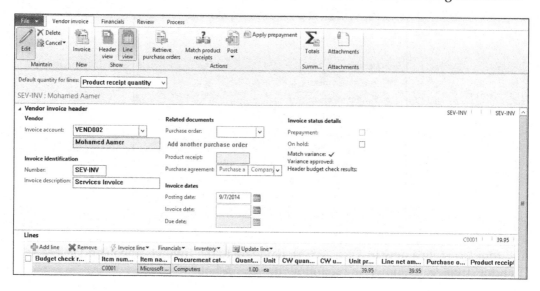

An advance payment is a regular business scenario where vendors are required to pay some amount of money as a down payment regardless of whether there is a purchase order; this might occur with a partner with whom they have regular business. In order to perform an advance payment transaction on Microsoft Dynamics AX 2012, navigate to **Accounts Payable** | **Common** | **Payments** | **Payment journal** and create a new journal; then move to **Lines**, enter the vendor ID, and enter the amount, then switch to the **Payment** tab and check the **Mark prepayment journal voucher** checkbox.

After this, the default posting profile value to the prepayment posting profile will be changed, as shown in the following screenshot:

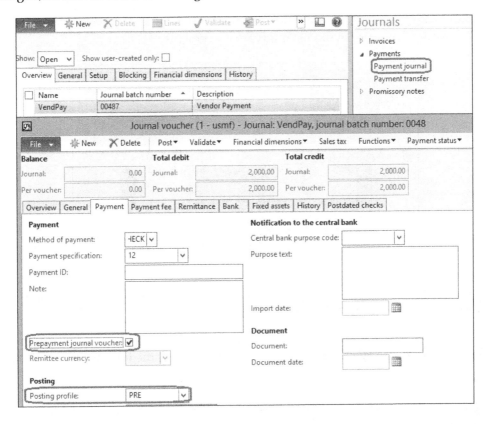

The prepayment posting profile is created under **Accounts payable posting profile**. Under **Accounts payable parameters | Ledger and sales tax**, assign the prepayment posting profile.

Vendor settlement

A settlement is an accounting transaction that occurs on accounts payable, accounts receivables, and general ledger. This transaction is used mainly to settle vendor invoices against vendor payments or advance payments.

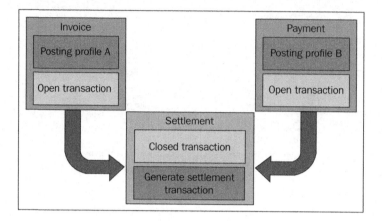

It is necessary to classify posting profiles of the vendor and customer in the opening balance as it will affect the settlement process.

The settlement transaction affects vendor and customer balances, and it is reported in the vendor or customer statement report that identifies the following:

- The vendor
- The open (unsettled) invoice and payments
- The closed (settled) invoice and payments
- The vendor balance

A settlement transaction can occur during a payment or collection transaction if the accountant marks the invoice that will be paid or collected. On the other hand, the settlement can be performed at the vendor or customer level, and these transactions can be unsettled.

The settlement transaction should take into consideration the currency as it can be performed in the company's home currency by an equivalent amount, which is calculated based on the currency exchange rate, or it can be settled in the same currency of the invoice by identifying the currency in the payment process.

The vendor settlement mechanism in Microsoft Dynamics AX

A vendor settlement in Microsoft Dynamics AX is a transaction that occurs to settle vendor advance payments against vendor invoices on a monthly basis.

Vendor settlements have the following effects:

- The first one is at the vendor level, which occurs when the vendor transaction closes
- The second is the financial entry, which occurs only if the posting profile of the advance payment and invoice are different

Here, I will illustrate the mechanism of vendor advance payment, invoices, and vendor settlement financial entries:

- The vendor advance payment posting profile is advanced, and the financial entry will be:
    ◦ Dr. Advances to vendor 1200 EGP
    ◦ Cr. Bank 1200 EGP
    ◦ Open transactions: 1200 EGP advance payment

- The vendor invoice posting profile is **General**, and the financial entry is:
    ◦ Dr. Expense 1000 EGP
    ◦ Cr. Payables 1000 EGP
    ◦ Open transactions: 1200 EGP advance payment and 1000 EGP vendor invoice

- The vendor settlement is as follows:
    ◦ Dr. Payables 1000 EGP
    ◦ Cr. Advances to vendor 1000 EGP
    ◦ Open transactions: 200 EGP advance payment
    ◦ Closed transactions: 1000 EGP advance payment and 1000 EGP vendor invoice

If the posting profiles of the advance payment and invoicing are different, a settlement financial entry will be created.

Summary

This chapter covered the Accounts payable module in Microsoft Dynamics AX 2012 R3, its integration with other modules, procurement, and inventory, and then looked into exploring the vendor master data and the characteristics that affect vendor transactions. We also learned about the controls for invoice matching, three-way matching for products and two-way matching for services, putting vendors on hold, and invoice numbering. Then, we moved on to exploring the accounts payable transactions vendor invoice, the prepayment invoice and its processing, advance payments, and the settlement mechanism.

In the next chapter, we will discuss accounts receivable master data, control, and transactions.

5
Understanding Accounts Receivable

The Accounts receivable module is the module that represents a customer's data and their transactions. The Accounts receivable cycles are customer invoicing, customer payment, and settlement. These business processes manage and control the execution of customer sales processes. These processes are based on sales activities and product delivery cycles in the sales and marketing processes, which manage and control the execution of the Order to cash business processes.

In this chapter, we will cover the following topics:

- Understanding the Accounts receivable module's integration with other modules
- Exploring customer master data characteristics
- Exploring Accounts receivable controls
- Exploring Accounts receivable transactions

Understanding the Accounts receivable module's integration with other modules

The Accounts receivable module manages and controls customer transactions from the accounting point of view, where recording customer master information and the basic transactions related to customer invoicing, payment, and settlement happen. The Accounts receivable function is integrated with other business functions.

The integration points with Accounts receivable are as follows:

- **Sales and marketing module**: This is where goods and services are quoted to the customer, and then the sales order is created

- **Inventory and warehousing module**: This is where goods are delivered to customers, and invoicing is based on the delivered goods from the warehousing module

- **Cash and bank management**: This is where customer payment and settlement against invoices are done

The full life cycle of the **Order to Cash** is shown in the following diagram:

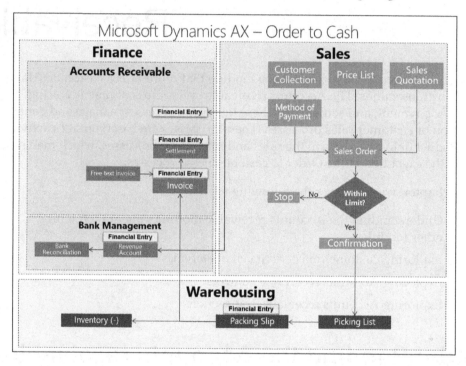

The normal practice of enterprise organizations is that no sales orders are created directly. This can lead to creating unnecessary sales orders and exposing the company to uncontrolled open orders. This business process must be controlled since it is the source point of company revenues. On the other hand, the unnecessary sales order can significantly impact the cost of goods sold and customer balances, in addition to the company's profitability.

The selling process typically goes through specific internal procedures to deliver items or services from the sales department. The sales process begins either by automatic orders of sales based on a sales quotation for a specific customer, or by entering the sales order manually.

> The **Sales Quotation** is a document representing the company's offer to the customer, and indicates the item or service, price, receipt date, and other information. The quotation is sent to the customer to evaluate the company's offer. The customer then replies to the sales agent by either confirmation or rejection. The confirmed sales quotation is a document that is ready to be converted to a sales order document.

The following are the **Sales Quotation** statuses:

- **Created**: The sales quotation has been created, but has not been sent to the customer. The sales quotation can be modified if its status is **Created**.

- **Sent**: The sales quotation status is updated once the sales quotation document is sent to the customer.

- **Confirmed**: This status shows when the sales quotation has been confirmed by the customer.

- **Lost**: This status will be displayed once the sales quotation has been refused by the customer.

- **Canceled**: This status will be displayed once the sales quotation and all sales quotation lines have been canceled.

The sales order has several types in Microsoft Dynamics AX 2012 R3. They are listed as follows:

- **Sales order**: This is a commitment document sent to a customer to deliver the required goods or services to them.

- **Journal**: This is a draft document that does not accept any further transactions nor affects inventory or finance.

- **Subscription**: This is a recurring sales order to supply the same item, quantity, and price. The system recreates the sales order after invoicing.

- **Returned order**: This document represents the **Returned Material Authorization (RMA)** and handles quantity returns and the customer credit note.

- **Item requirements**: This is a type of the sales order, which relates the sales order to project requirements.

- **Sales agreement**: A sales agreement is a document that is sent to a customer to deliver goods or services over a specific time period and includes prices. This is a new function introduced in Microsoft Dynamics AX 2012 R3 and it replaces Blanket Order in AX 2009.

The following are the types of sales order statuses:

- **Open Order**: This indicates that the sales order is at one of the following stages: newly created, not totally received, or not totally invoiced

- **Delivered**: This indicates that the sales order is fully delivered

- **Invoiced**: This indicates that the sales order is fully invoiced

- **Canceled**: This indicates that the ordered quantities in the sales order have been canceled

The following are the types of sales order document statuses:

- **None**: This indicates that the sales order is created and no further documents have been posted

- **Confirmation**: This indicates that the sales order has been confirmed

- **Picking list**: This indicates that the picking list document has been posted on the sales order

- **Packing slip**: This indicates that the packing slip document has been posted on the sales order

- **Invoice**: This indicates that the sales order invoice has been posted

The delivery of goods from the company warehouse occurs by the following two steps:

- The preliminary step is the picking list that assigns inventory dimensions such as serial number and batch number, in addition to the quality inspection if required. The preliminary step of the picking list does not affect the on-hand inventory. The packing slip transaction decreases the physical quantities in the on-hand inventory.

- The final step in a sales order is posting the invoice that represents the revenue recognition of the sales order, or in other words, the **cost of goods sold (COGS)**.

The packing slip document does not reflect any transactions on the customer balance.

The customer payment is the document that represents that the company is receiving an amount of money from the customer who receives goods or services from the company. The customer payment process is executed based on the customer invoices. The normal practice in enterprise organizations is that the customer collection will have two different scenarios: collection after issuing the sales order invoice, or advanced collection before creating a sales order.

The advanced collection can be assigned to a specific sales order. Each collection transaction is settled against a customer invoice. This affects the company's cash position and cash projection of future customer collection. The customer pays the amount of money after issuing the sales invoice. Then the Accounts receivable accountant records the collection transactions and settles them against an invoice. The invoice could be settled automatically if the advanced collection is linked to a sales order.

The bank accountant executes the check collection process and bank reconciliation accordingly, as shown in the following diagram, which illustrates the customer collection, invoice, and settlement document integration:

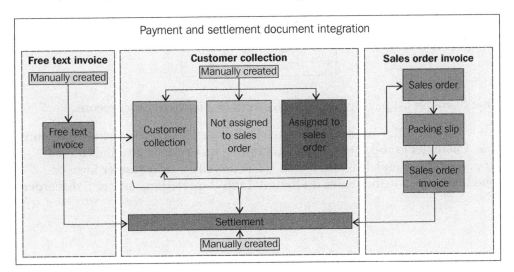

Each transaction is represented in a document type in Microsoft Dynamics AX, with the document containing the details of the transaction. The transactions data, whether inherited from the master data, entered manually, and/or automatically inherited from another transaction, is linked with a specific reference. The integration between the collection and other customer transaction documents gives us visibility to trace what the original sales order and packing slip that are related to the invoice are, together with who confirms the sales order.

Exploring customer master data characteristics

The customer record has essential information that directly affects Accounts receivable transactions. In the following section, we will cover the basic information that should be considered when creating a new customer record.

In order to create a new customer record, you should navigate to **Accounts Receivable | Common | Customers | All customers**, as shown in this screenshot:

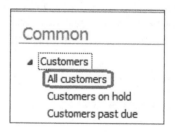

On the customer list page, press *Ctrl + N* to create a new customer record.

As shown in the following screenshot, the mandatory fields are **Customer account**, **Name**, **Customer group**, and **Country/region**. You can either save the entered information and complete it afterwards, or go directly to a **Customer** form or transaction form, whether **Sales quotation**, **Project quotation**, and/or **Sales order**.

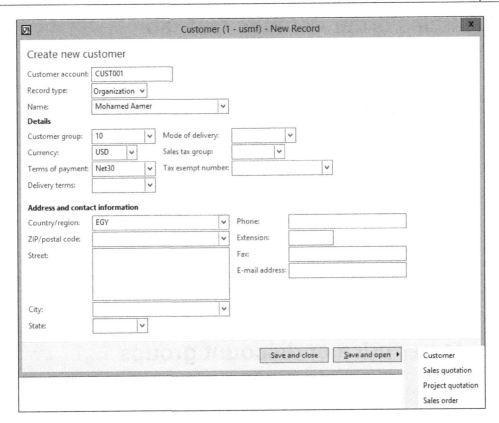

We can see the following in the preceding screenshot:

- The **Customer account**, whether assigned manually or automatically through the number sequence.

- **Group** is a mandatory field that represents the customer group that the particular customer belongs to, and this is considered as the integration point between Accounts receivable and the general ledger through the posting profile. However, the posting profile could be on the level of the customer code.

- **Country/region** represents the country that this customer belongs to.

- The **Currency** field is mandatory, and it represents the default currency for the particular customer transaction. However, it could be changed on the transaction level as per the business case.

Click on **Save and open**, and then select **Customer**. This will open the customer master data form.

The Sales order defaults fast tab

In the customer creation form, go to the **Sales order defaults** fast tab. In this section, we will explore the **Discount** field group.

The Discount field group

The **Discount** field group represents the discount and pricing options that could be applied on the particular customer. The **Discount** field group consists of the discount and pricing groups to which the customer belongs, as shown in this screenshot:

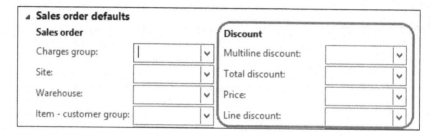

Customer price or discount groups

The customer price and discount groups consist of four pricing groups, as shown in the following diagram:

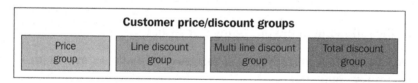

In order to create the customer price or discount groups, the user shall navigate to **Inventory management | Setup | Price/discount | Customer price/discount groups**, as shown in this screenshot:

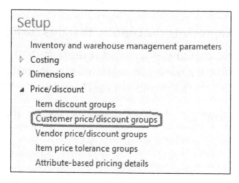

The **Customer price/discount groups** form shows the **Price/discount** options, and should be able to create groups for each **Price/discount** options.

 The price or discount must be activated by navigating to **Sales and marketing** | **Setup** | **Price/discount** | **Activate price/discount**.

The following screenshot shows the definition of the price discount group options:

- **Price group**: This represents the customer's price group used for price proposals upon sales, and this price group is attached to the customer master data.

- **Line discount group**: This represents the sales line discount used for sales, which is attached to the customer master data.

- **Multiline discount group**: This represents the multiline discount group used to control discounts across several sales lines. It is attached to the customer master data.

- **Total discount group**: This represents that the total discount group is attached to the customer master data in a field called total discount group.

In the created **Major accounts** value for **Price group**, navigate to **Trade agreements** | **Create trade agreements**, as shown in the following screenshot:

The **Trade agreements** journal will pop up. Create a new journal by pressing *Ctrl* + *N*, selecting a journal name, and then clicking on **Lines**. As shown in the following screenshot, we will create a journal line (or lines) by selecting under **Relation** the **Price (sales)** value. Then we select the **Account code** field as **Table**. To make this price related to a particular customer, on item relation, select **Table** to make this price correspond to a particular item when sold to a mentioned customer from a specific warehouse.

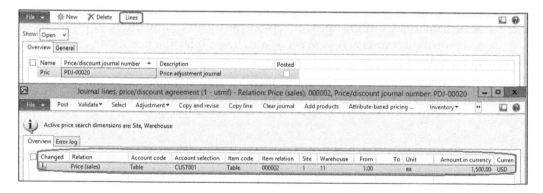

As shown in the next screenshot, the purpose of this setup is to recall the sales price on the sales line automatically from the posted trade agreements journal:

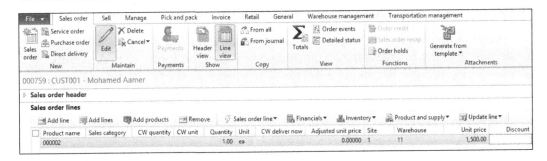

The Payment fast tab

In an opened customer form, move to the **Payment** fast tab, and under the payment field group, there is some required information for customer payment arrangements. The available options are as follows:

- **Terms of payment**
- **Method of payment**
- **Payment specification**
- **Payment schedule**
- **Payment day**
- **Cash discount**

The preceding options are displayed like this:

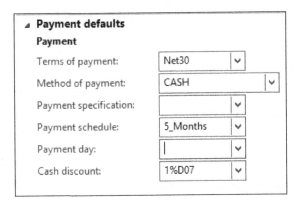

Terms of payment

The **Terms of payment** field represents the calculated due date to pay to the customer. In order to access the terms of payment creation form, go to **Accounts Receivable | Setup | Payments | Terms of payment**, as shown in the following screenshot:

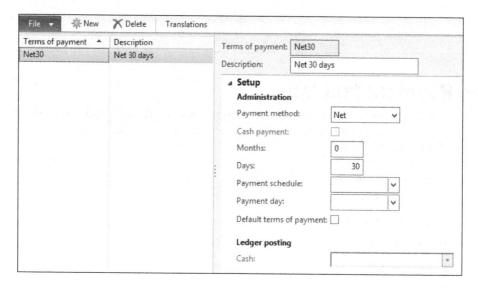

Identify the due date base in the **Payment method** combo box, which contains six options. Assume that the customer invoice is posted on January 1, 2015, and the number of days is **20**, the due date will be changed based on the selected payment method option, as shown in the following diagram:

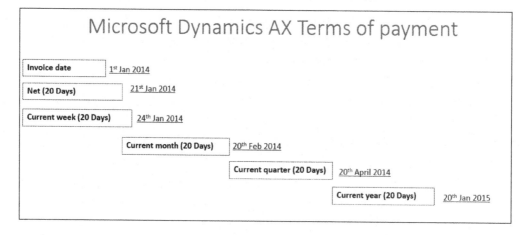

We can see the following in the preceding diagram:

- **Net**: The due date will be calculated from the invoice posting (January 1 + 20 days = **21st Jan**).

- **Current week**: The due date will be calculated from the end of the week in which the invoice was posted (January 4 + 20 days = **24th Jan**).

- **Current month**: The due date will be calculated from the end of the month in which the invoice was posted (January 31 + 20 days = **24th Feb**).

- **Current quarter**: The due date will be calculated from the end of the quarter in which the invoice was posted (March 31 + 20 days = **20th April**).

- **Current year**: The due date will be calculated from the end of the year in which the invoice was posted (December 31 + 20 days = **20th Jan**).

- **Cash on delivery**: This represents the cash payment upon delivery. With this option, a ledger account must be specified, which will be used when posting the sales order invoice.

Method of payment

The method payment represents the way of receiving payment from the customer by check, bank transfer, credit card, or cash. In order to access the **Method of payment** form, navigate to **Accounts Receivable | Setup | Payment | Terms of payment**. As shown in the following screenshot of the method of payment form, the required controls will be applied on the transaction. In this case, the **CASH** method of payment is used.

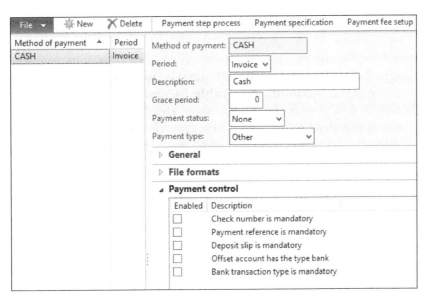

Payment specification

The payment specification represents the codes according to the agreement with the bank that is specified for the selected method of payment. The payment specification is tied with the method of payment.

Payment schedule

The payment schedule represents the installment that will be used after invoicing. To access the **Payment schedule** form, navigate to **Accounts Receivable | Setup | Payment | Payment schedule**. We can identify an installment with a fixed number of months or a fixed amount, as shown in this screenshot:

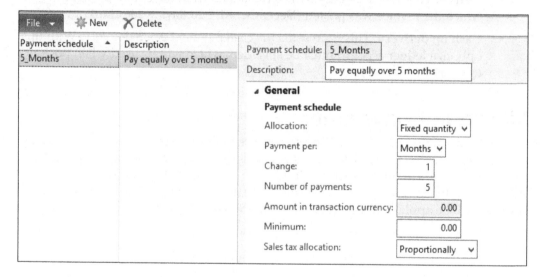

Assume that the sales order invoice is posted on January 1, 2014, its amount is $5,000, and it is assigned a payment schedule for 5 months, with the terms of payment as net 30 days. Navigate to **Accounts Receivable | Common | Sales orders | All sales orders**. Then open a sales order by navigating to **Header view**, and under the **Price discount** fast tab, assign a payment schedule. It can be automatically inherited from the customer master data and can be modified on the sales order header.

In order to check the payment installment dates, from the ribbon, navigate to **Invoice | Bill | Payment schedule**. The **Payment schedule** form will pop up. Then go to the **Payment lines** tab. The following screenshot shows the payment schedules, which are divided into five installments for five months:

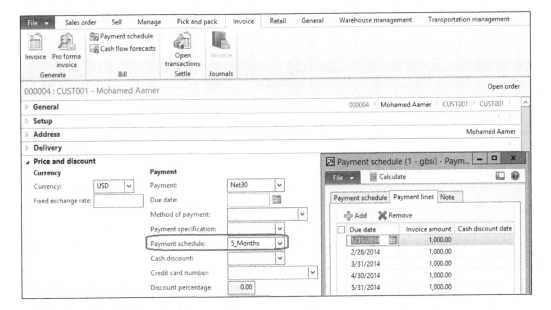

Cash discount

Cash discount represents the discount that will be applied during customer payment if the payment is made before the due date. This encourages the customer to pay before the due date. Cash discount has the flexibility to assign the next cash discount, which could be a deal with the customer. In order to create the cash discount record, navigate to **Accounts Receivable | Setup | Payment | Cash discount**.

As shown in the following screenshot, which represents the **Cash discount** form, the **Setup** fast tab identifies the discount percentage, number of months, and number of days. It is important to assign the main account for customer discounts.

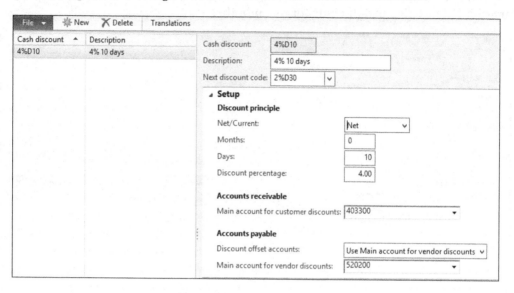

Assume that an invoice has been posted on January 1, the cash discount is 4 percent if the invoice is paid within 10 days, and the terms of payment are net 20 days. The invoice amount is $1,000. The sales tax is 6 percent, which becomes equal to $60 (*invoice amount * sales tax*) (*1000 * 6%*).

The total invoice amount is $1,060 (*invoice amount + sales tax*) (*1000 + 60*).

The cash discount is 4 percent of the invoice amount "before sales tax" $ 40 is the discount amount, which is calculated based on the invoice amount which is $1000, and note that the invoice amount is excluded the sales tax (*invoice amount * cash discount*) (*1000 * 4%*).

The invoice amount after the cash discount is $960 (*invoice amount – cash discount amount*) (*1000 - 40*).

The total invoice amount to be paid is $1,020 (*invoice amount after cash discount + sales tax amount*) (*960 + 60*).

The cash discount date of the customer free text invoice is January 11, and its amount is -40.

We then go to the **Create payment transaction** section and settle it against the posted invoice on January 1. As shown in this screenshot, the payment amount is **1020**:

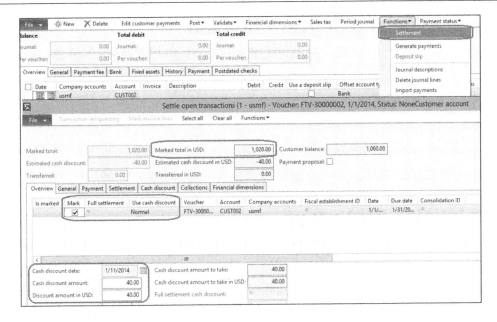

In order to apply the cash discount, the user should choose **Always** or **Normal** under the **Use cash discount** field.

In the following screenshot, the changed payment date, January 19, is visible and the cash discount goes to the next cash discount code. It is 2 percent during 30 days.

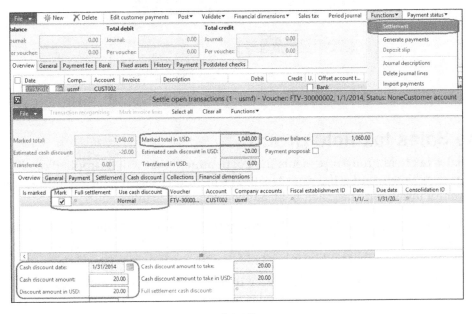

The Invoice and delivery fast tab

In this section, we will cover the **Invoice** and **delivery** and **Sales tax** field groups, as shown in this screenshot:

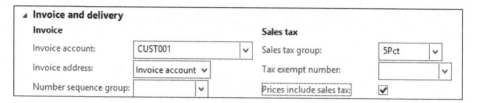

The Invoice field group

In the **Invoice** field group, the **Invoice account** field represents the account used in the invoicing process. The default invoice account is the customer code, but Microsoft Dynamics AX gives flexibility to point invoice posting to another customer. Assume that the company sends goods to two different customers, then the invoice will be issued to one particular customer out of the two.

The relation between the customer code and invoice account, where the customer invoice could be linked to one customer code or multiple customer codes, is shown in the following diagram:

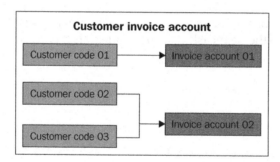

The Sales tax field group

The **Sales tax** field group represents the tax treatment that will be applied on the customer, which includes the sales tax, prices including sales tax or excluding, and tax exempt number if any. Each field can be explained as follows:

- **Sales tax group**: The **Sales tax group** section represents the assigned sales tax group to a particular customer. This record will be a default value on all transactions that will be inherited from the customer master data.

- **Price include sales tax**: The **Price include sales tax** field indicates whether the invoice amount includes sales tax or excludes it.

- **Tax exempt number**: The **Tax exempt number** field is used for reporting and statistical extractions.

> The **Sales tax group** could be set as default on the customer group level. Simply navigate to **Accounts Receivable** | **Setup** | **Customer** | **Customer group**. It can also be overridden by a user in the customer form.

Exploring Accounts receivable controls

The Accounts receivable module's controls are an essential task to be discussed during the analysis and design phases, in addition to being assessed on the operation phase for enhancements. Microsoft Dynamics AX 2012 R3 addresses the required basic business procedures for this module's controls. It is significant to the business to control the execution of Accounts receivable processes, since it directly affects company revenues. Therefore, it should be controlled and monitored. In the following section, we will explore:

- Customer hold activities
- Customer credit limit management

Customer hold activities

In the daily business operations in Accounts receivable, the accounting manager may need to stop transactions on a specific customer. The on-hold function for customers in Microsoft Dynamics AX 2012 is located at the customer level. To access this function, navigate to **Accounts Receivable** | **Common** | **Customers** | **All Customers**, select a customer, and go to the **Credit and collection** fast tab.

As shown in the following screenshot, the on hold function has several options based on customer transaction type, whether it is **Invoice**, **All**, **Payment**, **Requisition**, **Never**, or **No** (**No** is the default value). These options are used to prevent the customers from executing particular transactions or to stop the customers entirely.

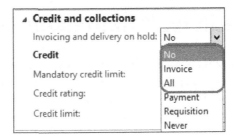

The customer on hold stats has the following options for customer transactions:

- **No**: This option means that the customer is allowed to execute all transaction types
- **Invoice**: This option means that the customer is prevented from executing invoices transactions only
- **All**: This means that the customer is prevented from executing any transaction
- The other options **Payment**, **Requisition**, and **Never** are related to the Accounts payable module

If an end user tries to select a customer with an on-hold status, the system will prevent the transaction from proceeding to the creation step. This is shown in the following screenshot, where a user tried to create a sales order:

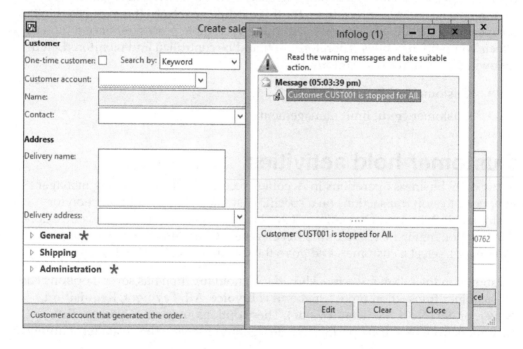

Customer credit limit management

There is a common practice in some business domains where the sales are only on a cash basis. The customer pays an amount of money up front, and this payment creates a balance in the customer account. This account is allowed to receive only those goods that are covered by this amount of money. Then the settle sales invoices are calculated against advanced collections.

Microsoft Dynamics AX manages the customer credit limit on the customer level, and there are two ways that affect customer balance additions, partly where there is an increase in the customer balance, which consists of a cash transaction (customer advanced collection) and a non-cash transaction credit limit. The second way is a transaction that deducts the customer balance. Here is a diagram that illustrates the customer balance elements:

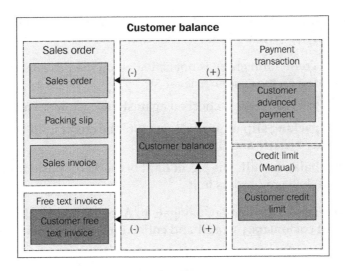

In order to activate and configure the credit limit, navigate to **Accounts Receivable | Setup | Accounts receivable parameters | Credit Rating**. The following screenshot denotes the credit rating options:

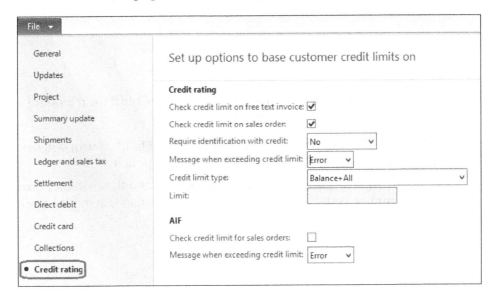

In the **Credit rating** section, identify whether the message to be displayed when the credit limit is exceeded is just a warning message or an error message. The difference in both of them is as follows:

- The warning message will not stop the transaction
- The error message will prevent the transaction from being executed

The **Credit limit type** field has four different options that represent the base of credit limit calculation; the options are listed as follows:

- **None**: The credit limit check is not activated on the module level, and could be overridden on the customer level
- **Balance**: The credit limit is checked against the customer balance
- **Balance + packing slip or product receipt**: The credit limit is checked against the customer balance and the deliveries
- **Customer balance + all**: The credit limit is checked, considering the open orders and delivered orders in it

On the customer master information, navigate to **Accounts receivable | Common | Customers | All customers | Credit and collections**, as shown in the following screenshot:

The **Credit** field group has the activation checkbox and the **Credit limit** amount on the customer level. These are explained as follows:

- **Mandatory credit limit**: If this is checked, the credit limit control will be applied on the customer. Otherwise, it will not be applied.
- **Credit limit**: This specifies the credit limit amount, and the customer cannot let this amount exceed. If the amount is zero, the customer should deposit the amount through payment transactions.

The sales order amount created during the sales order transaction by navigating to **Accounts Receivable | Common | Sales order | All sales orders** is $1,000 for the **CUST003** customer ID. Then navigate to **Manage | Check credit limit**. Microsoft Dynamics AX displays the **Infolog** window to indicate that the credit limit has been exceeded. The credit limit could be an automatic action as well.

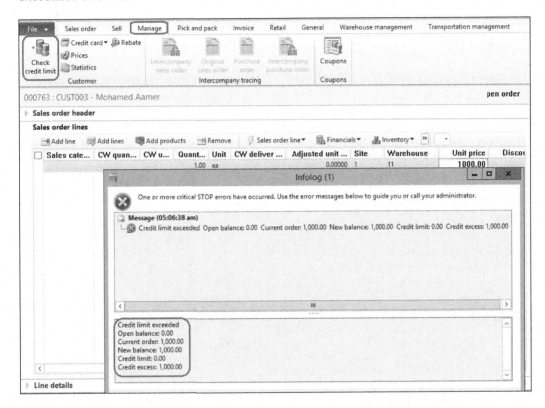

Now we can see the following information:

- **Open balance: 0.00**: This shows the current customer balance from customer advanced collections and open sales orders

- **Current order: 1,000.00**: This is the current sales order amount

- **New balance: 1,000.00**

- **Credit limit: 0.00**: This is the non-cash credit limit that is assigned to the customer

- **Credit excess: 1,000.00**: This is the amount that exceeds the customer balance

Credit limit equations

The following are the credit limit equations:

- *Open balance = – customer advanced collection + open sales order amount*
- *New balance = Open balance + current order*
- *Credit excess = New balance – credit limit*

Then post a prepayment transaction with $250, which affects the customer balance by $250. Check the same sales order balance; it will give the upcoming results.

In order to post the prepayment transaction, navigate to **Accounts receivable | Journals | Payments | Payment journal**. Create a new journal by pressing *Ctrl + N*. Then go to the lines. Select the customer and enter 250 in the credit side, as shown in this screenshot:

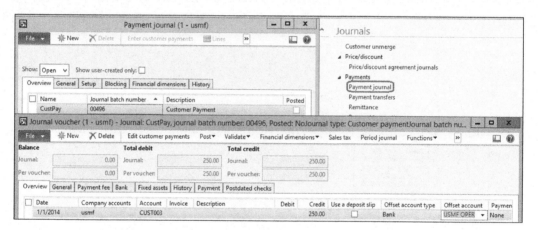

Then move to the **Payment** tab and select the **Prepayment journal voucher** checkbox. The posting profile will be automatically updated to be the **PRE** posting profile, as shown in the following screenshot:

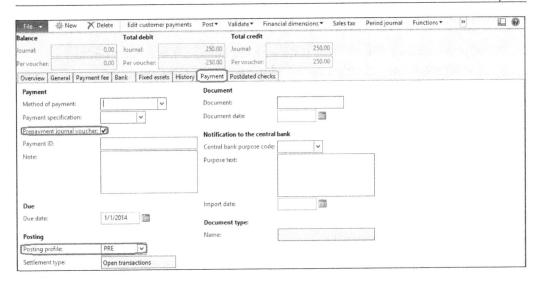

Go to the sales order in order to check the credit limit by navigating to **Accounts Receivable | Common | Sales order | All sales orders**, and then go to the **Manage** ribbon and select the **Check credit limit** option, as shown in the following screenshot:

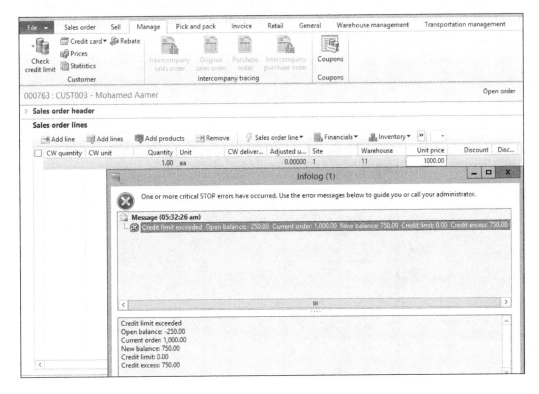

We can see the following results:

- **Open balance: -250.00**: This is the current customer balance from the customer advanced collections and open sales orders

- **Current order: 1,000.00**: This is the current sales order amount

- **New balance: 750.00**

- **Credit limit: 0.00**: This is the non-cash credit limit that is assigned to the customer

- **Credit excess: 750.00**: This is the amount that has exceeded the customer balance

Assume that a credit limit of $150 has been added to a customer, the current balance is $400, and the remaining is $600.

 In case the credit limit is added to the customer master data, it will be recalculated automatically.

As shown in the following screenshot, navigate to **Accounts Receivable | Common | All customers | Customers**. Then navigate to **Customer | Balance** from the ribbon.

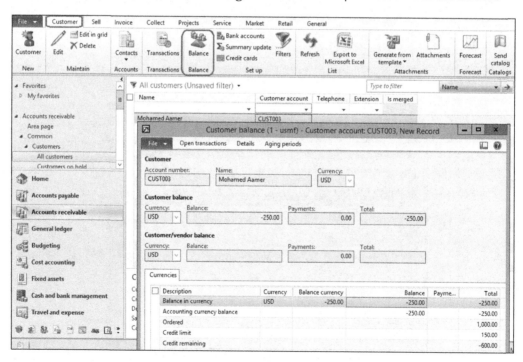

While checking the sales order credit limit, we get the **Infolog** window, like this:

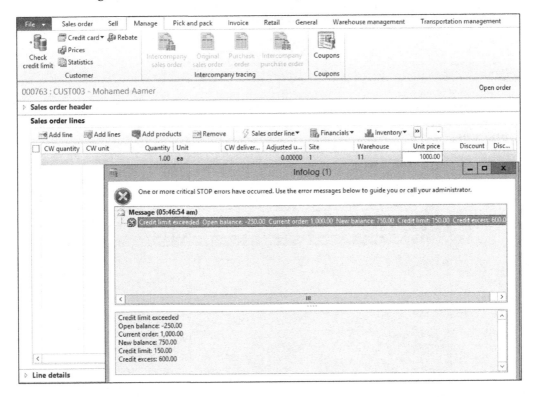

We can see the following results:

- **Open balance: -250**: This is the current customer balance from the customer advanced collections and open sales orders

- **Current order: 1,000.00**: This is the current sales order amount

- **New balance: 750.00**

- **Credit limit: 150.00**: This is the non-cash credit limit that is assigned to the customer

- **Credit excess: 600.00**: This is the amount that has exceeded the customer balance

Assume that there is another sales order of $1,000 created, and then check the sales order credit limit, as shown in the following screenshot:

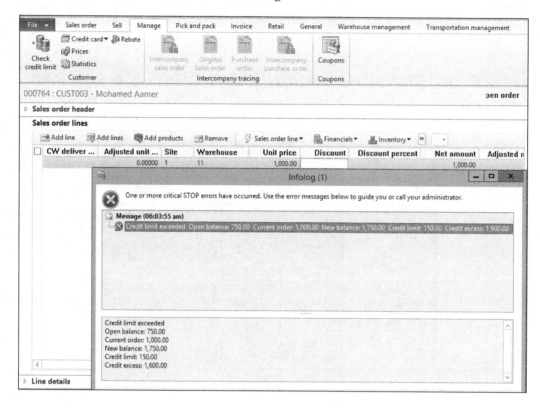

We can see the following results:

- **Open balance: 750.00**: This is the current customer balance from the customer advanced collections and open sales orders

- **Current order: 1,000.00**: This is the current sales order amount

- **New balance: 1750.00**

- **Credit limit: 150.00**: This is the non-cash credit limit that is assigned to the customer

- **Credit excess: 1600.00**: This is the amount that has exceeded the customer balance posting profile

Posting represents the integration point between the general ledger and subledger, and it automatically generates the financial entries according to the posting profile's setup. The Accounts receivable posting profiles are assigned on the module parameters. Navigate to **Accounts Receivable | Setup | Accounts receivable parameters | Ledger and sales tax**. Then perform the following steps:

1. In the **General** fast tab, select a **Posting profile** value for the general Accounts receivable transactions. In other words, this represents the Accounts receivable ledger account.

2. In the **Prepayment journal voucher** field group, select a **Posting profile with prepayment journal voucher** value. In other words, this represents the advances from the customer ledger account.

The Accounts Receivable module posting profile are assigned in the accounts receivable parameters, as shown in the following screenshot:

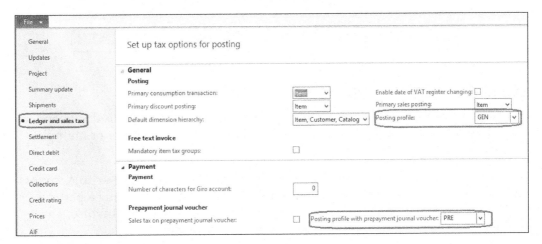

Exploring Accounts receivable transactions

The following section will explore the types of transactions of the Accounts receivable module. The transactions are divided into the following main categories:

*   **Invoicing**: The invoicing is divided into sales order-related and free text invoices. The **Sales Order Invoice** represents the invoices that are normally attached to a sales order (or sales orders). The sales order invoice could be the final invoice of the sales order. In that case, it is issued after delivering the goods. The free text invoice correction function is a newly introduced feature in Microsoft Dynamics AX 2012.

- **Payment**: The second category is payment. This category consist of two types. The first type is prepayment transactions, which are considered as customer advances from clients of which could be assigned to sales order. The second type is customer payment, which is settled against customer invoice.

The following diagram will make things clearer:

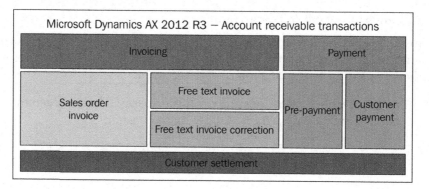

Sales order invoice

The sales order invoice document represents revenue recognition. This document is posted from the sales order form. It could be related to one sales order or multiple sales orders.

In order to post a sales order invoice from the sales order form, navigate to **Accounts Receivable | Common | Sales order | All sales orders**. After choosing a particular sales order, go to the **Invoice** ribbon and then navigate to **General | Invoice**. The following screenshot illustrates the sales order invoice menu:

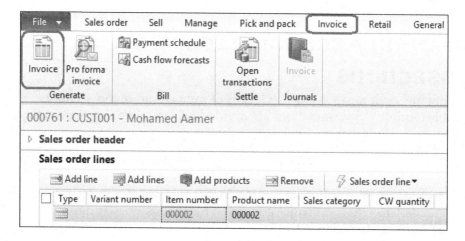

On the customer invoice form, the sales order and packing are retrieved automatically. Click on **OK** to generate the invoice transaction. Here is a screenshot showing the customer invoice form:

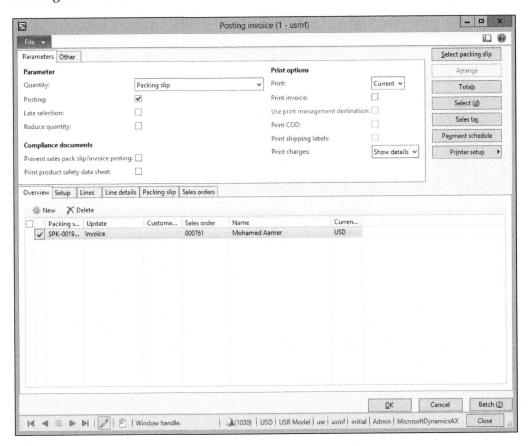

The preceding screenshot depicts the relation between the customer invoice, packing slip, and sales order. The sales order has more than one packing slip, and the invoice may cover one sales order with more than one packing slip. In some business cases, the customer invoices cover packing slips occurring on more than one sales order. The following diagram illustrates the relation between the sales order, packing slip, and invoice:

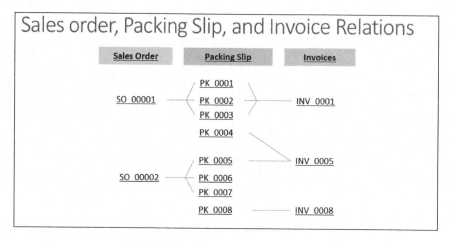

This business scenario shows which invoice covers more than the packing slip and sales order. This can be managed on Microsoft Dynamics AX 2012 R3 by navigating to **Accounts receivable | Periodic | Sales update | Invoice**.

This opens the filtration query, as shown in the following screenshot. The user can retrieve information based on values on the query (this could be a packing slip, customer ID, and so on). Assume that a company invoices its customers on a weekly basis for delivered goods, and this requires identifying the delivered packing slips within the specific period to be invoiced.

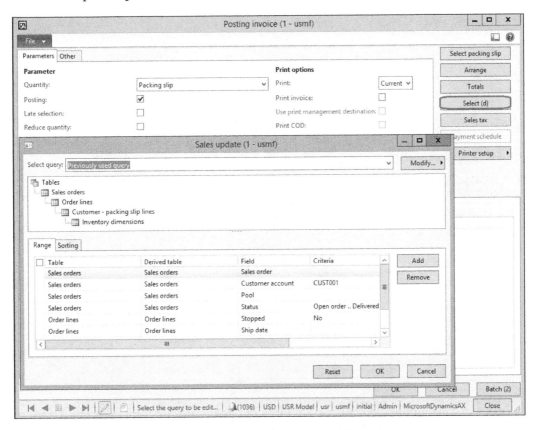

As shown in the next screenshot, there are two lines that have been retrieved according to the entered query — two sales orders with two different packing slips. The following posting invoice form represents two different invoices for each line.

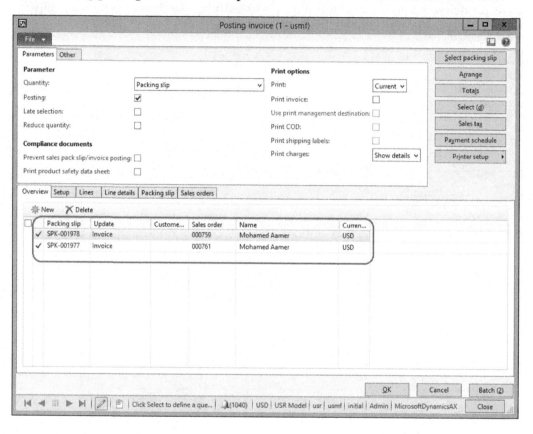

In order to consolidate the multiple invoices in one invoice document, go to **Arrange**. The following screenshot illustrates the consolidate option:

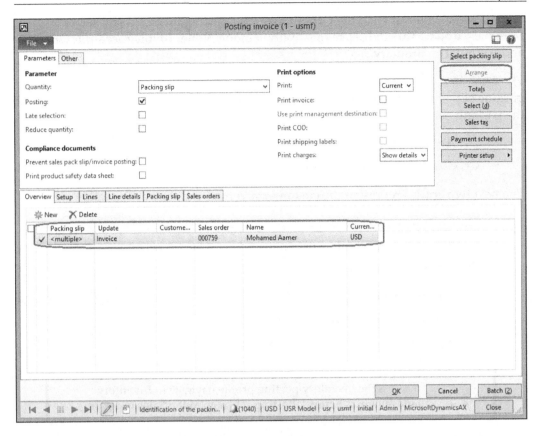

In order to activate the **Arrange** function, the **Summary update** should be identified by navigating to **Accounts receivable | Setup | Accounts receivable parameters | Summary update**. The **Default value for summary update** field can have **None**, **Invoice account**, **Order**, or **Automatic summary** values, as shown in this screenshot:

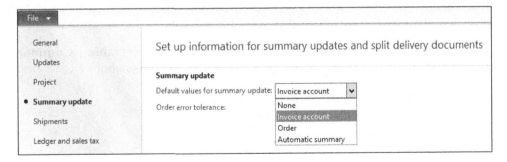

Alternatively, you can go to the **Other** tab on the posting invoice form, select **Summary update for**, and select one option among **None**, **Invoice account**, **Order**, and **Automatic summary**.

The generated sales order invoice mainly consists of the following entries: reversal of packing slip entry, cost of goods sold entry, and revenue entry. The financial entry of the packing slip is as follows:

- **Dr. Accounts Receivable – not invoiced**
- **Cr. Customer accrued account**

The next two entries represent the customer revenue, and they are as follows:

- **Dr. Customer accrued account**
- **Cr. Accounts Receivable – not invoiced**
- **Dr. Customer balance**
- **Cr. Sales revenue**
- **Dr. Cost of goods sold (COGS)**
- **Cr. Inventory**

 To access the inventory posting profile navigate to **Inventory management** | **Setup** | **Posting**. Then go to the **Sales order** tab.

Free text invoice

The free text invoice represents the service invoices that are issued to the customer and are not related to inventory items or sales orders. The free text invoice is not attached to a sales order. It consists of a header and lines for the ledger main account. The free text invoice document could be used for services such as training fees.

In order to access the free text invoice navigate to **Accounts receivable** | **Common** | **Free text invoice** | **All free text invoices**, as shown in this screenshot:

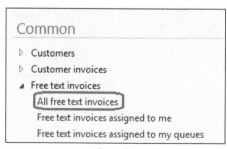

As shown in the following screenshot, in the free text invoice form, we will select a customer account. In the invoice lines, we will select the offset main account, sales tax, and amount. The line view is the default view. To switch to the header view, click on **Header view** in the ribbon. The header view shows information regarding the customer such as terms of payment, method of payment, and posting profile.

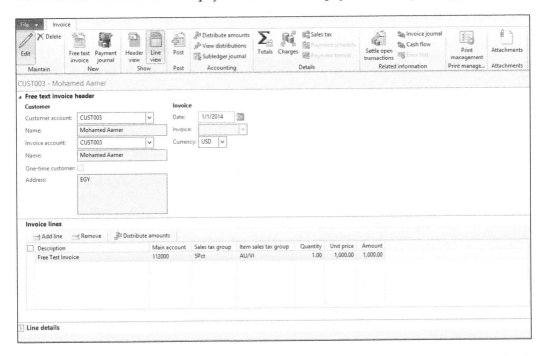

Free text correction

The free text invoice correction is a new functionality introduced in Microsoft Dynamics AX 2012. It represents a business process used to correct posted free text invoices, assuming that after issuing a training service invoice, the customer has realized that there is an error in the issued invoice and it needs to be corrected.

As shown in the following screenshot, to access the free text invoice correction, navigate to **Account Receivable | Common | Free text invoices | All free text invoices | Correct invoice**. In the **Correct Invoice** ribbon, select the **Reason code** value and enter a value in the **Canceling invoice date** field:

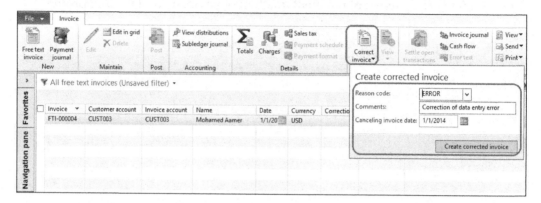

As shown in the next screenshot, the free text invoice correction form will pop up. There is an indication that this invoice form is for correction (**You are correcting a free text invoice**). Edit the amount and post the entry.

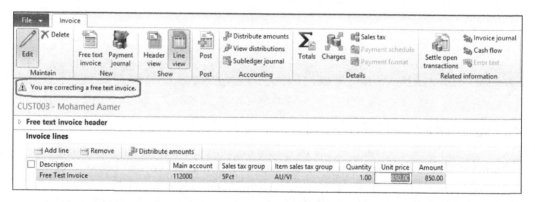

In order to post the free text invoice correction, go to the ribbon and click on **Post**. Behind the scenes, Microsoft Dynamics AX posts both the canceled transaction and the corrected transaction. The following screenshot shows the **Infolog** window with the posted transactions:

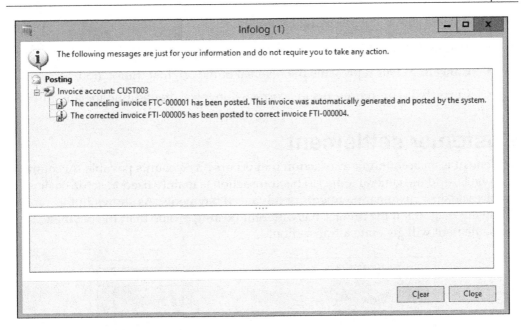

In the next screenshot, we can see the free text invoice. Navigate to **Accounts Receivable | Common | Free text invoices | All free text invoices**.

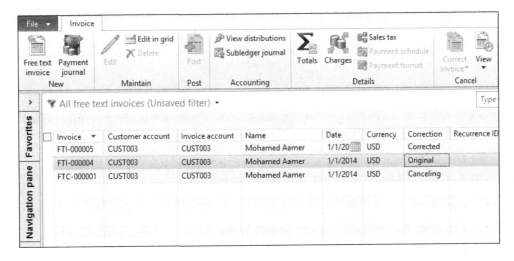

This screenshot shows the following transactions:

- **Original**: This represents the original transaction
- **Canceling**: This represents the reversal of the original transaction
- **Corrected**: This represents the corrected invoice after editing the amount

Customer settlement

Settlement is an accounting transaction that occurs on Accounts payable, Accounts receivable, and the general ledger. This transaction is mainly used to settle customer invoices against customer payments or advanced payments. As shown in the following diagram, if the invoice has different posting profile than the payment, the settlement will generate a transaction:

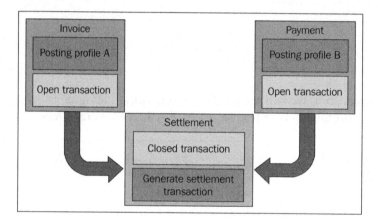

It is necessary to classify the posting profiles of the customer in the opening balance, as it will affect the settlement process.

The settlement transaction affects customer balances, and it is reported in the customer statement report, which identifies the following:

- Customer
- The open (unsettled) invoice and collections
- The closed (settled) invoice and collections
- Customer balance

A settlement transaction could occur during a payment or collection transaction if the accountant marks the invoice that will be paid or collected. On other hand, the settlement could be performed on the vendor or customer level, and these transactions could be unsettled.

The settlement transaction should take into consideration the currency because it could be performed in the company's home currency by an equivalent amount that is calculated based on the currency exchange rate, or it could be settled in the same currency as that of the invoice by identifying the currency in the payment process.

Customer settlement mechanism – Dynamics AX

In Microsoft Dynamics AX, customer settlement is a transaction used to settle customer advanced collections or collections against customer invoices, and this function is done on a monthly basis.

Customer settlement has the following effects:

- The first effect is at the customer level. It closes the customer transaction.
- The second effect is on the financial entry, which occurs in case the posting profiles of the advanced collection and invoice are different.

Next, I will illustrate the mechanism of the customer advanced collection, invoices, and customer settlement financial entries as follows:

- The customer advanced collection posting profile is **Prepayments**, and the financial entry will be as follows:
    - Dr. Banks: 1200 EGP
    - Cr. Customer deposits: 1200 EGP
    - Open transactions: 1200 EGP Advanced collection
- The customer invoice posting profile is **General**, and the financial entry is this:
    - Dr. Receivables: 1000 EGP
    - Cr. Sales revenue: 1000 EGP
    - Open transactions: 1200 EGP Advanced collection, and 1000 EGP sales invoice
- The customer settlement's entry is as follows:
    - Dr. Customer deposits: 1000 EGP
    - Cr. Receivables: 1000 EGP
    - Open transactions: 200 EGP Advanced collection
    - Closed transactions: 1000 EGP advanced collection, and 1000 EGP sales invoice

In case the posting profiles of advanced payment and invoicing are different, a settlement financial entry will be created.

Summary

This chapter covered the Accounts receivable module in Microsoft Dynamics AX 2012 R3 and its integration with other modules. We then explored the customer master data, the controls for customer credit limits, and the on-hold function. We looked at the Accounts receivable transactions customer invoice, free text invoice, and its processing and settlement mechanism.

In the next chapter, we will discuss fixed assets master data and transactions.

6
Exploring Fixed Assets

The fixed assets module represents the tangible assets, intangible assets, and equipments. This module manages and controls the execution of fixed assets transactions. These transactions are based on fixed assets journals, or through other modules such as Procurement and sourcing, and Accounts receivable. This chapter will cover the following topics:

- Understanding fixed assets integration with other modules
- Exploring fixed assets master data characteristics
- Exploring fixed assets transactions

Understanding fixed assets integration with other modules

The fixed assets module manages and controls fixed assets transactions that records fixed assets master information and the basic transactions related to fixed assets acquisition, depreciation, and disposal. The fixed assets function is integrated with other business functions. The first integration point is with the Procurement and sourcing business functions that executes assets acquisition through normal procurement and purchase order processing, then the reception, and finally, the invoice. The second integration is with Accounts receivable that executes fixed assets disposal sales. There is a transaction document that moves an inventory item to be a fixed asset.

The integration of fixed assets document integration is as shown in the following diagram:

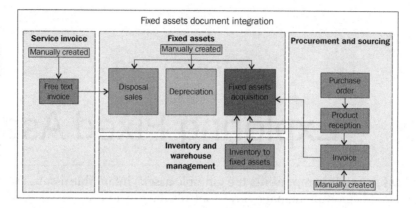

Each transaction is represented in a document type in Microsoft Dynamics AX with the document that contains the details of the transaction. The transaction data, whether inherited from the master data, entered manually, and/or automatically inherited from another transaction, is linked with a specific reference. The integration between fixed assets and other transaction documents gives visibility for tracing what are the original documents that are related to the asset transactions and who posted it.

There is a list of fixed assets transactions besides the basic transactions of acquisition, depreciation, and disposal sale or scrap. The following screenshot shows fixed assets transactions in Microsoft Dynamics AX 2012 R3. This can be accessed from the fixed assets posting profile under **Fixed assets | Setup | Fixed assets posting profiles**.

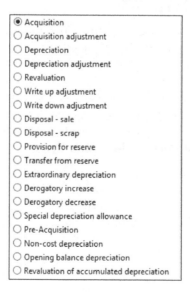

Exploring fixed assets master data characteristics

The fixed assets master data records have essential information that directly affects the asset transactions. The following section will cover the basic information that should be considered when creating a new fixed asset record. The following diagram shows the basic characteristics of fixed assets. There are more generic and higher levels of assets master data, depreciation profile, value model, and the asset group that represents the logical grouping of assets. The fixed asset record is the lowest level that represents the asset itself.

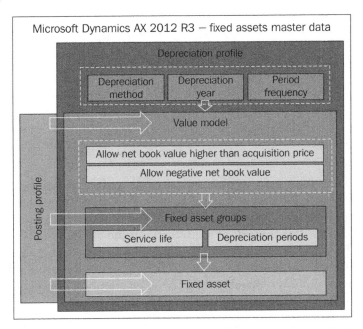

The depreciation profile

The depreciation profiles in Microsoft Dynamics AX 2012 R3 represent the rules that manage the depreciation principles that will be applied on the fixed assets. For example, the straight line depreciation method or the reducing balance depreciation method. The depreciation profile rules contain the depreciation method, depreciation year, and period frequency. In order to access the depreciation profile, go to **Fixed assets | Setup | Depreciation | Depreciation profiles**.

The depreciation method

The depreciation method represents the method that can be applied for depreciation calculation. The following screenshot shows the supported depreciation methods in Microsoft Dynamics AX 2012 R3:

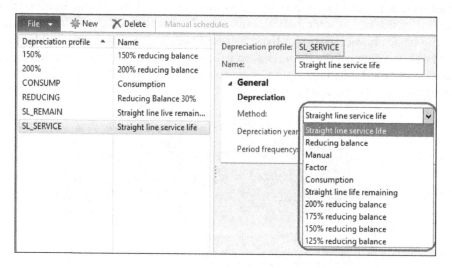

The depreciation method is an accounting principle that identifies the calculation method of distributing the cost of the fixed assets over the service line of the asset. The depreciation method is normally decided based on business requirements that might be built on law. It is important to understand the business requirements during the analysis and design phases. This requires a close cooperation between the implementation team and financial controller to ensure the proper design deployment and operation of fixed assets. The most common depreciation method is the straight line service life. Consider the following example.

Let's assume that a company acquired a car as a fixed asset at 20,000 USD and the service life for this car is 5 years. The depreciation calculation will be as follows.

Depreciation months are 60, that is, 5 years multiplied by 12 months.

The depreciation for each month will be equal to allocation, that is, 20,000 USD divided by 60 months, which is equal to 333.333 USD per month.

The form contains two types of fields based on the selected depreciation method. The first type is constant fields, which are shared with all the methods, and the second type is dynamic fields, which are activated based on the depreciation method selection.

Constant fields

Constant fields refer to depreciation year and period frequency. These fields are interrelated, which means that the values in period frequency are based on the depreciation year. The depreciation year represents the basis of calculation of depreciation whether calendar or fiscal.

The period frequency represents the ledger accruals during the calendar year, as follows:

- In case the selected depreciation year is a calendar year, Microsoft Dynamics AX 2012 R3 considers the calendar year starting from January. The available values are yearly, monthly, quarterly, and half-yearly.

- In case the selected depreciation year is year, Microsoft Dynamics AX 2012 R3 considers the fiscal year setup that might start at July. The available values are yearly and fiscal period.

Dynamic fields

Dynamic fields are activated based on the selection of the depreciation method:

- **Percentage**: It represents the percentage of depreciation calculation
- **Full Depreciation**: It represents that the fixed asset will be fully depreciated when the remaining service life reaches zero
- **Factor**: It represents the percentage value of origin that constitutes the depreciation
- **Interval**: It represents the interval to run the depreciation. This field will be active if the selected depreciation method is factored.

The value model

The value models represent the financial value of the fixed asset that belongs to the value model, and it can be the integration point between fixed assets and the general ledger in the posting profile. In order to access the value model, go to **Fixed assets | Setup | Value models**. The following screenshot shows the value model form:

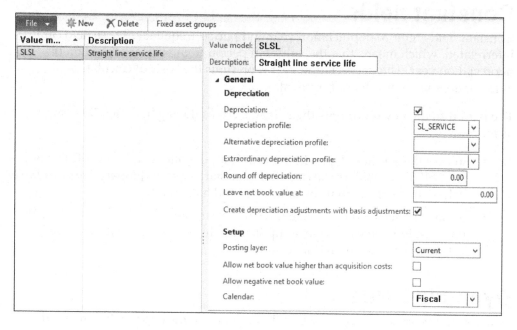

The depreciation profile is attached to the value model, and it identifies whether the assets that belong to this value model will be depreciated or not. The depreciation can be overridden on a fixed asset level.

The value model identifies the control point on the assets belonging to a value model and checks whether to allow the net book value to go higher than the acquisition cost. Assume that there is a fixed asset with an acquisition price of 1250 USD and the depreciation amount is 187 USD. In case the user is going to reverse a depreciation transaction and modify the amount to be 300 USD, the system will throw an info log message indicating that the net book value will be higher than the acquisition cost, as shown in the following screenshot:

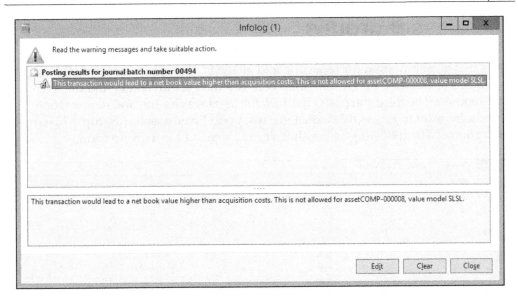

The second control point on the value model denotes whether to allow a negative net book value for assets that belong to this value model. Assume that there is a fixed asset with an acquisition price of 1250 USD and the depreciation amount is 187 USD. In case the user is going to post a depreciation transaction and modify the amount to be 1251 USD, the system will throw an info log message to indicate that the net book value will be in negative, as shown in the following screenshot. In case we allow a negative net book value, the net book value will be equal to -1251.

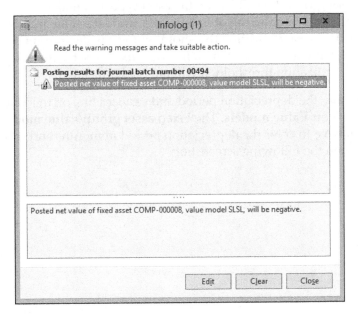

Fixed asset groups

The fixed asset group has three purposes. The first is a logical grouping of fixed assets that is mainly used for reporting and analysis. The second purpose is considered as another integration point between the general ledger and the fixed asset module. The third purpose identifies the asset service life and depreciation periods. In order to access fixed asset groups, go to **Fixed assets | Setup | Fixed asset groups**. The following screenshot shows the fixed asset group form:

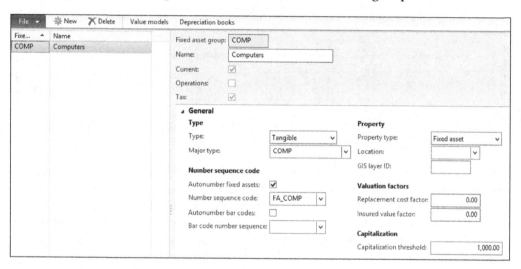

On the fixed asset groups form, identify the asset type and major type, in addition to identifying the auto-numbering of fixed assets, and attach the number sequence that will be used. The capitalization threshold represents the minimum amount of acquisition cost that will be depreciated. In case a fixed asset acquired has an amount less than the capitalization threshold, it will not be depreciated.

In order to identify the depreciation period and services life, on the **Fixed asset group** form, click on **Value models**. The **Fixed asset group/value model** form will open; here you have to enter the depreciation period in months and services life in years, as shown in the following screenshot:

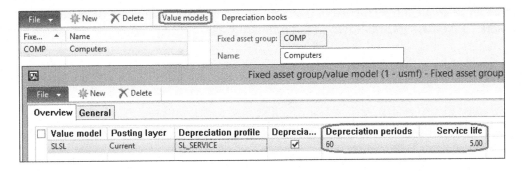

Fixed assets

Fixed assets can be equipments, cars, and/or buildings. They represent the lowest level of assets master data, which contains the fixed asset record, the unique ID, description, grouping, and specific characteristics for fixed assets. In order to create a fixed asset record, there are two ways. You can either create a record manually or automatically through purchase order posting. The method of creation differentiates the acquisition document. The following diagram shows the creation methods and acquisition documents:

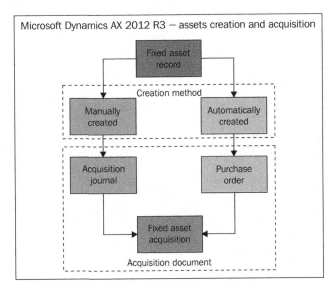

In order to create a new record of fixed assets, go to **Fixed assets | Common | Fixed assets | Fixed assets**, as shown in the following screenshot:

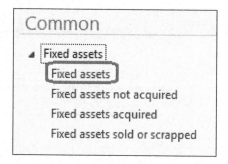

Press *Ctrl + N* to create a new record. Here, the **Fixed asset group** and **Number** fields are the mandatory fields. When the user selects the **Fixed asset group** value, the number is automatically created. Enter the **Name** and **Search name** of fixed assets under **Description**, as shown in the following screenshot:

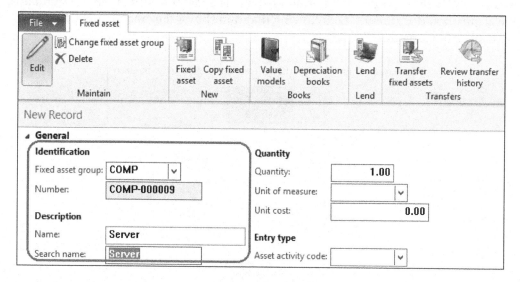

Under **Value models**, there are two types of data. The first type of data is populated automatically, which represents the value model assigned to the fixed asset group. These fields contains depreciation, service life, and depreciation periods. This is shown in the following screenshot:

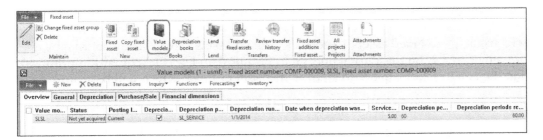

The second type of field can be identified manually. For this, navigate to the **General** tab to identify acquisition date and price. This is shown in the following screenshot:

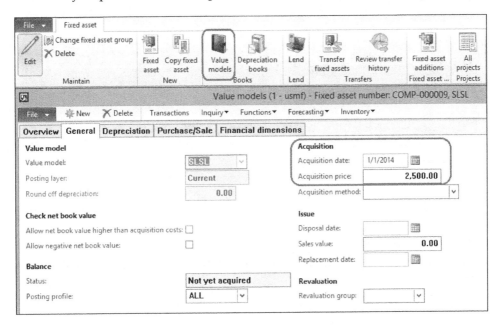

Exploring fixed assets transactions

In this section, we will explore fixed assets transactions starting from acquisition transactions by acquisition journal, acquisition through purchase order, depreciation, disposal scrap, and fixed assets reversal transactions.

In order to record and post an acquisition journal, as shown in the following screenshot, go to **Fixed assets** | **Journals** | **Fixed assets**. Create a new journal by pressing *Ctrl + N* on the journal line, go to **Proposal** and select **Acquisition proposal**, and then go to select a query to identify the asset number, which will be acquired.

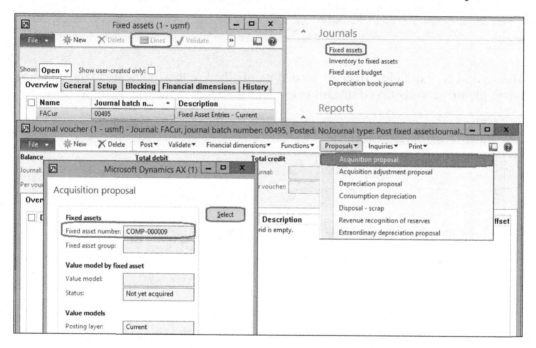

Note that if the acquisition price is not identified, the acquisition proposal will not populate the asset.

In order to acquire fixed assets through a purchase order, a parameter must be activated first. This gives the company the control to acquire the assets through the procurement department and enables it to apply the segregation of duties between the procurement, reception, invoicing, and payment process. As shown in the following screenshot, go to **Fixed assets | Setup | Fixed assets** and then click on **Purchase orders**:

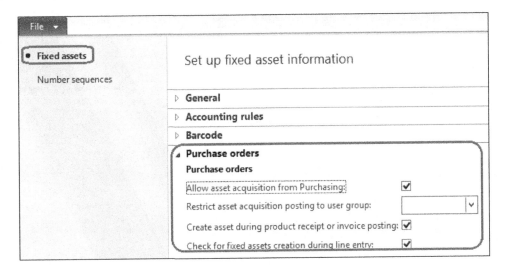

The following options are available under the **Purchase order** tab:

- Allow asset acquisition from purchasing
- Restrict asset acquisition posting to a user group
- Create asset during product receipt or invoice posting
- Check for fixed assets creation during line entry

In the course of the execution of a fixed asset acquisition through a purchase order, go to **Procurement and sourcing | Common | Purchase order | All purchase order**. Then, create a new record by pressing *Ctrl + N*, select vendor, go to purchase lines, select service item, and then enter warehouse and price details. Now, go to the **Fixed assets** tab, as shown in the following screenshot:

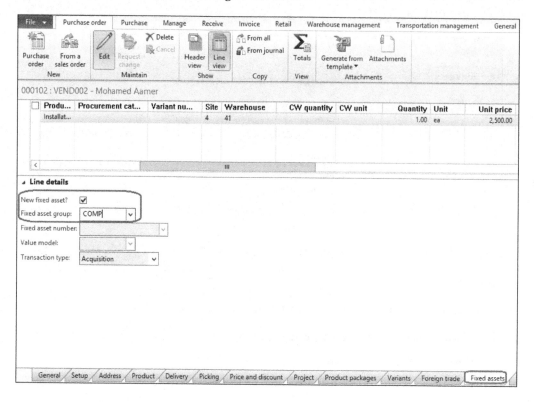

If the fixed asset is new, check the **New fixed asset** checkbox and select a **Fixed asset group**. If this transaction is to capitalize on already created fixed assets, uncheck the **New fixed asset** checkbox, select **Fixed asset group** and **Fixed asset number**, and identify the **Transaction type** whether it is **Acquisition** or **Acquisition adjustment**. The Value model field is populated automatically. The process of the purchase order normally goes from confirmation to product receipt to invoice. After posting the purchase order invoice, the fixed asset record will be created and the asset acquisition transaction will be posted.

An acquisition entry has the following:

- Dr. Fixed assets
- Cr. Vendor balance

As shown in the following screenshot, select the purchase order line after posting the invoice, then go to the asset value model by right-clicking on the asset number and then click on **View details**. Now, click on the value model in the fixed asset form.

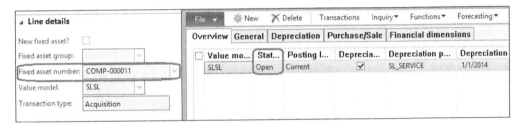

 The status changing from **Not acquired yet** to **Open** represents the acquired fixed assets, and this asset will be included in the next depreciation run.

As shown in the following screenshot, in order to run fixed assets depreciation, go to **Fixed assets | Journals | Fixed assets**, create a new record and go to **Lines**. Then, go to **Proposals** and select **Depreciation proposal**. Now, identify the depreciation date, find the asset number by clicking on the **Select** button, and decide whether to summarize the depreciation in one line or for separate lines for each month.

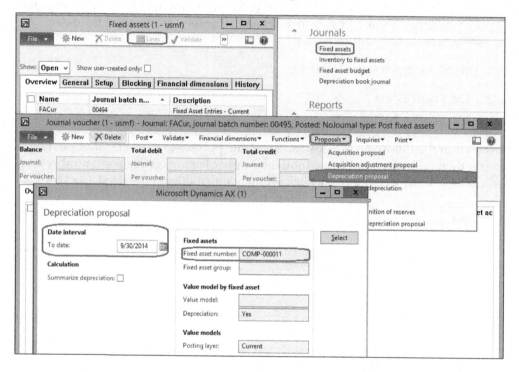

Assume that the acquired fixed assets price is 2500 USD, the acquisition date is January 1, 2014, and the depreciation period is 60 months. The depreciation for each month is calculated as 2500 USD divided by 60 months, which is equal to 41.67 USD. The depreciation will run on till September 30, 2014.

The following screenshot illustrates the depreciation for each month:

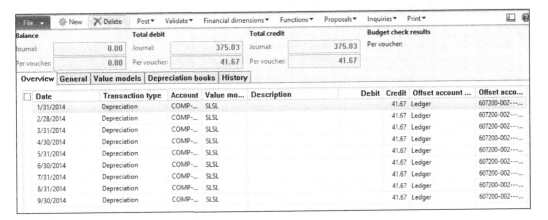

In case the **Summarize depreciation** checkbox is checked, the depreciation will be created in one line on September 30, 2014 as 375.03 USD.

The depreciation entry has the following:

- Dr. Depreciation expense
- Cr. Accumulated depreciation

The posted transaction of fixed assets are located on the value model, and in order to inquire about the posted transaction, go to **Fixed asset**, select a particular asset ID, go to the **Value model** ribbon, and then click on **Transactions**. As shown in the following screenshot, updates have occurred on the **Date when depreciation was last run** field, and the **Depreciation periods remaining** field that represents the equation, depreciation periods minus ran depreciation periods, that is 60 minus 9, which equals 51.

The **Transactions** button shows the posted transactions on the asset depending on whether it is acquisition or depreciation.

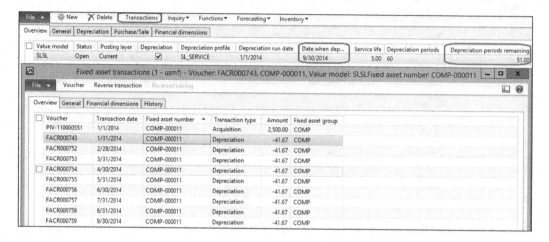

As shown in the following screenshot, the inquiry illustrates the acquisition price, depreciation, and net book value. The net book value represents the equation acquisition price minus depreciation, that is, 2500 minus 375.03, which equals 2124.97.

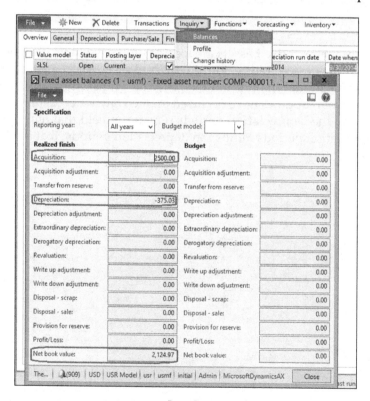

Fixed asset disposal sale

Assume that the disposal sale transaction occurred in a company that decided to sell a car, which is a fixed asset. This transaction that took place of selling a fixed asset occurred through the free text invoice in Accounts receivable. The posting profile of a disposal sale considers the following:

- **Depreciation (prior years)**: The total depreciations of prior years will be reversed; the ledger account is the accumulated depreciation account, and the offset account is the fixed assets gain/loss account.

- **Depreciation (this year)**: The total depreciations of the current year will be reversed; the ledger account is the accumulated depreciation account, and the offset account is the fixed assets gain/loss account.

- **Acquisition value**: The acquisition value will be reversed; the ledger account is the fixed assets account, and the offset account is the fixed assets gain/loss account.

- **Net book value**: The ledger account is the fixed assets gain/loss account, and the offset account is also the fixed assets gain/loss account.

In order to set up a fixed assets posting profile, go to **Fixed assets | Setup | Fixed assets** and select **Disposal | Sale**, as shown in the following screenshot:

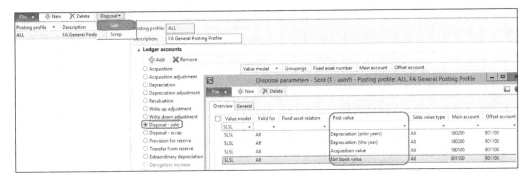

The generated entry will be as follows:

- Dr. Accumulated depreciation account
- Dr. Fixed assets gain/loss account
- Dr. Accounts receivable
- Cr. Fixed assets gain/loss account
- Cr. Fixed assets gain/loss account
- Cr. Fixed assets account

There are some scenarios in daily business that require reversing fixed asset transactions. This can be executed from the fixed asset journal, as shown in the following screenshot. Now, go to **Function** and select **Retrieve fixed asset transactions**. Then, select **New voucher number per transaction** in order to generate a new voucher number, and check **Invert sign** to invert the transaction sign from the original one. To select a particular fixed asset, click on the **Select** button and add the asset number.

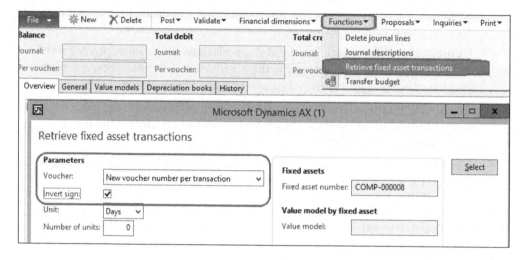

The following screenshot illustrates the retrieved fixed asset transaction with an invert sign. You can see a minus sign on the debit side, which means it is a credit, and a minus sign on the credit side a means debit.

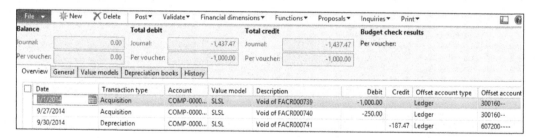

	Date	Transaction type	Account	Value model	Description	Debit	Credit	Offset account type	Offset account
	1/1/2014	Acquisition	COMP-0000...	SLSL	Void of FACR000739	-1,000.00		Ledger	300160--
	9/27/2014	Acquisition	COMP-0000...	SLSL	Void of FACR000740	-250.00		Ledger	300160--
	9/30/2014	Depreciation	COMP-0000...	SLSL	Void of FACR000741		-187.47	Ledger	607200----

Summary

In this chapter, we covered the fixed assets module in Microsoft Dynamics AX 2012 R3. We explored the fixed asset characteristics and its integration with other modules. We then explored the fixed assets master data and the required data to acquire, depreciate, and dispose an asset. Next, we explored the fixed asset transactions acquisition, whether through an acquisition proposal journal or through the purchase order, monthly depreciation, disposal sales, and fixed asset transaction reversals.

In the next chapter, we will discuss the cash flow management integration concept, basic configurations, and transactions.

7
Functioning of Cash Flow Management

Cash flow management is a tool that predicts a company's future cash requirements. Cash flow management mainly covers the cash out and cash in events. Cash out is generated from the company's expenditure against the goods or services purchased, whereas cash in is generated from the company's revenue against the sale of goods or services. It gives the company's management a vision of the cash position in order to efficiently manage vendor payments in a specific period, and also the customer collections during the same period to protect the company's cash situation. In this chapter, we will cover the following topics:

- Understanding cash flow integration with other modules
- Exploring cash flow forecast configuration
- Working with cash flow transactions
- Forecasting cash flow by currency requirements
- Forecasting the main account's cash flow

Understanding cash flow integration with other modules

The integrated modules of cash flow management are **Accounts payable**, **Accounts receivable**, and **General ledger**. The Accounts payable module manages the vendor payments process, the Accounts receivable module manages the customer collections process, and the General ledger module identifies the cash and cash-equivalent accounts. The following figure shows the integration of the cash flow modules:

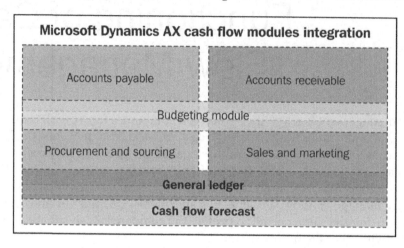

The modules that are integrated in cash flow forecast management are divided into the following groups:

- Vendor expenditure management has the following elements:
    - **Accounts payable**: This identifies the vendors' terms of payment, settlement periods, vendors' posting profiles, accounts used for vendor settlement, and vendor invoice transaction execution
    - **Procurement and sourcing**: This identifies the transactional execution of vendor purchase orders and receptions
- Customer collections management has the following components:
    - **Accounts receivable**: This identifies the customers' terms of payment, settlement periods, customers' posting profiles, accounts used for customer settlement, and customer invoice transaction execution
    - **Sales and marketing**: This identifies the transactional execution of customer sales orders, issuances, and invoicing

- **Budgeting**: This identifies the budget distributions based on specific time intervals (years, months, and days)

- **General ledger**: This identifies the cash and cash-equivalent accounts that represent the liquidity account

- **Cash flow forecast**: This represents the cash flow position for purchase and sales order transactions

With the Microsoft Dynamics AX consultant, the implementation of cash flow forecast management is a mutual effort between the controller, accounting manager, treasury, budgeting, procurement, and sales.

Cash flow forecast configuration

The cash flow forecast configuration and setups are combined with the integrated modules of cash flow management. The following figure explains the cash flow forecast configuration in detail:

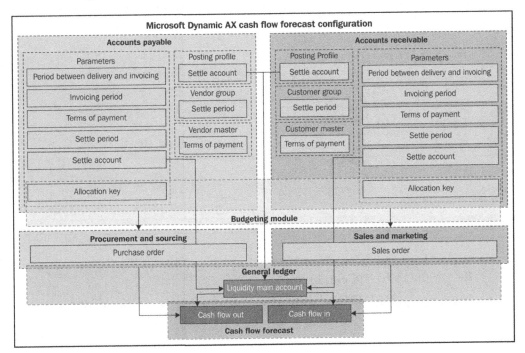

The main configuration and setup of cash flow forecast in Microsoft Dynamics AX are performed in the following modules:

- Accounts payable
- Accounts receivable
- Budget
- General ledger

Accounts payable

The Accounts payable module is further subdivided as follows:

- **Parameters**: This identifies the company-wide parameters for Accounts payable. For the parameters of Accounts payable, navigate to **Accounts payable | Setup | Accounts payable parameters**. Now go to **Ledger and sales tax** and click on **Cash flow forecast**, as shown in the following screenshot:

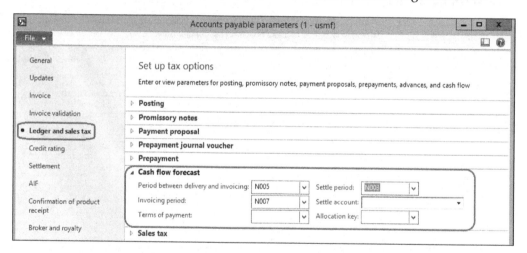

- **Period between delivery and invoicing**: This identifies the period between the product's receipt and invoice.
- **Invoicing period**: This identifies the period of receiving the vendor invoice.

- **Terms of payment**: This identifies the period between the vendor invoice posting and the due date.

- **Settle account**: This represents the liquidity account.

- **Allocation key**: This represents the allocation key used for budget reduction with regards to purchase level.

- **Settle period**: This identifies the period between the vendor payment due date and the date of payment execution. The terms of payment values are commonly used in the Accounts payable's cash flow forecast, where we can set the number of days or months that identify the payment due date. To see the Accounts payable's terms of payment, navigate to **Accounts payable | Setup | Payment | Terms of payment**, as shown in the following screenshot:

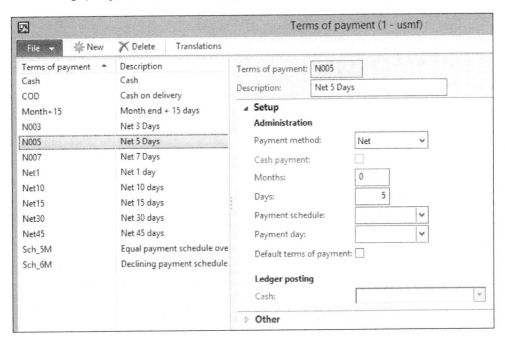

- **Vendor posting profiles**: This is an integration point between the Accounts payable sub ledger and general ledger, where identifying a particular ledger account will be used while posting a transaction for a specific vendor. The **Settle account** column in the following screenshot represents the liquidity accounts that are used for vendor payments. For the Accounts payable posting profiles, navigate to **Accounts payable | Setup | Vendor posting profiles**. The following screenshot displays the **Vendor posting profiles** page in detail:

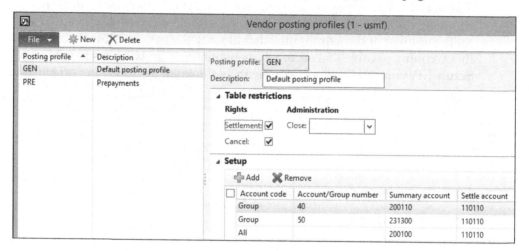

 The **Settle account** column in **Vendor posting profile** overrides the **Settle account** column under module parameters.

- **Vendor groups**: This represents the vendor's classification and the posting profile assigned to a specific vendor group in order to identify the **Settle period** column that is used in cash flow management logic. To see the Accounts payable vendor groups profile, navigate to **Accounts Payable | Setup | Vendor | Vendor groups**. The following screenshot shows the **Vendor groups** screen as an example:

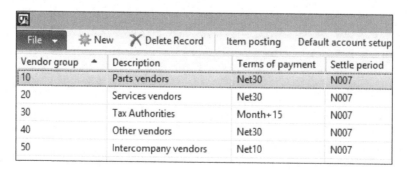

The **Settle period** column in vendor groups overrides the **Settle period** column under module parameters.

- **Vendor master**: In the **Vendor master** data information, which is captured and recorded during the creation of vendors and has an effect on the vendor's aging and cash flow forecast as well, the terms of payment under the payment section is considered as a default value. It is proposed when the vendor is selected in transaction, and can be changed on a transactional level without modifying the master data record. For the Accounts payable vendor master data, navigate to **Accounts payable | Common | Vendors | All vendors**, then press **Edit** on a particular vendor and go to the **Payment** fast tab:

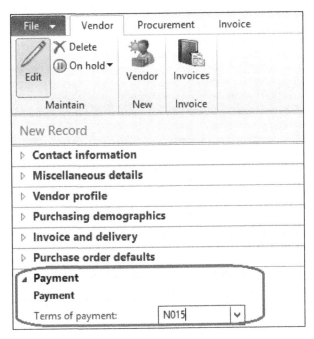

Accounts receivable

The Accounts receivable module is subdivided as follows:

- **Parameters**: This identifies the company-wide parameters for Accounts receivable. For Accounts receivable parameters, navigate to **Accounts receivable | Setup | Accounts receivable parameters**, then go to **Ledger and sales tax**, and click on **Cash flow forecast**. The following screenshot shows **Ledger and sales tax** in detail:

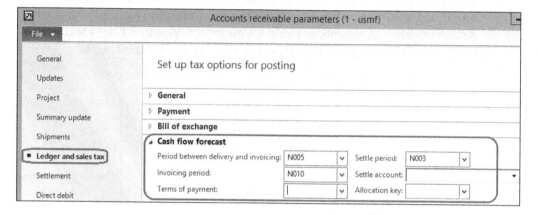

- **Period between delivery and invoicing**: This identifies the period between the product's issuance and invoicing.

- **Invoicing period**: This identifies the period of issuing the customer invoice.

- **Terms of payment**: This identifies the period between the customer invoice posting and due date.

- **Settle account**: This represents the liquidity account for settling payments.

- **Allocation key**: This represents the allocation key used for budget reduction with regard to the volume of orders.

- **Settle period**: This identifies the period between the customer payment due date and payment execution. The terms of payment values are commonly used in the Accounts receivable module's cash flow forecast, where we can set the number of days or months that identify the payment due date. To see the terms of payment, navigate to **Accounts receivable | Setup | Payment | Terms of payment**, as shown in the following screenshot:

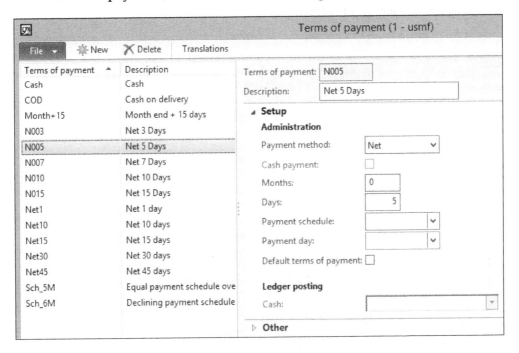

- **Customer posting profiles**: This is an integration point between Accounts receivable and General ledger, where identifying the ledger account will be used when posting a transaction on a customer attached to a particular posting profile. The **Settle account** column in the following screenshot represents the liquidity accounts that are used for customer payments. To see the posting profiles, navigate to **Accounts receivable | Setup | Customer posting profiles**.

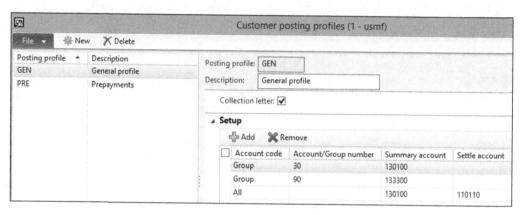

 The **Settle account** column in **Customer posting profile** dominates the **Settle account** column under module parameters.

- **Customer groups**: This represents the customer classification and the posting profile assigned to a specific customer group. You can also see the **Settle period** column in the following screenshot. It is used in the cash flow management logic. In order to see the customer groups, navigate to **Accounts receivable | Setup | Customers | Customer groups**.

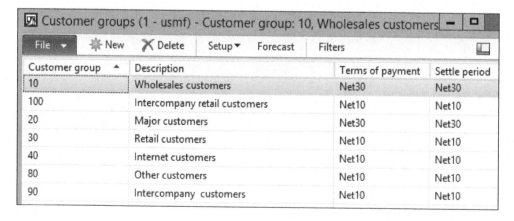

- **Customer master**: In the customer master's data information, which is captured and recorded during the creation of a customer and has an effect on customer aging and cash flow forecast as well, in terms of payment under payment section in customer master data. This terms of payment is considered as a default value proposed when the customer is selected in a transaction, and the value could be changed on a transactional level without modifying the master data record. For this, navigate to **Accounts receivable | Common | Customers | Customers | All customers**, select a particular customer and press **Edit**, then move to the **Payment** default fast tab:

Budget

The core concept in the Budget module is the allocation key. This distributes the budgets for a specific period by a weight of allocation percentage, which could be days, months, and or years. To access the budget allocation key window, navigate to **General ledger | Setup | Periods | Periods allocation categories**. Click on **Lines** to enter an allocation percentage for each period.

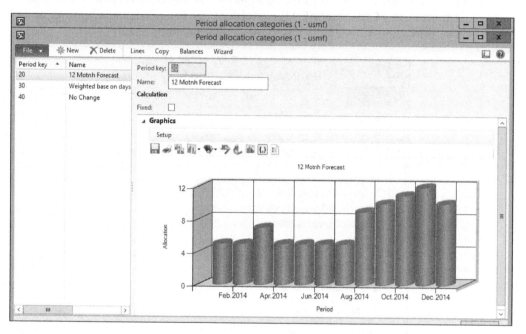

General ledger

The general ledger is subdivided as follows:

- **Main accounts**: The **Set up cash flow forecasts** screen, which is shown in the following screenshot, represents the dependency of other accounts that will affect the company's cash flow, for example, sales tax payment. To see the main account's cash flow, navigate to **General ledger | Setup | Chart of accounts | Chart of accounts**, and select **Main account**. Then select **Companies** in **Select the level of main account to display**. Now click on **Cash flow forecast** under the **Setup** tab, as shown in the following screenshot:

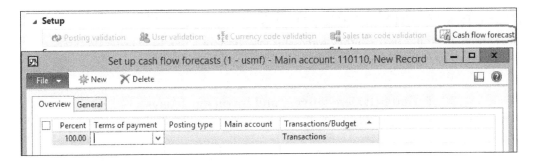

- **Liquidity accounts**: This lists the cash and cash-equivalent accounts that are used to calculate the cash flow forecast. In order to access the following screenshot, which illustrates the liquidity accounts form, navigate to **General Ledger | Setup | Posting | Liquidity**:

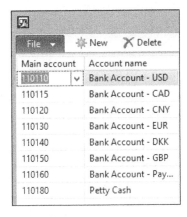

Cash flow transactions

The transactions that affect the cash flow forecast are purchase and sales orders. The cash flow transactions also depend on the configuration of the company-wide parameters and the master data setup.

Purchase order cash flow forecast

This section illustrates the cash flow forecast transaction for a **purchase order (PO)**. The order's data is as follows:

- Configuration of the Accounts payable module's parameters:
    - ○ **Period between delivery and invoicing**: 5 days
    - ○ **Invoice period**: 7 days
    - ○ **Settle period**: 3 days

- Vendor master data:
    - ○ **Terms of payment**: 15 days

- Purchase order data:
    - ○ **Purchase order date**: January 1
    - ○ **Purchase order quantity**: 1 Piece
    - ○ **Currency**: EGP
    - ○ **Default currency**: USD
    - ○ **Exchange rate**: 1 USD = 5 EGP
    - ○ **Purchase price**: 5,000 EGP = 1,000 USD

The purchase order was created on January 1. Based on the setup of the period between delivery and invoice, which is 5 days, the date will be January 6 (by adding 5 days to the PO line date). Based on the setup of the invoicing period, which is 7 days, the date will be January 13 (PO line date plus 5 days plus 7 days). Then, based on the setup of the terms of payment, which is 15 days, the date will be January 28 (PO line date plus 5 days plus 7 days plus 15 days). Finally, based on the setup of the settle period, which is 3 days, the date will be January 31 (PO line date plus 5 days plus 7 days plus 15 days plus 3 days).

The following figure represents the cash flow forecast transaction in detail:

Microsoft Dynamics AX cash flow forecast

Period between delivery and invoicing (5 days)	January 6
Invoicing period (7 days)	January 13
Terms of payment (15 days)	January 28
Settle period (3 days)	January 31

The **Cash flow forecasts** tab can be viewed under **Purchase order**. In the ribbon, navigate to the **Invoice** section, go to the **Bill** group, and select **Cash flow forecasts**, as shown in the following screenshot:

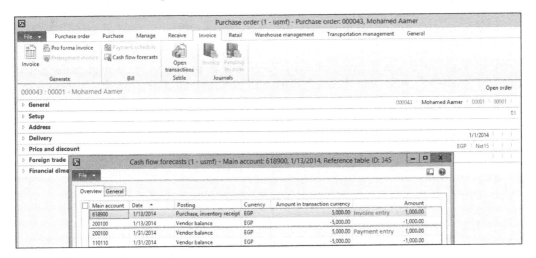

The invoice entry date is calculated based on the **Period between delivery and invoicing** and **Invoice period** (5 days plus 7 days). Then the invoice entry date will be January 13. The payment entry date is calculated based on the number of days in **Terms of payment**, **Settle period**, and **Invoice date** (13 days plus 15 days plus 3 days). Thus, the payment entry date will be January 31.

Cash flow forecast by currency requirement

Microsoft Dynamics AX has a function that fulfills the currency requirement. This function is the **Currency requirement** inquiry form. For cash flow forecast currency requirements, navigate to **General ledger | Periodic | Currency requirement | Currency requirement**. The following screenshot shows the **Currency requirement** screen:

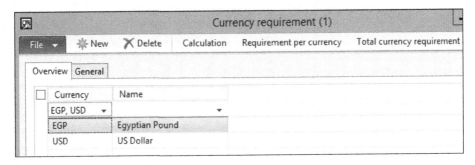

> In some cases, the **Cash flow forecast** requirements are not calculated properly, thereby requiring you to run a **Cash flow forecast** job. This job can be run manually or an automatic batch job can be set up to do it.

The **Requirement per currency** tab represents **Cash flow forecasts** for a specific currency code for a specific period. With reference to the previous transactions, select the **EGP** currency code, and the cash flow will be illustrated in a graph, as shown in the next screenshot:

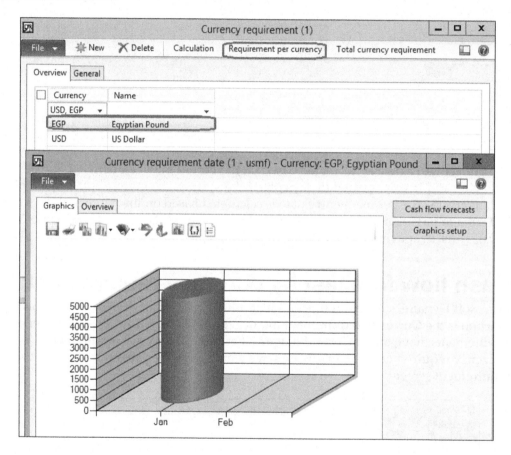

The **Overview** tab, which is shown in the following screenshot, represents the cash flow requirements per period:

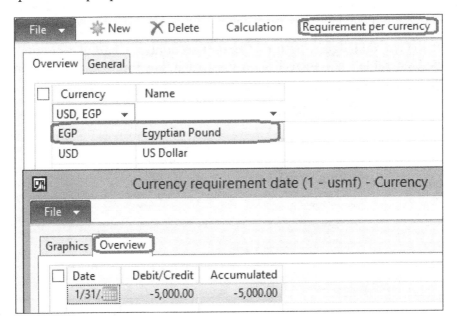

In the **Currency requirement** form, the **Total currency requirement** button represents the cash flow forecast requirements by company, and the default currency is USD. This gives a clear vision for the projection of *cash in* and *cash out* for a specific period.

Main account cash flow forecast

Main account, which has a setup for cash flow forecast, shows the cash flow of forecasts that are related to the main account.

Navigate to **General ledger** | **Setup** | **Chart of accounts** | **Chart of accounts** under the **General** tab, and then click on **View cash flow forecast**, as shown in the following screenshot:

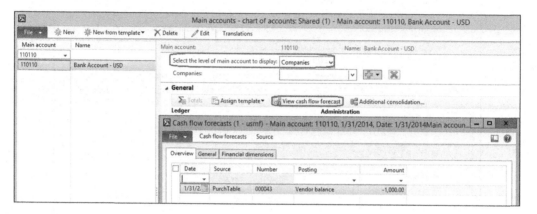

Summary

In this chapter, we covered the basics of cash flow forecast configurations and setups in Microsoft Dynamics AX, and the integration points between modules used to facilitate cash flow functions. We also showed a practical example of a cash flow transaction and inquiries, in addition to a forecast by currency and main account.

In the next chapter, we will discuss cost management from the inventory perspective, as it is the most significant cost for an organization, and requires control and monitoring.

8
Working with Cost Management

The costing function is one of the most critical subjects in the ERP implementation, specifically inventory costing. In the competitive and emerging markets of today, we aim at getting the best usage from the current company resources in order to ensure that they are translated into company profitability and more potential cash flow. On the other hand, the inventory cost affects the company reporting in the balance sheet and income statement along with the cost of goods sold and cost of production. This function requires intensive workshops during the implementation life cycle to contest the business costing model and how it will be mapped to Microsoft Dynamics AX.

In this chapter, we will cover the following topics:

- Understanding the business costing model
- Configuring inventory costing
- Exploring the inventory costing background (physical and financial update)
- Understanding inventory recalculation and closing
- Working with inventory marking
- Exploring inventory reconciliation

Understanding the business costing model

The highest significant cost of organizations is encumbered in the inventory costing. In this sense, one of the main objectives of ERP implementation is to manage, reduce, and control inventory costing. The inventory significantly affects the company's bottom line and profitability as well. The companies that carry inventory as a raw material for production bear the cost of inventory, which in turn affects the cost of production in addition to the goods in the process and the **cost of goods sold (COGS)** accordingly. The companies that carry inventory as stock for sales bear the inventory cost, which in turn affects the cost of goods sold.

The main driver of inventory cost is the purchase cost from the vendor in addition to all the costs that are paid until the goods are received into the company's warehouse, such as freight, customs duties, and loading. All these are known as miscellaneous charges, which is a function name in Microsoft Dynamics AX.

The company's profitability is directly impacted by the inventory cost. Therefore, it is essential for the organization to effectively manage the procurement activities and financial cost control that monitors inventory costs. The following figure shows Microsoft Dynamics AX inventory costing:

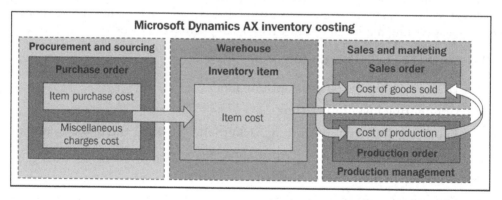

The implementation team ascertains the inventory costing strategy for the company. It is a joint effort between the financial controller, inventory and warehousing manager, and application consultant during the analysis phase of the implementation. The financial controller sets the inventory valuation method and inventory posting profiles. The inventory and warehousing manager sets the inventory item coding structure and item groups for inventory classifications. The application consultant maps the controller as well as the inventory and warehousing manager's requirements to Microsoft Dynamics AX 2012.

Configuring inventory costing

The configuration and setup of inventory costing are combined between the integrated modules of inventory and warehousing management, product information management, and financial controls. A collection of all types of setup is shown in the product master form, depicted in the following figure:

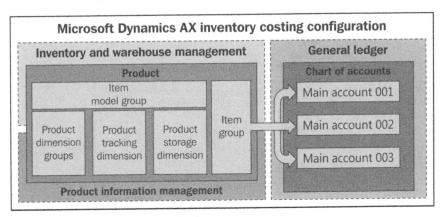

The blocks in the preceding figure are defined as follows:

- **Item model group**: This identifies the inventory valuation method
- **Product dimension groups**: This identifies the product's attributes
- **Product storage dimension groups**: This identifies the product's location
- **Product tracking groups**: This identifies the product's tracking information

Item model group

The main configuration and setup of inventory costing in Microsoft Dynamics AX is in **Item model group**, where we identify the inventory costing valuation method. For inventory model group, navigate to **Inventory and warehouse management | Setup | Inventory | Item model group**. Microsoft Dynamics AX 2012 R3 supports the following inventory valuation methods:

- **FIFO**: This is first-in, first-out
- **LIFO**: This is last-in, first-out
- **LIFO date**: This is the last-in, first-out date
- **Weighted avg.**: This is the weighted average
- **Weighted avg. date**: This is the weighted average date

- **Standard cost**: This is the standard cost
- **Moving average**: This is the moving average cost

The following screenshot shows all the inventory valuation methods:

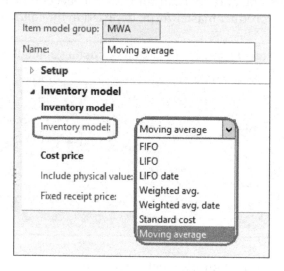

In the following section, we will highlight some of the item module group configurations:

- **Inventory policy**: This indicates whether the item or the service is stockable or nonstockable. Stockability indicates that the item will be tracked in the inventory transaction, and included in the inventory costing and its calculation.

- **Physical negative inventory**: This is a control point that prevents the inventory quantities to be issued from the warehouse if there is no available quantity. If the business requires issuing quantities more than the quantity available in the warehouse, this should be coordinated with the controller and the stock manager, as the inventory balance will be in negative.

- **Financial negative inventory**: This is allowed, by default, to issue quantities that are not financially updated yet. This is a control point that can prevent issuing inventory quantities from the warehouse without a financial update, which means the final cost must be known before issuing the items.

- **Post physical inventory**: This option posts the physical inventory to the **General ledger** module, and this requires a configuration on Accounts payable parameters and Accounts receivable parameters by checking the **Post product receipt in ledger** checkbox. If the **Post physical inventory** checkbox is unchecked, the physical transactions will not be posted in the ledger, regardless of the configuration in the AP/AR parameter setup forms.

- **Post financial inventory**: This option posts the financial inventory update to the **General ledger** module if this checkbox is checked. The posting will be as follows:

    ○ **Purchase order invoice update**: If this checkbox is checked, the amount of the items is posted to the inventory receipt account; otherwise, the amount of the items is posted to the purchase expenditure for product account.

    ○ **Sales order invoice update**: If this checkbox is checked, the amount of the items is posted to the inventory issue and the consumption accounts; otherwise, no posting occurs in the item consumption account or the issue account.

These fields are shown in the following screenshot:

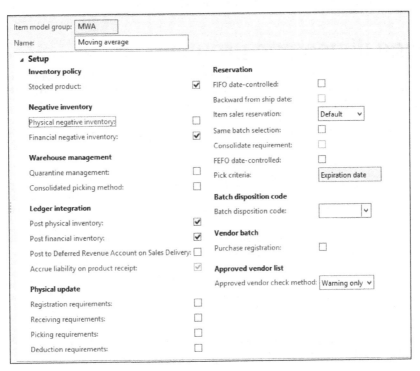

Product dimension groups

Product dimension groups represent the items' characteristics that identify the key differences of the item. For example, a polo shirt item has two dimensions, namely, size and color. The size and color can be small and blue or medium and blue. The following screenshot shows a product dimension group screen that represents the item attributes **Configuration**, **Size**, **Color**, and **Style**:

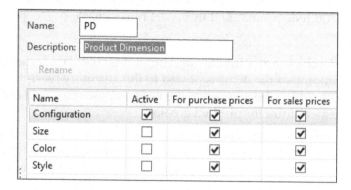

For product dimension groups, navigate to **Product information management | Setup | Dimension groups | Product dimension groups**.

Storage dimension groups

As you can see in the following screenshot, the storage dimension groups screen sorts the required stock, keeping a note of the location, whether it is **Site**, **Warehouse**, **Location**, or **Pallet ID**. This assists in the reporting of inventory quantities and cost.

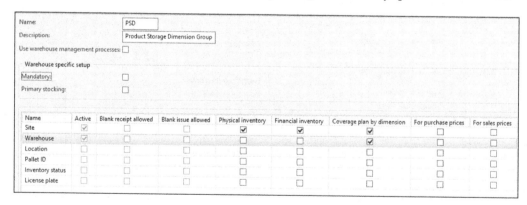

To access the storage dimension window, navigate to **Product information management | Setup | Dimension groups | Storage dimension groups**.

Tracking dimension groups

The tracking dimension is a lower-level assortment of products, irrespective of whether it is a serial number for electronic inventory items or a batch number. For tracking dimension groups, navigate to **Product information management | Setup | Dimension groups | Tracking dimension groups**, as shown in the following screenshot:

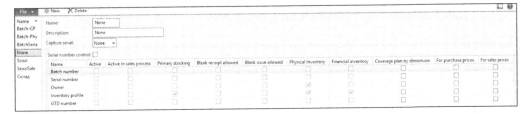

Item groups

As you can see in the following screenshot, **Item groups** is the product classification for inventory items, and it is the integration point between the inventory and financial modules. The classification of **Item groups** should be a joint effort between the stock manager and the controller. In order to access **Item groups**, go to **Inventory and warehouse management | Setup | Inventory | Item groups**.

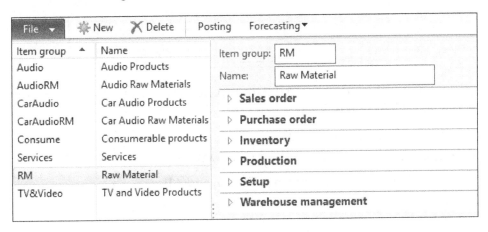

The inventory posting profile consists of the following possible inventory transactions:

- **Sales order**: This is a sales and marketing module transaction
- **Purchase order**: This is a procurement and sourcing module transaction
- **Inventory**: This is an inventory and warehousing management module transaction
- **Production**: This is a production management module transaction

The posting profiles are the integration point between the subledgers and the general ledger. It is a set of ledger accounts that are used to generate the automatic ledger entry in which a transaction occurs. It is possible to select different ledger accounts for each type of subledger transaction. Microsoft Dynamics AX offers flexibility in the setup of posting profiles. The posting can be on four different levels, as shown in the following figure:

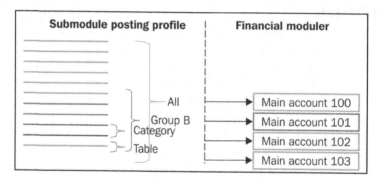

The posting domination levels are **All**, **Group**, **Category**, and **Table**. The preceding figure can be explained as follows:

- **Group B** dominates over **All**
- **Category** dominates over **Group B** and **All**
- **Table** dominates over **Category**, **Group**, and **All**

If the posting profile is for **All** and there are some groups that have been identified for a specific main account, then these will be excluded from the **All** setup. At the same time, if there is a category relation selected for a specific main account, then these categories will be excluded from the **All** and **Group** posting profiles. If there is a table relation selected for a specific main account, it will apply the **Table** posting profile. In order to access the inventory posting profile, go to **Inventory and warehouse management** | **Setup** | **Inventory** | **Posting** | **Posting**. The following screenshot illustrates an example of all of these posting domination levels:

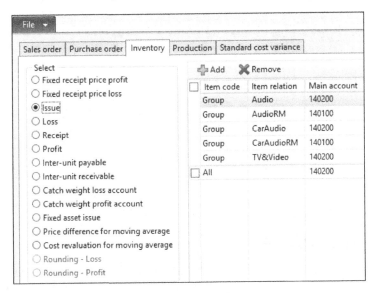

Exploring the inventory costing background

For highlighting the inventory costing model in Microsoft Dynamics AX in order to understand the inventory valuation methods, there are three main concepts – physical and financial update, inventory recalculation and closing, and marking.

Physical and financial updates

The physical and financial update considers real-life business scenarios where there is a difference between the reception costs and invoices. It works in uncertain business environments.

Physical update

The physical update represents the inventory transaction, whether it is a product receipt for a purchase order or a packing slip for a sales order. The reception price inherits from the item purchase price in the purchase order and identifies the item cost price in the warehouse. The cost of goods sold is retrieved from the inventory cost price and the physical issuance that occurred from the sales order. The following figure shows the physical and financial updates:

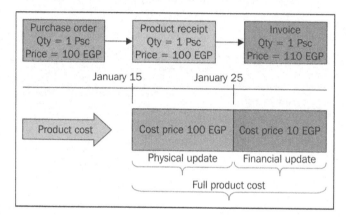

Financial update

The financial update represents the invoice posting either for a purchase order or a sales order. The sales order invoice only has an effect on sales revenue and cost of goods sold. While on the other hand, the purchase order invoice affects the inventory cost if there are changes in purchase price, be it an increase or a decrease.

 If your business requires considering the miscellaneous charges in the event of product reception, there is the Inventory II solution offered by FSB Development (http://www.fsbdev.com/).

The default mechanism of the financial update for purchase orders in Microsoft Dynamics AX is that the financial update dominates the physical update in order to allocate the final item addition cost that will be reflected in the inventory. The physical update can be considered as an estimated cost, and the final cost is reflected in the purchase order invoice that will affect inventory cost in the warehouse submodule and main account in the chart of accounts as well.

Understanding inventory recalculation and closing

The inventory recalculation is a normal procedure in the Microsoft Dynamics AX environment that calculates the inventory cost in the warehouse and adjusts the inventory issuances according to the inventory value model (the valuation method).

The inventory cost in Microsoft Dynamics AX is a running average cost. In order to apply the valuation method, the recalculation process should be run. The normal mechanism of the inventory cost calculation applies the inventory valuation method that is attached to the product master by running the recalculation function. The recalculation function mainly affects two areas: the item cost in the warehouse and the inventory adjustment entries for product issuances from the inventory that generates the inventory financial transaction entries.

> The inventory adjustment entries are generated when the issuance cost of the item is different from the current cost of the inventory items in the warehouse, according to the inventory model group (the valuation method). The entries are generated based on the original issuance transactions.
>
> For example, if COGS of the sales order is 100 EGP and the current cost in the warehouse is 110 EGP, the recalculation process generates an entry by 10 EGP (Dr. COGS 10, Cr. Inventory 10).

The commonly applied valuation method is **Weighted Average Cost**, where the inventory issuances are valued at the average cost of the items that are received during that period and also the on-hand inventory.

> The formula for weighted average is *Weighted average = (Received quantity * Received cost) + (On-hand quantity * On-hand cost) / (Received quantity + On-hand quantity)*

The inventory cost is also considered as a tentative cost. The inventory issuances carry the current running average cost. The actual cost is applied after the recalculation process is done and is based on the inventory valuation method that is configured in **Item model group**. The adjustment transactions represent the difference between the running average cost and the configured costing valuation method. To access the inventory closing window, navigate to **Inventory and warehouse management | Periodic | Closing and adjustment**. The following figure explains the inventory recalculation and closing concept:

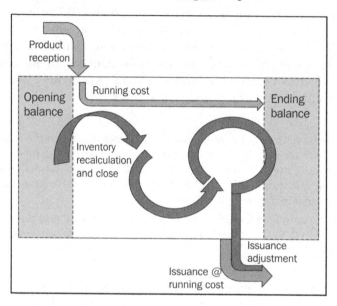

Working with inventory marking

During daily business in inventory management, there are some transactions that need to be returned to the inventory at the same cost at which they were issued. Each inventory transaction is associated to a unique **Lot ID**. Any inventory transaction is assigned to a Lot ID with a unique identification that helps in inventory cost and inventory transaction tracking; this is used to specify the transaction's cost. The marking function can be used with **Sales order** to specify the cost of goods sold for the marked line in the **Sales order** lines, and it can be used in the issuance return (inventory addition) from the movement journal, production order, and/or **bill of material (BOM)** journal. The following diagram shows the relation of the inventory marking between inventory issuance and receptions:

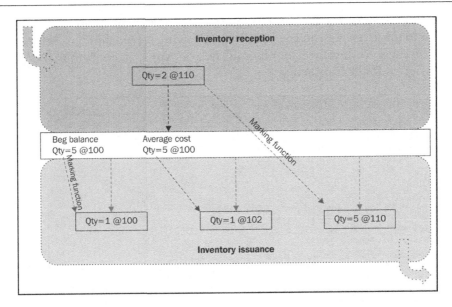

To access the marking function window, navigate to **Sales and marketing |
Common | All sales orders | Sales order**. Then, go to **Sales order lines**, click on
Inventory, and select **Marking**. This can be seen in the following screenshot:

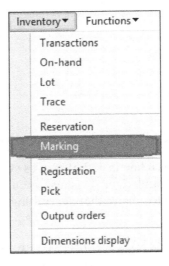

The **Marking** form lists all the relevant transactions for the inventory item, which will be set to mark on. As you can see in the following screenshot, the **Set mark now** checkbox is checked, and the users should click on **Apply** to confirm that the cost will be assigned to the transaction:

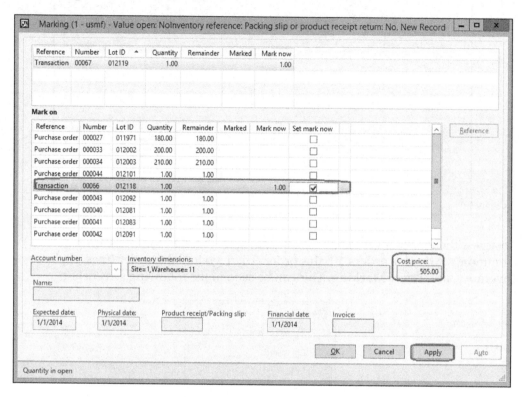

Exploring inventory reconciliation

The inventory reconciliation is a key task that proves system integrity between the general ledger and inventory subledger. This task occurs on a monthly basis as a check point after month close to ensure that everything is properly reconciled with this contentment routine.

In Microsoft Dynamics AX 2012 R3, a set of reports are concerned with inventory and general ledger reconciliation. In the following section, we will explore the inventory value report.

Inventory value report setup

The inventory value report setup gives the option to have versions of the report based on the purpose of the report focus. The report can concentrate on the reconciliation between inventory and inventory account, **work in progress (WIP)** account, **deferred cost of goods sold (deferred COGS)** account, and **cost of goods sold (COGS)** account, in addition to report design for columns and rows.

As shown in the following screenshot, to access inventory value report setup, go to **Inventory management | Setup | Costing | Inventory value reports**:

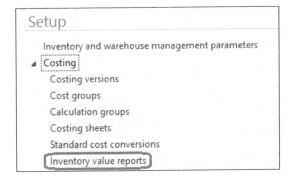

The following screenshot shows the inventory value report setup form. In order to create an inventory report, click on **New** or press *Ctrl + N* and enter the report ID and report description. On the **General** tab, you can predefine the date interval for the report as this is considered as a proposed value when generating the report in the second stage, and the user can select other date intervals as per their needs.

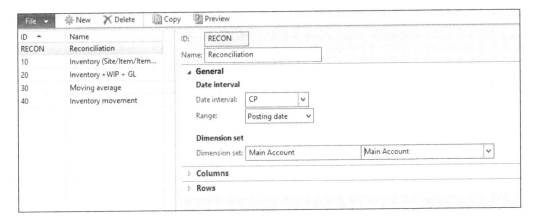

To set up date intervals, go to **General ledger | Setup | Periods | Date intervals**.

Now, identify the report date under the **Range** combobox, whether it is based on **Posting date** or **Transaction time**. Now, identify **Dimension set** that will be used in the report.

To set up a dimension set, navigate to **General ledger | Setup | Financial dimensions | Financial dimensions sets**.

When designing report columns in the **Columns** tab, the first part is **Financial position** that represents the inventory submodel values for **Inventory, WIP, Deferred COGS, COGS**, and/or **Profit and loss**, which will be showed in the report.

The second part is **Compare on-hand inventory value to cumulative accounting values**, which represents the ledger account for **Inventory, WIP, Deferred COGS**, and/or **COGS**.

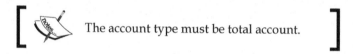 The account type must be total account.

The third part is **Inventory dimension**, which is the inventory breakdown by inventory dimensions and storage dimensions.

The other parts represent summarization of the report, including transactions not posted to ledger, calculate average cost price, and/or total quantity and value.

The following screenshot shows the **Columns** tab:

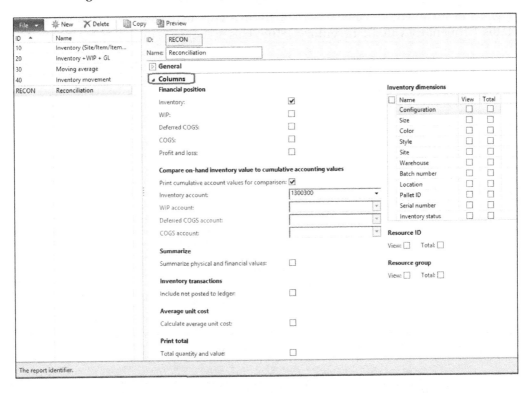

The **Rows** tab, where report rows can be designed, represents the cost elements that are required to be shown in the report row and also shows whether the level is **Totals** or **Transaction**, as shown in the following screenshot:

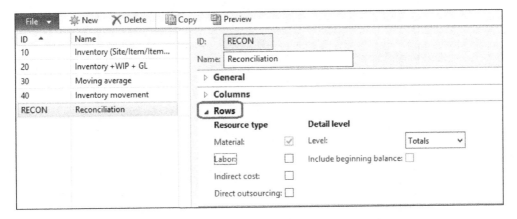

Inventory value report generation

To generate an inventory value report, go to **Inventory management | Reports | Status | Inventory value | Inventory value**. This is shown in the following screenshot:

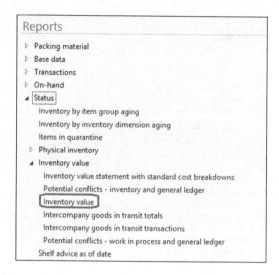

The inventory value report form, where we can select the required selection criteria and filtration, is shown in the following screenshot:

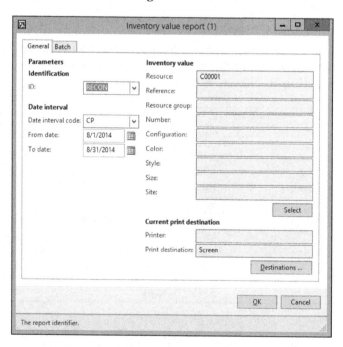

As shown in the following screenshot (which denotes the report print out), the report is divided into two sections – the first section represents the inventory submodule values, and the second section denotes the ledger account amount and the difference, if any:

File
1 of 1 100% Find | Next

Inventory value

Contoso Entertainment System USA

From	8/1/2014
To	8/31/2014

	Resource	Reference	Inventory: Financial quantity	Inventory: Financial amount	Inventory: Physical quantity posted	Inventory: Physical amount posted
Material						
	C00001	Ending balance	10.00	1,000.00	0.00	0.00
Material Totals			10.00	1,000.00	0.00	0.00

	Sum Inventory: Financial quantity	Sum Inventory: Financial amount	Sum Inventory: Physical quantity posted	Sum Inventory: Physical amount posted
Report summary	10.00	1,000.00	0.00	0.00

Inventory Ledger account	Account name	Amount	Percent
1300301	Raw Material	1,000.00	
	Total	1,000.00	
	Discrepancy	0.00	0.00

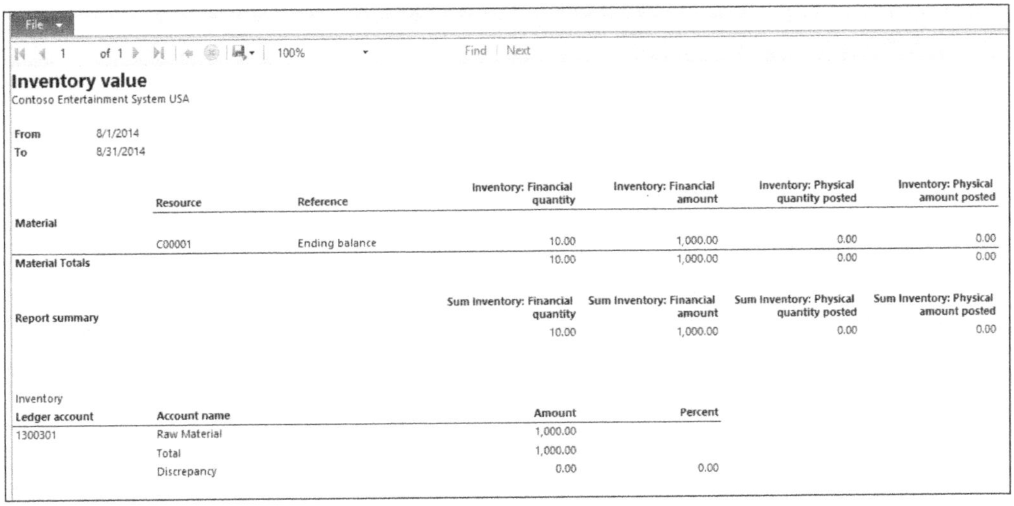

Summary

In this chapter, we covered the business model of inventory costing based on the business domain, the required configuration, and setup of Microsoft Dynamics AX in the inventory management module, as well as the integration concepts with the general ledger to map business requirements. The difference between the physical and financial updates model of Microsoft Dynamics AX is the inventory transaction with marking functions, in addition to recalculations and closing processes. We also covered the inventory value report, its setup, and generation.

In the next chapter, we will cover financial dimensions and practice practical reporting in Microsoft Dynamics AX.

9
Exploring Financial Dimensions

One of the major objectives of an ERP implementation is to provide clear business insights that can provide support for the organization's top management in the decision-making process. This requires analyzing the numbers, understanding them clearly, and then being able to examine the same numbers from different perspectives. Hence, a detailed structure is required to decide how an organization wants to analyze their numbers.

In this chapter, we will cover the following topics:

- Understanding the concept of financial dimensions
- Understanding the ledger account segmentation
- Posting types in Microsoft Dynamics AX
- Exploring dimension reporting

Understanding the concept of financial dimensions

The main source of financial reporting is the main accounts. The components of financial reporting are a balance sheet, income statement, trial balance, cash flow, and so on. The normal scenario is that the main account's balances do not mean much when it comes to analysis. This is because the balance sheet account is a total of the posted transactions' amounts, and it is required to be able to dig into this total breakdown. In other words, it provides us with information on how this amount is allocated, for example, among business units and departments. This allocation gives the lowest level of analysis to break down the same balance for a main account by more than one dimensional perspective.

The following diagram shows the financial dimension allocation for the **Main Account**:

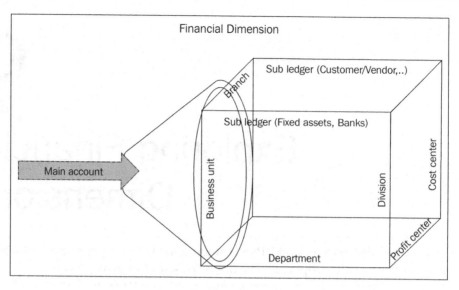

Financial dimensions provide us with a deeper analysis of the transactions posted on the general ledger accounts, where the financial dimension gives the controller an analytical view of the transactions that occurred on the expenses account. For example, one can analyze the account balance according to the financial dimensions assigned to the main account.

The Microsoft Dynamics AX 2012 financial dimension allows an organization to reach the lowest level of breakdown and analysis. There are three main standpoints to consider while discussing the financial dimension:

- The first standpoint is the required breakdown analysis for each main account in the chart of accounts in order for it to be utilized at the reporting level.

- The second standpoint is the controls and validations while doing the data entry in order to certify that the keyed-in transactions are allocated to the required dimensions before the transaction is posted. This directly affects the accuracy of reporting.

- The third standpoint is the reconciliation between the subledger and the general ledger, and the ability to break down the balance using the subledger (customers, vendors, items, banks, and so on).

These standpoints are shown in the following diagram:

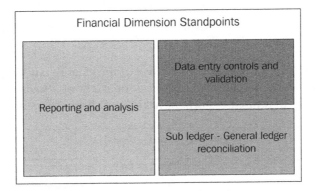

The role of the Microsoft Dynamics AX consultant is to clarify the best usage of financial dimensions to the concerned parties. The key process owners who ascertain the financial dimensions' requirements are the **Chief Financial Officer (CFO)** and the financial controller. The three main standpoints of financial dimension can be summarized as follows:

- **Reporting and analysis**: This is used to identify reporting needs and data entry results

- **Data entry controls and validations**: This is used for data entry filtration

- **Subledger and general ledger reconciliation**: This is used for reconciliation of transactions between the subledger and the general ledger

The implementation team ascertains the financial dimensions' requirements during the analysis phase to understand what the business needs are at the reporting and analysis stage, and then identifies the required number of financial dimensions and how to utilize these dimensions.

 Microsoft Dynamics AX 2012 R3 supports an unlimited number of financial dimensions.

According to the business domain, every business needs to build the structure of their chart of accounts and financial dimensions. They also need to identify which subledger should be tracked at the general ledger level. To build the structure of the chart of accounts and financial dimensions, follow the ensuing steps:

- Classify the required dimensions for each main account, whether it is mandatory or optional.

- Categorize the financial dimensions that are interrelated and are dependent on each other to filter dimensions based on the previously selected value.

- Categorize the intra-related dimensions. These are not dependent on the previously selected dimension.

Microsoft Dynamics AX 2012 supports the use of the existing subledger master data to define financial dimensions. The following diagram illustrates the usage of financial dimensions in reporting and analysis, in addition to reconciliation:

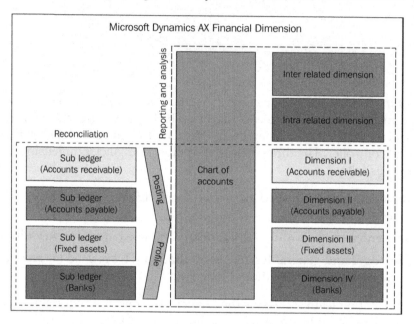

The heart of a financial dimension is the chart of accounts, as shown in the previous diagram. It should be carefully structured and set to the required dimension validation of each main account. It is important to consider this structure of the chart of accounts and dimensions' validation in the opening balance upload, as it will affect reporting and analysis in addition to an automatic transaction, such as the exchange rate adjustment.

Changing the financial dimension's structure and validation during operations should be wisely planned, evaluated, and executed as it may affect some historical transactions and some automatic transactions (for example, exchange rate adjustment, inventory adjustment, and settlement). It is recommended that you apply it at the beginning of a month when all historical transactions, along with the old structure and validation, are closed.

Understanding the ledger account segmentation

The following section covers the newly introduced segmented ledger account entry in Microsoft Dynamics AX 2012 and the financial dimensions' assignment in a one-line voucher entry.

Segmented ledger accounts

Microsoft Dynamics AX 2012 introduced the segmented ledger account where the main account and the financial dimension are combined in a single line. This gives more flexibility and control to the data that is entered than the previous versions.

The data entries are considered as the major sources of information quality. During the analysis phase, the implementation team exploring the reporting requirements as well as the process owners and top management require reliable information, and this information is generated by the data entry. It is required to control the data entry to ensure that the entered data is formatted in the correct way. The application consultant can fulfill these requirements to ensure the quality of data entry by performing the following tasks: by defaulting some values from the master data that are automatically populated in the transaction, by changing fields to be mandatory for reporting, and by identifying the required financial dimensions to the transaction level.

Microsoft Dynamics AX 2012 offers a very powerful entry mechanism that is built on the account structure. The segmented entry control is a function that simplifies the data entry and controls the complex combination of accounts and financial dimensions.

It is a simple cheat sheet window that gives the user hints on which segment should be entered, in addition to the lookup for that segment.

To access the general journal, navigate to **General ledger | Journal | General journal lines**. The following screenshot shows the simple cheat sheet in detail:

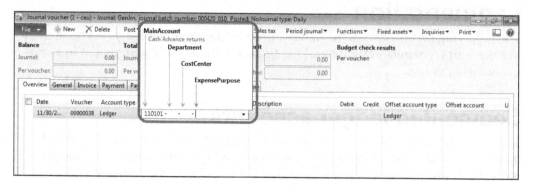

Financial dimensions entry

In this section, we will explore the further enhancement of segmented entries that gives more flexibility to Microsoft AX 2012 to accommodate the one-line entry to allocate the segments. This was followed in previous versions of Microsoft Dynamics AX, where the default application assigned dimensions to both the sides (debit and credit), enforcing the end users to use the double-line entries to have different financial dimensions for each side.

Microsoft AX 2012 covers this point completely. If an entry is created in a one-line style, the voucher created is that of a debit (vendor) or credit (bank) and requires the assigning of different segments. Here is a new feature where we will be able to assign different financial dimensions for **Account** and **Offset account**. Navigate to **General ledger | Journals | General Journal**, and then go to **Lines**. In the general journal form, click on the **Financial Dimension** button. There are two options here, **Account** and **Offset account**, as shown in the following screenshot:

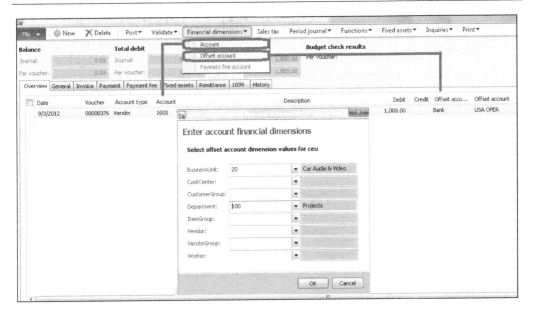

Creating financial dimensions

There was an obstacle facing the implementation team in assigning master data to financial dimensions such as vendors, customers, fixed assets, items, and banks, and the best-case scenario to tackle this is an automatic (online) assignment in order to keep consistency of assigning the default financial dimension to the master data. The solution for this requirement is that it will either be maintained manually or by an automatic trigger (customization). Microsoft Dynamics AX 2012 has bridged this gap. Microsoft Dynamics AX 2012 has two types of financial dimensions, as shown in the following diagram:

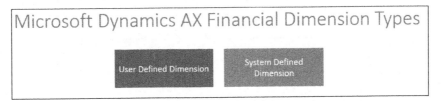

The first type is the user-defined dimension, which was used in Microsoft Dynamics AX 2009 to allow users to add an unlimited number of dimensions (business unit, cost center, purpose, profit center, and so on) as per the outcome of the analysis. The second type is the system-defined dimension. It helps in assigning the master data to newly created dimensions such as vendors, customers, fixed assets, and items.

The steps to create a new dimension are as follows:

1. Navigate to **General ledger | Setup | Financial dimensions** as shown in the following screenshot:

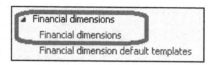

2. Within **Financial dimensions**, navigate to **Financial dimensions**, as shown in the following screenshot:

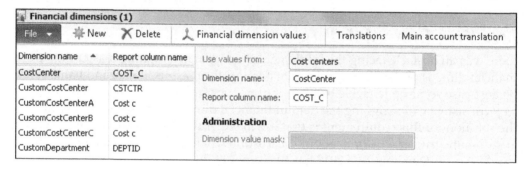

3. Create a new financial dimension by clicking on **New** in the **Financial dimensions** window, as shown in the following screenshot:

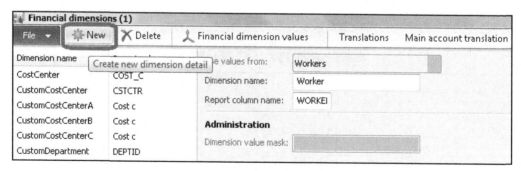

4. Select the dimension type.

5. If you want to add a user-defined dimension, select **<Custom dimension>**, as shown in this screenshot:

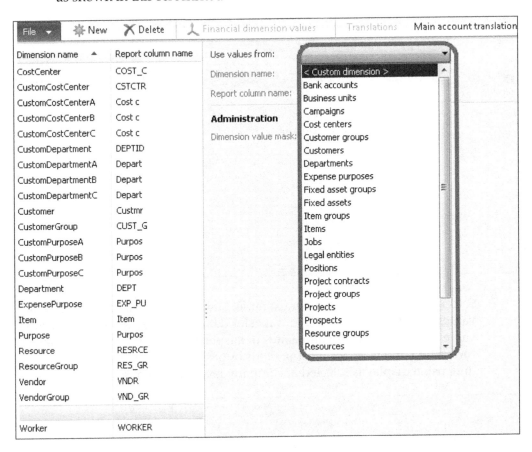

6. Enter the user-defined dimension list and configure the dimension value by its dates of activation and/or suspension by filling in the **Active from**, **Active to**, and **Suspended** fields, as shown in the following screenshot:

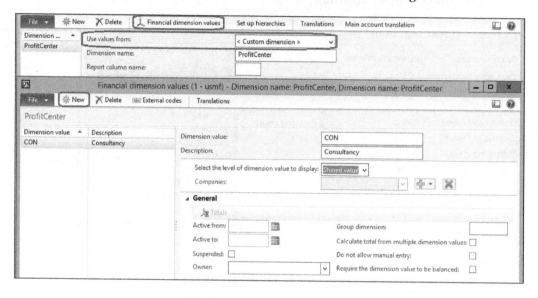

7. Select the subledger values, for example, `Customers`. Then select the financial values called from the customer's master data and configure the dimension value by its dates of activation and/or suspension. The **Financial statement formatting** and **Cost accounting** fields only show when the level of dimension display is selected at company level instead of shared level.

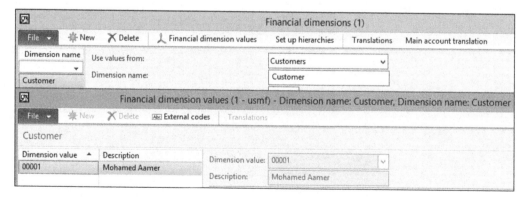

Configuring the account structure

The account structure's configuration identifies the required dimensions for the main account. The account structure is attached to the company's ledger setup (refer to *Chapter 1, Getting Started with Microsoft Dynamics AX 2012*). As you can see in the following diagram, an account structure is a combination of the main account and financial dimensions:

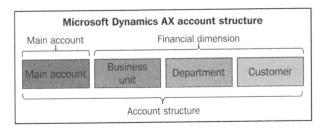

Microsoft Dynamics AX 2012 provides flexibility to add the account structure for the main accounts with any combination of financial dimensions.

Navigate to **General ledger | Setup | Chart of accounts | Configure account structures** to configure the account structures. As you can see in the following screenshot, **Configure account structures** should be in the edit mode to be edited:

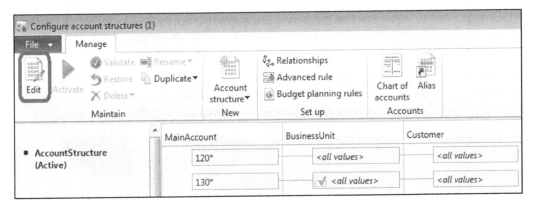

Add a segment (financial dimension) to the account structure that is already defined (regardless of whether it has user-defined or system-defined dimensions) by clicking on the **Add segment option**, as shown in the following screenshot:

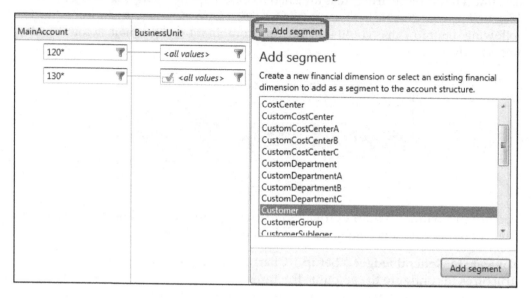

 The green tick shown in the preceding screenshot needs to be checked in order to activate the proper segment.

Microsoft Dynamics AX 2012 provides an option to identify the main account by identifying one specific account and/or a part of the main accounts. This is done by selecting **Specify which values are allowed**, as shown in the following screenshot. This provides the availability to use the filtration option.

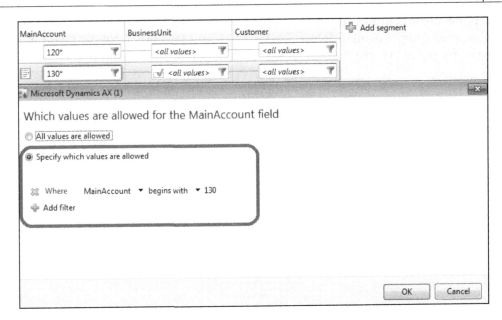

As you can see in the following screenshot, it is possible to arrange the order of the dimensions by moving the segments to the left or right, or by right-clicking to move the segment:

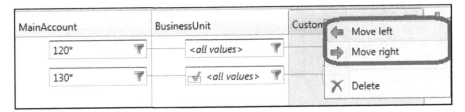

Accepting a blank (null) value in the dimension is possible. The feature of accepting a value or keeping it blank is introduced in Microsoft Dynamics AX 2012, and it is allowed for users to leave the dimension blank, as shown in the following screenshot:

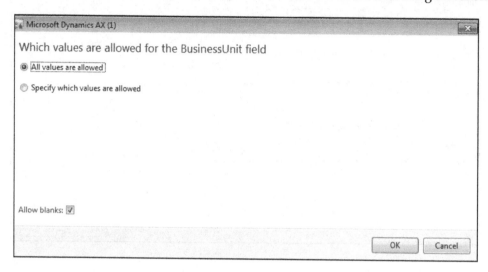

To apply the account structure configuration, it must be activated as shown in the following screenshot:

Advanced rules structure

There is a limitation in the account structure—you can have only ten dimensions, but more dimensions may be required. The **Advanced Rules Structure** can add an unlimited number of dimensions. The concept of the advanced rules structure is to create an advanced rule structure record, add the required segments to it, and activate it. This also involves attaching it to the account structure. The following diagram illustrates the concept of advanced rules structure:

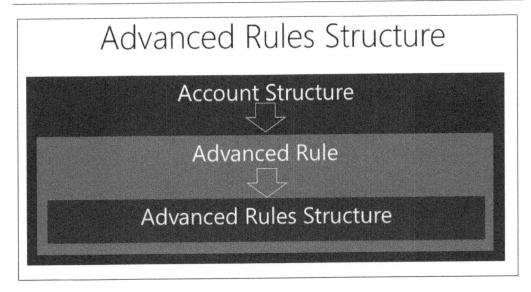

In order to create an advanced rules structure, navigate to **General Ledger | Setup | Chart of accounts | Advanced rules structure**, as shown in the following screenshot. Click on the **New** button to create a new record. Now, in the right-hand corner of the window, click on **Add segment** to add dimension segments, and then click on **Activate**.

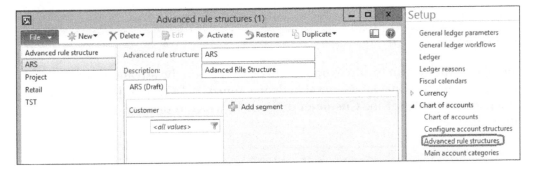

In order to attach the advanced rule structure to the account structure, navigate to **General ledger | Setup | Chart of accounts | Configure account structure on the account structure form**. Ensure that it is in the edit mode, and then click on **Advanced rule** in the ribbon. Create a new record by clicking on the **New** button.

After entering the ID and description in the right-hand corner under the **Advanced rule structures** tab, click on **Add** and select the **Advanced rule structure** value. Then make sure you activate the account structure configuration.

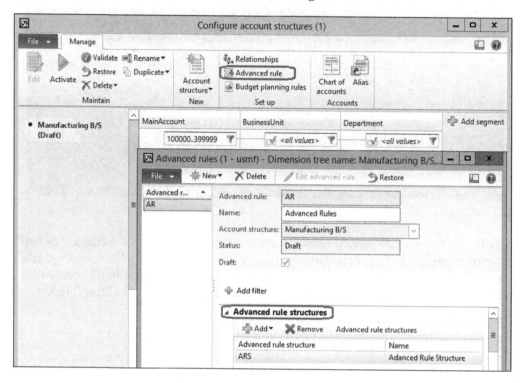

This allows the system to add extra dimensions based on the advanced rule structure. If you navigate to **General Ledger | Journals | General journal in the voucher line**, you'll see the **Customer** dimension, which is defined in the advanced rule structure:

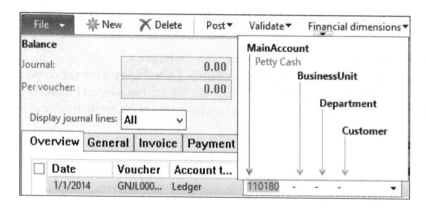

Fixed dimension

In some cases, there is a business requirement to fix a particular dimension on a specific main account. A fixed dimension is on a company level. In order to activate the fixed financial dimension, the account should be specified for a particular company.

In order to set up a financial dimension on the main account, navigate to **General ledger | Setup | Chart of accounts**, and then select the account structure. Then click on **Edit**. This will open the main accounts in the edit mode. As shown in following screenshot, select a specific account, then select **Companies** in **Select the level of main account to display**, and then select the company ID in the **Companies** field. This will show the **Financial dimension** tab.

Here the dimension could be **Not fixed**, which means the dimension value will be as proposed, or **Fixed value**, which means the dimension value will be always used for this main account. When we select a fixed value, a dialog box will always pop up.

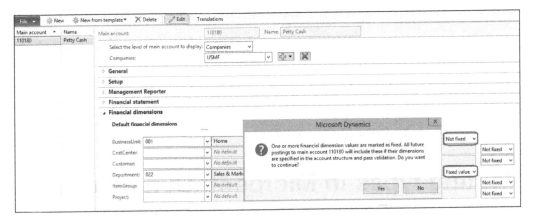

The result of this setup when we create and post the general journal looks like what is shown in the following screenshot. Navigate to **General Ledger | Journals | General Journal**, but do not select the **Department** value with the `110180` account. Now post the journal. Under the voucher inquiry, the system fixes the **Department** dimension value on the account as per the main account setup.

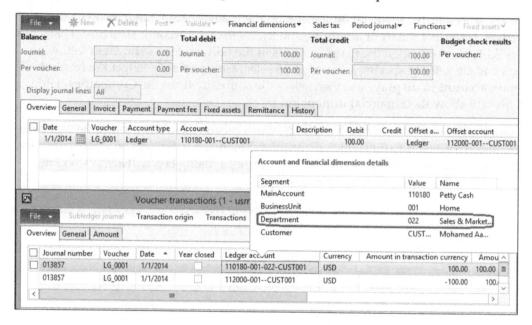

Posting types in Microsoft Dynamics AX

In Microsoft Dynamics AX, there are two ways to post transactions to the main account. The first type is through the posting profile, which represents the integration point between the general ledger and subledger, and generates the financial entries automatically according to the posting profile's setup. The second type is the journal entries, which post directly to the ledger accounts.

The posting profile concept

Posting profiles are the point of integration between the subledger (fixed assets, accounts payable, inventory, banks, accounts receivable, project, and production) and the general ledger. The posting profile is a set of main accounts that are used to generate the automatic ledger entry in which a transaction has occurred. It is possible to select different main accounts for each type of subledger transactions. Microsoft Dynamics AX offers flexibility in setting up posting profiles. Posting could be on three different levels:

- **All**: Any transaction occurring on any subledger such as customers, vendors, and/or items will be redirected to the main account, which is assigned to all the customers, vendors, and/or items

- **Group B**: Any transaction for a particular customer, vendor, and/or item inherits the posting profile of the customer, vendor, and/or item group to which they are assigned

- **Table**: Any transaction that occurs for a subledger, vendor, and/or item will be directed to the ledger account, which is assigned to the posting profile

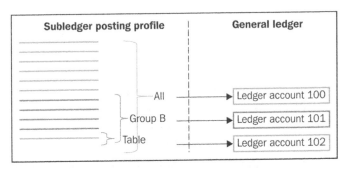

The common question during the design phase is which level out of **All**, **Group B**, and **Table** will prevail over the other levels. Customers can be assigned to a specific group, but in some exceptions, the customer should be directed to another ledger account. The lowest level of all is Table, which specifies the customer ID and will prevail over Group B and All.

To access the posting profile, navigate to the following paths:

- For the Accounts payable posting profiles, navigate to **Accounts payable | Setup | Vendor posting profiles**

- For the Accounts receivable posting profiles, navigate to **Accounts receivable | Setup | Customer posting profiles**

- For the inventory posting profile, navigate to **Inventory and warehouse management | Setup | Posting | Posting**

 The ledger accounts specified in the posting profile must not allow a manual entry to be created in the general ledger, in order to preserve the integrity between the general ledger and subledger.

Journal posting

The journal model in Microsoft Dynamics AX is a journal header that contains voucher lines. Here, the default data in the journal name (header), such as currency and sales taxes, is copied to the voucher lines. This data can also be changed in the voucher lines. Every subledger has its own journal name based on the transaction type. Navigate to **General ledger | Setup | Journals | Journal names** to access the journal names.

The voucher line can be a ledger account, vendor account, customer account, fixed asset, bank, or project. If the selected account is an option other than the ledger account, the subledger posting profile will direct the posting to the ledger account.

The journal posting elements are the information listed as follows:

- **Journal posting controls**: The journal posting controls consist of embedded controls that cannot be changed or avoided. The voucher balance and other controls form the basic setup for each journal name that can be applied at any time. This can be explained as follows:

  - **Voucher balance and journal balance**: The basic accounting principle, which is a financial entry, must be balanced so that the debit side is equal to the credit side. Microsoft Dynamics AX prevents posting any transaction if there are any discrepancies between the transactions sides (debit or credit). This validation occurs on the voucher line as well as the journal.

  - **Transaction date**: The balance voucher must be posted on the same date as the transaction sides (debit and credit). Microsoft Dynamics AX applies the concept of one-line voucher entry and two-line entries. This control is validated if the entry appears on two lines.

  - **Offset account**: Fixing an offset account on a specific journal will prevent users from changing or modifying the offset account on the voucher line. It can be a proposal and it may be changed at the transaction level.

- **Blocking the journal name**: During the daily operations on the journal entries in Microsoft Dynamics AX, whether these journals are related to the general ledger, fixed assets, accounts payable, accounts receivable, inventory journals movement, transfer journals, or BOM, it is normal to have more than one journal name under the same journal type. Each journal name serves a specific business transaction based on the business requirements gathered in the analysis phase. Microsoft Dynamics AX gives this control to a private user group in the journal name configuration. This allows the use of that journal only for the appropriate user group.

- **Journal approvals**: Approval controls on the general ledger journals are divided into two levels. The first level is the one-step approval, and the second level is the workflow approval. The workflow approval requires an automatic batch job to run at a specific interval in order to ensure that the approvers receive the documents that require approval. The two levels of approval can be explained as follows:

  - **One-step approval**: This is considered as a simple configuration for the journal's approvals, as it assigns a user group to be the approval group for a specific journal name.

  - **Workflow approval**: This approval needs to configure a workflow approval step. This gives you the flexibility to add a complex approval matrix that will be triggered if the condition, which is configured in the workflow occurs on the journal. Thus, the workflow approval offers more control on journal posting.

Exploring dimension reporting

Overall, this chapter covers the financial dimension model from business and application angles. The required configuration for main accounts and the account structure directly affect the accuracy of the data entered, by controlling the dimensions' selection and validation.

The following section will explore the financial dimensions' reporting capabilities in a trial balance and dimension statement.

Financial dimension sets

Financial dimension sets are the result of reporting the transactions based on financial dimensions. They can be a combination of more than one financial dimension. Financial dimension sets are initially designed, along with the designing of financial dimensions in the design phase, to accommodate the reporting perspective, and they can be extended during the operations.

As you can see in the following diagram, the financial dimension set is used as a focal point in reporting, where it will be able to analyze numbers by one dimension focus or more than one focus:

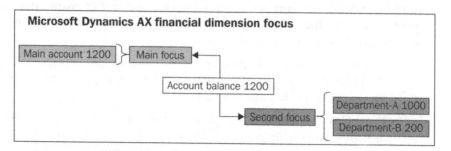

Identify the financial dimension set by selecting one or more dimensions from **Available financial dimensions**. The selected financial dimensions are used for analysis. The analysis could be, for example, *Main account + Department* or *Main account + Department + Cost Center*, as shown in the following screenshot:

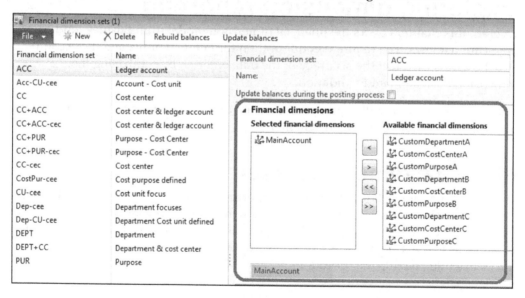

To access the financial dimension sets, navigate to **General ledger | Setup | Financial dimension | Financial dimension sets**.

Trial balance is one of the major financial reports where the trial balance report will be able to generate a transaction's trial balance for all the main accounts. In Microsoft Dynamics AX 2012, this report is converted to a form.

To access **Trial balance**, navigate to **General ledger | Common | Trial balance**, as shown in the following screenshot:

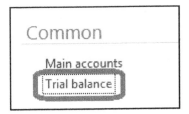

Identify the reporting date of the trial balance by entering the following dates:

- **From date**: In this field, enter the start date of the report date range
- **To date**: In this field, enter the end date of the report date range

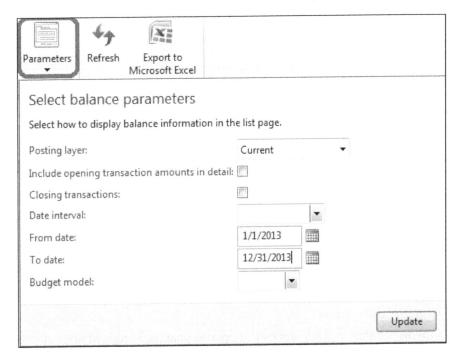

 The date range of **Trial balance** should be within one fiscal year. Thus, the info log message should be displayed in the following format: From date is in fiscal year 20XX. To date is in fiscal year 20XX. Dates must be in the same fiscal year.

For example, From date is in fiscal year 2010. To date is in fiscal year 2010. Dates must be in the same fiscal year.

Identify **Financial dimension set** as a focus option, as shown in this screenshot:

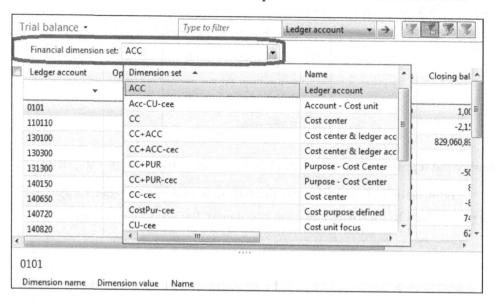

Trial balance is broken down by the selected **Financial dimension set**, as shown in the following screenshot:

Trial balance contains the following information:

- **Ledger account**: This shows the main account or the account structure dimension.

- **Opening balance**: This shows the opening balance amount after closing the fiscal year.

- **Debit**: This shows the transaction of the amount debited on that account (monthly movement).

- **Credit**: This shows the transaction of the amount credited on that account (monthly movement).

- **Closing balance**: This shows the closing balance for that account at the end of the fiscal period. The date range is calculated as the sum of the net difference and the opening balance.

As you can see in the following screenshot, the **Dimension** statement is the most commonly generated report by the controller to examine the main balance, along with the dimensions' allocation. Navigate to **General ledger | Reports | Transactions | Dimension statement** to access the dimension statement.

The financial dimensions' report filtration identifies the following parameters:

Parameter	Description
Primary financial dimension set	This is used to select the primary financial dimension set for the report.
Secondary financial dimension set	This is used to select the secondary financial dimension set for the report.
Date interval	This is used to select the current date interval for the report.
From date	This is used to enter or select the start of the date range to print transactions for.
To date	This is used to enter or select the end of the date range to print transactions for.

Parameter	Description
New page	Select this checkbox to insert a page break between each account.
Posting layer	This is used to select how the posting layer or combination of posting layers should be included for the selected column such as the following: • **Current**: This column will contain transactions that are included in the current posting layer • **Operations**: This column will contain transactions that are included in the current posting layer or the operations posting layer • **Tax**: This column will contain transactions that are included in the tax posting layer • **Operations minus tax**: This column will contain the net transactions from the operations posting layer minus the tax posting layer • **Only operations**: This column will contain transactions that are included in the operations posting layer • **Only tax**: This column will contain transactions that are included in the tax posting layer • **Operations plus tax**: This column will contain transactions that are included in the operations posting layer or the tax posting layer • **Total**: This column will contain transactions that are included in the current posting layer, operations posting layer, or tax posting layer
Include the opening transaction amounts in detail	Select this checkbox to include the opening transactions from the line of the report that lists the opening balance. Opening transactions are displayed in the report details.
Closing transactions	Select this checkbox to display the closing transactions. Clear this checkbox to display the closing transactions in the closing balance in the summary form.

The following screenshot shows the **Statement by dimensions** report query:

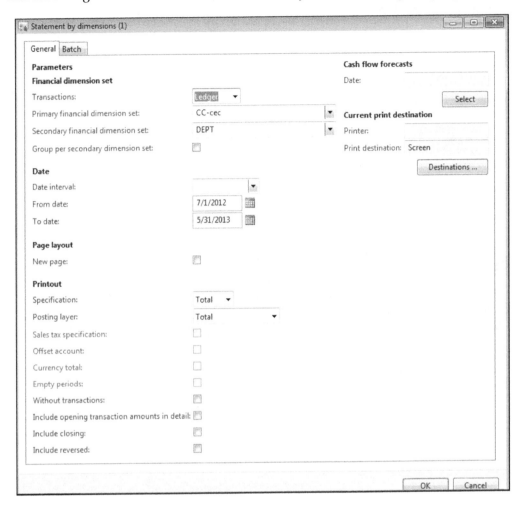

As you can see in the next screenshot, the dimension statement breaks down the account balance by department:

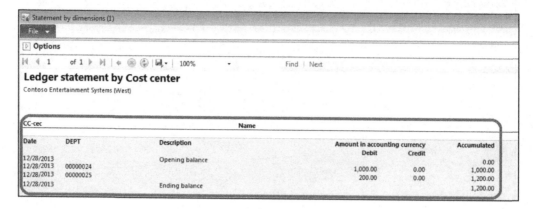

Summary

In this chapter, we covered the business concept of financial dimensions and segmentation of ledger accounts. We also covered Microsoft Dynamics AX posting profile types, journal posting and its controls, and financial dimensions reporting.

In the next chapter, we will explore financial reporting and analysis, planning reporting needs, information source blocks, and discovering Microsoft Dynamics AX reporting options.

10
Exploring Financial Reporting and Analysis

The main principles of reporting are the reliability of business information and the ability to get the right information at the right time for the right person. Reports that analyze ERP data in an expressive way represent the output of the ERP implementation. Reporting is considered as the cream of the implementation and the next level of value that the solution stakeholders should aim for. This ultimate outcome results from building all reports based on a single point of information.

In this chapter, we will cover the following topics:

- Planning reporting needs for ERP
- Understanding the information technology value chain
- Understanding Microsoft Dynamics AX information source blocks
- Discovering Microsoft Dynamics AX reporting
- Reporting options
- Reporting currency

Planning reporting needs for ERP

The Microsoft Dynamics AX implementation teamwork should challenge the management's reporting needs in the analysis phase of the implementation with a particular focus on exploring the data required to build reports. These data requirements should then be cross-checked with the real data entry activities that end users will execute to ensure that business users will get vital information from the reports.

On several projects, there are no well-defined reports except the financial reports (trial balance, income statement, and balance sheet) that are in place during analysis. Later, for live operations on such projects, the implementation team determines the need for more data and starts chasing the required information inside the application by completing the missing information and fields, and/or redesigning the data entry process. This may lead to an increase in the data entry time due to additional steps for data validations and the surprise discovery that there are not enough end user resources to execute the updated requirements. Hence, there should be a balance between the sum of required data entry values that directly affect the reporting quality, and the total number of end user resources that perform the data entry process.

Another word of caution is that the solution architect may recognize during the operation that some transactions are performed by one end user, but typically, these transactions are performed by two or three end users to attain the segregation of duties and control. For example, in the procurement cycle, there is one user who creates the inventory item, purchase order, and reception, but these transactions are normally performed by three different users. In this kind of resource-constrained situation, the segregation of duties and control concepts are breached, and the ERP solution is negatively impacted for the end users and key users. In these situations, the root cause of the concern is not the functionalities of ERP but the lack of allocated resources.

The two other important models of reporting are as follows:

- **Pulling reports**: Pulling of reports refers to the active requesting of reports by operational managers for the lowest transactional level such as purchasing, warehousing, sales, marketing, and financial entries. The middle management layer will pull reports to serve procurement, commercial/sales, and controllership.

- **Pushing reports**: Pushing of reports refers to the Business Intelligence (BI) capabilities that serve the top management, such as offering KPIs, balance score cards, and analytics/comparison views.

The various reporting levels of Microsoft Dynamics AX are shown in the following diagram:

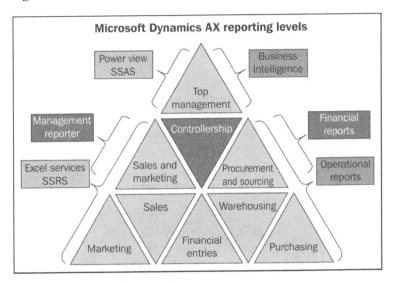

Microsoft Dynamics AX 2012 R3 and the supporting Microsoft technology stack offer a diversity of reporting capabilities, including ad hoc reports for the transactional level, developed by Microsoft Excel 2013, Excel Services, and Microsoft **SQL Server Analysis Services (SSAS)**. The Microsoft Dynamics **Management Reporter** offers the controllership in the middle management the ability to create and run financial reports. For the BI solutions built for Microsoft Dynamics AX, customers should begin with **Excel Power View**, SSAS, and **PerformancePoint Services** in SharePoint. The different levels of management are as follows:

- **Operational management**: The operational managers are involved in monitoring the performance of each business unit and managing employees

- **Middle management**: The middle managers are focused on the internal firm's performance, including revenues and costing management, resource allocation, and the development of short-term plans

- **Top management**: The top managers are focused on strategic business decisions that affect long-term plans, future performance, and the firm's overall objectives

Understanding the information technology value chain

In this section, we will explore reporting and data management in ERP from the management's information system perspective, with its dependent layers.

The model of a management information system is most applicable to the **Information Technology (IT)** manager or **Chief Information Officer (CIO)** of a business. Business owners likely don't care as much about the specifics as long as these aspects of the solution deliver the required results. The information technology value chain is shown in the following diagram:

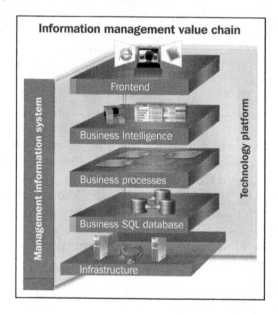

ERP implementations in enterprises have multiple components for successful project delivery. The most common element is addressing business requirements at all enterprise levels from basic IT infrastructure to user interface technology.

Infrastructure

Infrastructure is vital and ensures the reliability of the solution, assuring the availability of daily business operations. It must also be able to sustain an agreed level of uptime.

Hardware sizing depends on elements as well as a number of transactions, users, locations, and the available connectivity for each location. The infrastructure must also meet the architectural requirements of the servers that will ride the application, database, and reporting.

Beyond the live production planning environment, each company should consider building at least three different environments, as follows:

- The first is a development environment for testing customizations and the new functionalities.

- The second is a training environment that is a replication of the live environment and can accept tested updates from the development environment.

- The third is a live production environment for live transactions. It is similarly important to consider clustering and load balancing.

Having a single reporting server improves the reporting performance with **SQL Server Business Intelligence** reporting or **SQL Server Reporting Services** (**SSRS**). Furthermore, there are automatic batch jobs for notifications, alerts, and running special processes that set more load on the application server. Therefore, assigning these batch jobs to a separate server is favored. Depending on the industry, external access to Microsoft Dynamics AX can have an important impact on server performance. For example, for external access from customers and vendors, a retail business should consider an integrated e-commerce solution with Microsoft Dynamics AX.

Database management

The relational database (Microsoft SQL Server) that stores all the ERP-related transactions is known as **Online Transactional Processing** (**OLTP**). For BI reporting with a SQL Server, SSAS can store the aggregations, measures, and dimensions. This results in a higher performance in querying reports. It is also important to consider backup and restore strategies.

Reports from Microsoft Dynamics AX are based on the SSRS approach that has been standardized with Microsoft Dynamics AX 2012.

Business processes

The comprehensive business processes will reflect the data requirements. The design of a business process should identify the data owner, and where and when the data was captured.

Business processes are transformed into business functions in Microsoft Dynamics AX. The applied access rights for users' security ensure the segregation of duties, data ownership, and accuracy of data validation. Similarly, the approval matrix in a workflow will define the control mechanisms in the business processes such as the required management approvals.

Business Intelligence

It is often useful to analyze and measure a company's business results against industry benchmarks and best practices as a technique to develop the most valuable indicators and reports.

The richness of Power View and Excel Services gives the Microsoft Dynamics AX 2012 Enterprise Portal significant power to perform analysis and increase business insights more than any earlier release could.

Frontend

The frontend pinpoints the devices that the organization will need to access the applications that are being used. The most commonly used device in many organizations is still the laptop. More widespread access from numerous locations over the Internet may require more planning for mobile devices (cellular phones, handheld devices, and tablets). For example, Microsoft has introduced Microsoft Business Analyzer for Windows 8 that gives access to the high-level reports of charts for Microsoft Dynamics AX.

Understanding Microsoft Dynamics AX information source blocks

In this section, we will explore the information sources that eventually determine the strategic value of BI reporting and analytics. These are divided into three blocks. The first block is the detailed transaction level, the second is BI, and the third is executive decisions. These three blocks are explained in the following sections.

Detailed transactions block

At its roots, BI depends on capturing accurate transactional data from business processes at the first level of detail and transforming these processes into a regular flow of meaningful entries in an ERP solution such as Microsoft Dynamics AX. Application consultants should consider the reports that are required by the customers and certify that the required data points are captured through the recording process for daily transactions. Whenever possible, the application consultant has a responsibility to also challenge the business process owners about the process, as it relates to using the data to make changes to optimize the business. The following diagram shows the detailed transactions block:

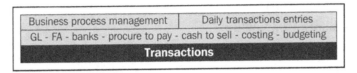

In some projects, consultants split their attention between business process workshops during business requirement gathering in the analysis phase, and the establishment of the data structure in forms during the design phase. It is vital to document the business process including the start point, end point, comprehensive steps of the process (if needed), the data path in each step, and exceptional cases for each process. On the other hand, the forms are a transformation of the business processes into the real work activities of employees (fields, grids, buttons, multiple selection, and so on).

The main processes that should be addressed in a typical ERP implementation include banks, fixed assets, procure to pay, cash to sell, costing, and budgeting, with the general ledger integration for each.

Business Intelligence block

BI is the second block in the information hierarchy that uses the raw data of transactions to provide valuable information to different levels of the organization. BI adds a layer of aggregation on transactions and makes it possible to create a comparative analysis for key measures such as actual versus budget comparisons.

The consultant should identify the measures needed and how they will be utilized from the transactional level. These measures are raw numbers aggregated from specific fields that result from a definite process or a combination of business processes.

Microsoft Dynamics AX 2012 is delivered with 14 cubes covering the following areas:

- General ledger
- Accounts payable
- Accounts receivable
- Sales
- Production
- Purchases
- Project accounting
- Expense management
- Environment sustainability
- Customer Relationship Management
- Workflow analysis
- Budget control
- Inventory valuation
- Retail

Measures need to be informative, not just as raw numbers, but as a source for analysis at the management level. The consultant should identify the analytic dimensions as well as the dimensions needed by the process owner to analyze numbers. The most common example is sales revenue, which can be analyzed by dimensions such as customer segmentations, geographical locations, warehouses, and customer demographics. The following diagram shows the BI block:

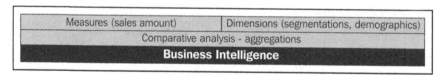

Now that we have seen the importance of the structure of reporting blocks based on the business processes and daily transaction data, it is worth exploring the common scenarios that consultants may face when the reporting requirements cannot be met by the data that is being captured. This missing data would lead a consultant to revisit the business process that includes the entry of daily transactions, and identify a need for the cleansing of historical data, which may lead to the loss of some information.

Executive decisions block

The third block in the information source is the executive decision support, where all of the information is summarized and numbers are transformed into KPIs, indicators, analytic views, and dashboards. The following diagram shows the executive decisions block:

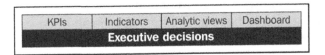

Executives do not have the luxury of time to drill down to all the comprehensive reports. They need a bird's-eye view of the overall enterprise performance to support them in taking critical business decisions. With the right low-level data, the ERP solution should be demonstrating its worth as a true decision support system that offers this visibility.

The conclusion is that when implementing a Microsoft Dynamics AX solution, there is no reliable information for executives without a solid BI platform that is based on a well-defined ERP. The ERP absorbs business processes, such as the daily transactions entered by workers with a high level of clarity.

Discovering Microsoft Dynamics AX reporting

The following section covers the Microsoft Dynamics AX reporting options. The reporting options are inquiry forms and SSRS reports.

Reporting options

Reporting in Microsoft Dynamics AX can be generated through two approaches, namely inquiry forms and predesigned standard reports, as shown in the following diagram:

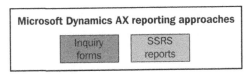

Inquiry forms

Inquiry forms are used for fast and easy reporting of transactions where the transactions are listed. Advanced filtration gives the facility to reduce the inquiry results to a number of specific results. If it is required that you show all the transactions, don't identify any filter.

As you can see in the following screenshot of the inquiry form, the advanced filtration and sorting capabilities can be accessed from all Microsoft Dynamics AX 2012 screens by pressing *Ctrl + F3*:

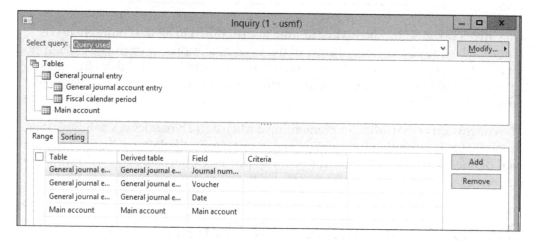

As you can see in the next screenshot, you can save a query by clicking on the **Modify** button. Now select **Save as** and add new tables to a data source in the inquiry filtration form by right-clicking on the **Tables** section. The two relations here are as follows:

- **1:n**: This represents the relation of one-to-many
- **n:1**: This represents the relation of many-to-one

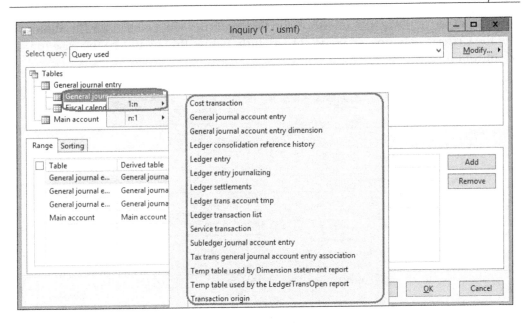

Under the **Range** tab, we will be able to add tables that are available in the data source, as shown in the following screenshot:

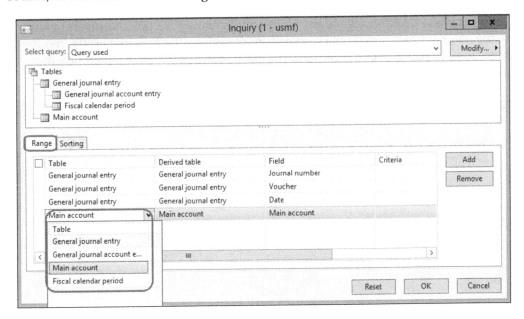

As you can see in the next screenshot, the **Field** column will be used for filtration, and the **Criteria** column will be used to identify values that would be the base for the filtration:

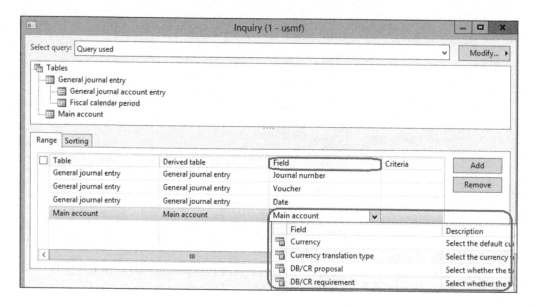

The inquiry will result in a standard Microsoft Dynamics AX 2012 form, and you can use the quick information on the transaction by moving the mouse over the required transaction, in addition to the personalization options, as shown in the following screenshot:

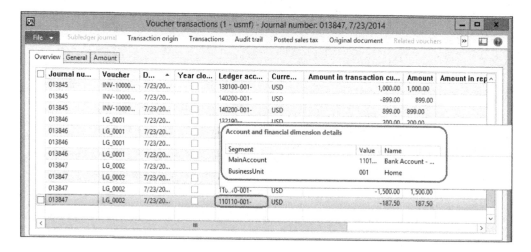

After the form generation, we can use wild character filtration by pressing *Ctrl + G*, and we see something like what is shown in the next screenshot:

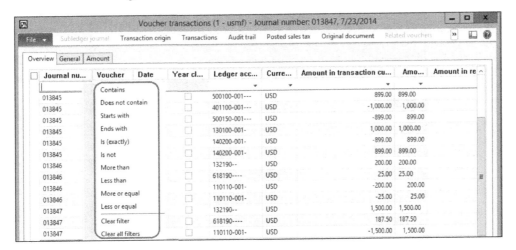

The wild characters used for filtration in grids are as follows:

- *: This character matches any character
- ?: This is used to check the must-have character
- ..: This specifies the "from" and "to" range
- !: This verifies that the grid does not have the character
- !A*: This verifies that the grid does not begin with the given character
- >/<: This checks for greater than and less than values
- ,: This checks the record we are looking for and another record
- D: This specifies the system date
- T: This specifies today's date.
- "": This is used to find a blank value

SSRS reports

SSRS reports are used to generate reports in the document format to be printed for filing, which are used as official supporting documents in the company's template or as external official documents. The normal advanced filtration is the base of SSRS report generation, and can sort report results. We can use the tables that are in the data source. We can also specify the fields that will be the base of the sorting and the available sorting option, either **Ascending** or **Descending**.

For the ledger transaction list, navigate to **General ledger | Reports | Transactions | Ledger transaction list**, and something that looks like this screenshot appears:

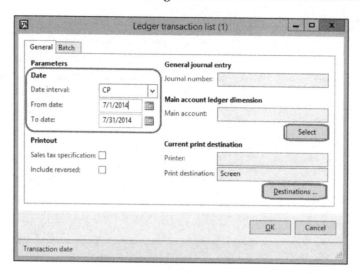

After completing the selection criteria, click on the **Select** button and navigate to the **Sorting** tab to identify the report sorting, as shown in the following screenshot:

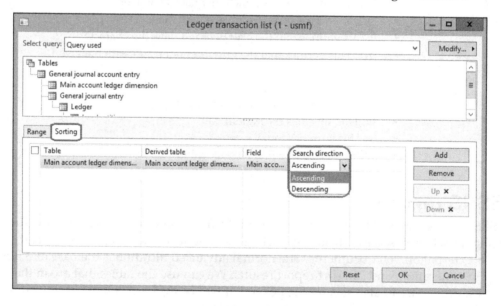

On the ledger transaction form, click on the **Destination** button to access the **Print destination** settings. Now identify the location of report printing, that is, **Print archive**, **Screen**, **Printer**, **File**, or **E-mail**. Also select **File format** from the drop-down list, which can be **Microsoft Excel**, **HTML**, **PDF**, **CSV**, and so on, as shown in the next screenshot:

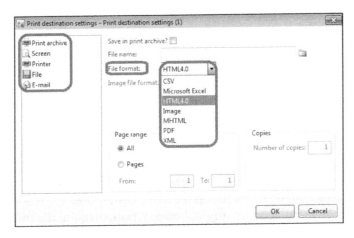

As you can see in the following screenshot, the generated report is based on SSRS, which gives more flexibility to the report layout:

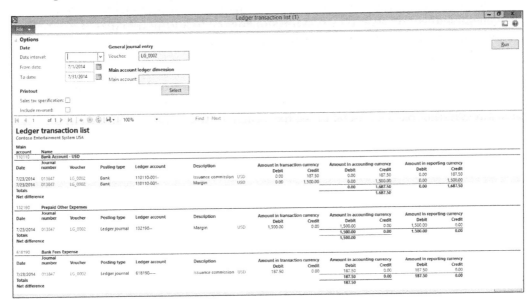

The report can be exported after report generation by the export function, as shown in this screenshot:

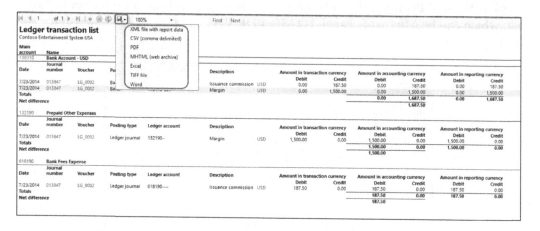

There are three major preferences for financial reporting that Microsoft Dynamics AX users should be familiar with: original transaction, original document, and audit trail.

The original transaction

The **Transaction origin** function fetches the transaction entries that are posted to the general ledger and their effect on the subledgers. In addition to that, this function can be performed to fetch any transaction entry. It is commonly used when you need to identify the subledger affected by that entry.

For voucher transactions, navigate to **General ledger | Inquiries | Voucher transactions**. Firstly, you will get an inquiry screen. Here, you do not have to give any criteria, so click on **OK** to see the voucher transactions, as shown in this screenshot:

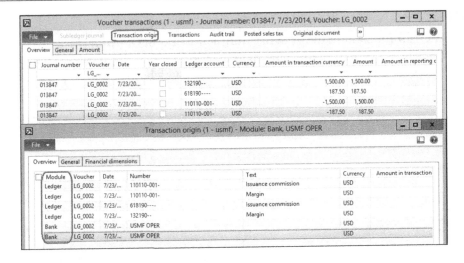

The Original document function

The **Original document** function fetches the transaction entries posted in the general ledger and reaches the original document that generated those entries.

As shown in the following screenshot, the **Original document** function in the voucher transaction inquiry form gives the ability to reach the original transaction document regardless of whether it is a general ledger entry, sales order, purchase order, or anything else:

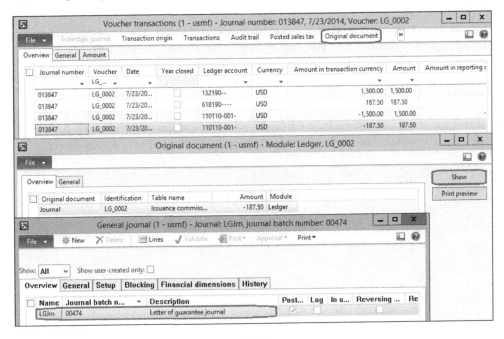

Audit trail

The **Audit trail** function in the voucher transaction inquiry form fetches the transaction entries posted in the general ledger and reports. It gives the facility to show who posted the transaction, when, and from which document type. Here is a screenshot that shows the **Audit trail** option of Microsoft Dynamics AX:

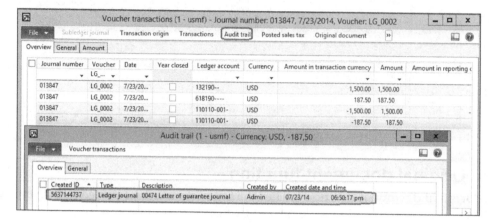

 There is a creation date and time that represents the actual date when the transaction was posted. However, this is not the financial posting date, which may be different from the creation date and time.

The main source of the transactions is transaction database. The transactions are replicated to cube database or database warehouse at every midnight. The report information is pulled out from cube DB and DB warehouse. If we are on July 1, the report will get information till the end of July. Assume that on July 1 a user posts a transaction dated on June 30.

If we run the report again on July 1 which pulls information from cube DB, it will not consider the posted transaction on June 30 since it is not considered in the replication. It will be included with effect from the next replication, which will take place on July 2 at midnight.

Reporting currency

Companies report their transactions in a specific currency that is known as **accounting currency** or **local currency**. It is normal to post transactions in a different currency, and this amount of money is translated to the home currency using the current exchange rate. This is a business need in enterprises that operate in a multinational environment. Each subsidiary has its local reporting currency, and at the same time, there should be a specific secondary reporting currency. All the transactions are translated into the reporting currency using the exchange rate.

To access the reporting currency, navigate to **General ledger | Setup | Ledger** and then you will see something like this:

Autoreports

The **Autoreport** wizard is a user-friendly tool. The end user can easily generate a report starting from every form in Microsoft Dynamics AX. This wizard helps the user to create a report based on the information in the form and save the report.

In this example, we will create an autoreport for vendor details as follows:

1. Open the **All vendors** list by navigating to **Accounts payable | Common | Vendors | All vendors**, as shown in this screenshot:

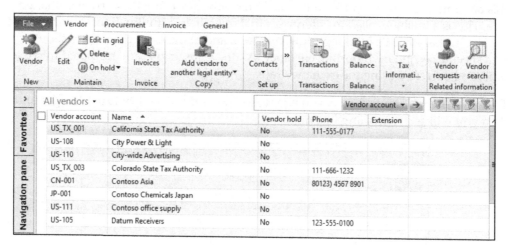

2. Navigate to **File | Print | Print... Ctrl + P**, as shown in the following screenshot:

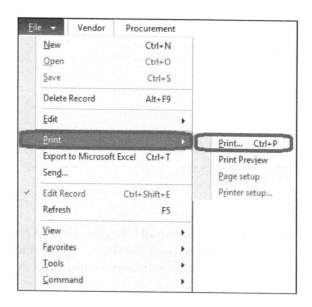

As you can see in the next screenshot, the **Autoreport** dialog box will pop up, and you can load a saved report or create a new report here:

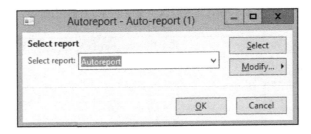

3. To create a new report, click on **Modify** and select **New**, as shown in the following screenshot:

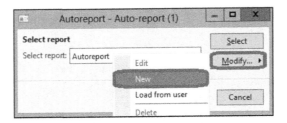

4. The autoreport wizard will pop up. Now click on **Next**, as shown in this screenshot:

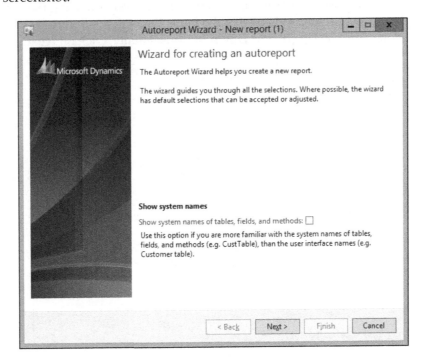

5. Enter the report name under the **Name** field, and click on **Next**.

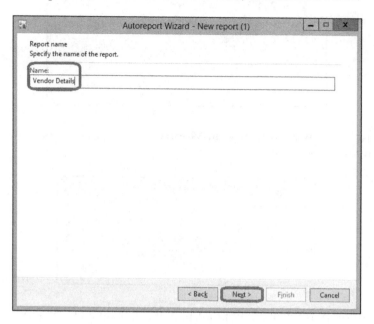

6. Select the report fields from the **Available fields** section using the left and right arrow buttons, and arrange the fields through the **Selected fields** section using the **Up (b)** and **Down** buttons. Finally, click on **Next**.

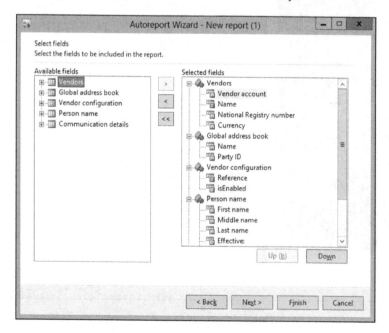

7. Select the numerical fields from the **Available fields** section, which contains total values, using the left and right arrow buttons. Then arrange the fields through the **Selected fields** section using the **Left** and **Right** buttons, as shown in the following screenshot, and click on **Next**:

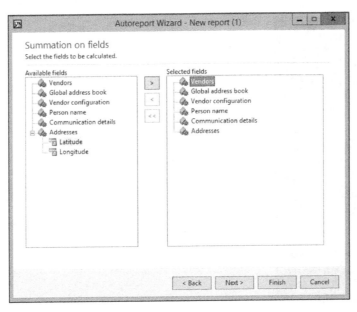

8. Specify the report template by selecting **Report layout template** and **Table style template**.

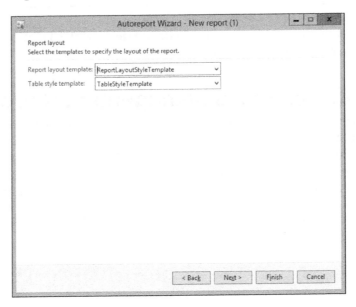

9. Click on **Finish** to close Autoreport wizard. You should be able to run the report after this step.

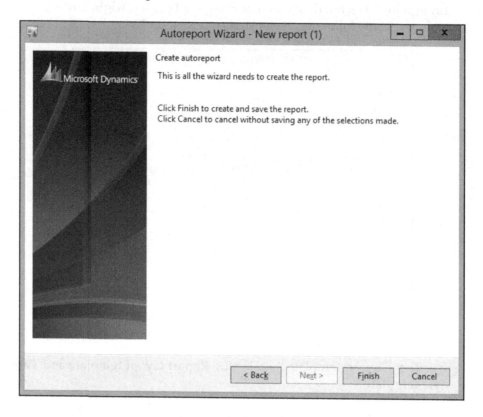

10. To generate the saved report, navigate to **File | Print | Print**, select the report name, and click on **Ok**.

Microsoft Dynamics Management Reporter

Microsoft has introduced Microsoft Dynamics Management Reporter as a financial reporting tool. It gives flexibility and insights to represent an organization's financial situation with high-level integration with the ERP. Microsoft Dynamics Management Reporter 2012 empowers financial decision makers by a set of 14 default reports. They are delivered as out-of-the-box reports. Here is the list of these reports:

- 12 Month Rolling Single Column Income Statement - Default
- 12 Month Trend Income Statement - Default

- Balance List - Default
- Balance Sheet - Default
- Cash Flow - Default
- Detailed Trial Balance - Default
- Expense Three Year Quarterly Trend - Default
- Income Statement - Default
- Ledger Transaction List - Default
- Ratios - Default
- Rolling 12 Month Expense - Default
- Rolling Quarter Income Statement - Default
- Summary Trial Balance - Default
- Weekly Sales and Discounts - Default

In addition to the designing tool used to build financial reports as per company requirements, the Management Reporter is considered the consolidation tool for Microsoft Dynamics AX 2012 where you can report the consolidated company financial reports from the management reports.

In Microsoft Dynamics AX 2012 R3, users can access the Management Reporter from general ledger financial reports menus. For this, you have to navigate to **General Ledger | Reports | Management Reporter**, as shown in this screenshot:

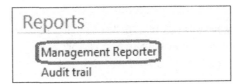

On the **Report Definition** screen, select the report the user wants to generate. Then click on **Generate** as shown in the following screenshot:

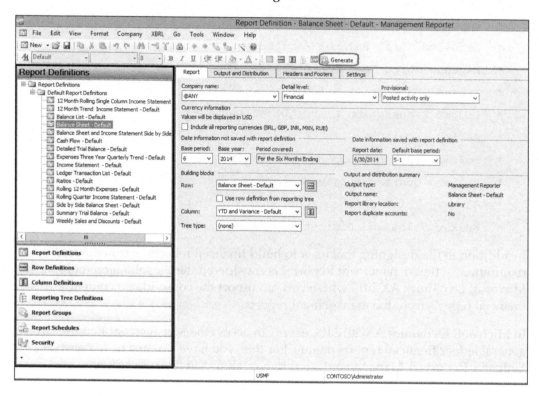

Microsoft Internet Explorer will open with the report. Here is a screenshot that represents the balance sheet as a summarized report:

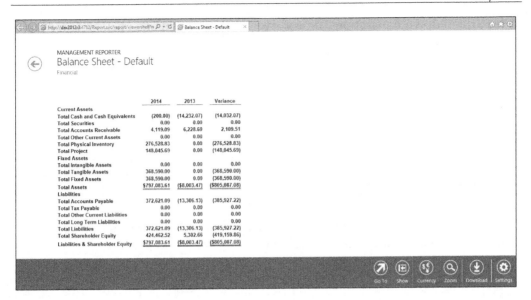

Microsoft Dynamics Management Reporter provides a drill-down capability to reach the lowest level of transaction and open the ledger entry on the Microsoft Dynamics AX 2012 client. In the following example, generate the **Expenses Three Year Quarterly Trend - Default** report title. When we mouse over on an amount, we can drill down to the details of that amount.

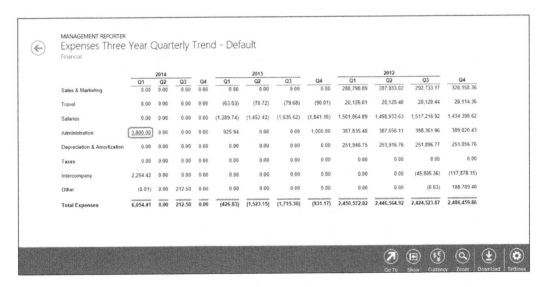

In the drilled-down transactions, mouse over on the amount and click on **Open in Microsoft Dynamics**.

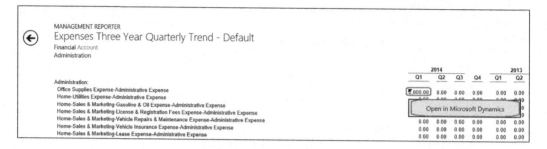

The Microsoft Dynamics AX 2012 R3 client will open with the voucher transaction form, as shown in the following screenshot:

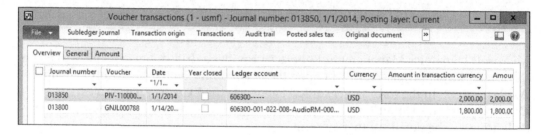

In the lower pane on the report are the function buttons, as shown here:

The function buttons can be summarized as follows:

- The first button is **Go to**. This represents a shortcut to reach a specific item on the report.

- The second button is **Show**. This shows the report in a summarized mode, or detailed mode, and shows the charts and comments pane.

- The third button is **Currency**. This represents a function used to convert the report to the selected currency.

- The forth button is **Zoom**. This presents the users with the zoom-in and zoom-out options for the report.

- The fifth button is **Download**. This represents the download option of the report, whether XPS format, Microsoft Office Excel, or Microsoft Dynamics Management Reporter Viewer.

Summary

In this chapter, we covered financial reporting from planning to consideration of reporting levels, where we ensured to gather the reporting requirements in the early stages of the implementation, and considered the differences of reporting in the different managerial levels.

We covered important points that affect reporting quality by considering the reporting value chain, which consists of infrastructure, database management, business processes, business intelligence, and the frontend. We also discussed the information source blocks, which consist of the detailed transactions block, business intelligence block, and executive decisions block.

Then we learned about the reporting possibilities in Microsoft Dynamics AX such as inquiry forms and SSRS reports, autoreport capabilities in Microsoft Dynamics AX 2012 R3, and Microsoft Dynamics Management Reporter.

Index

C

cash and bank management
about 164
bank account reconciliation 82-89
bank facility, letter of guarantee 90-101
controlling 74, 75
credit limit 75, 76
date activation 77, 78
exploring 82
general ledger reconciliation 80
status activation 78, 79
transaction currency 80, 81
cash discount
about 118-121, 177-179
Invoice and delivery fast tab 180
Invoice field group 180
Sales tax field group 180
cash flow
budgeting 229
customer collections management 228
forecast 229
general ledger 229
integrating, with other modules 228, 229
vendor expenditure management 228
cash flow forecast, configuration
about 229
Accounts payable module 230-233
Accounts receivable module 234-237
budget module 238
by currency requirement 241-243
general ledger 238, 239
cash flow, transactions
about 239
cash flow forecast, by currency
requirement 241-243
main account cash flow forecast 244
purchase order cash flow forecast 240, 241
chart of accounts. *See* **COA**
Check the invoice number used field
Accept duplicates option 138
Reject duplicate option 138
Reject duplicates within fiscal year
option 138
Warn in case of duplicates option 138
Chief Information Officer (CIO) 296

closing procedure
about 68-71
Finance department 69
Human resources department 69
Procurement department 69
Sales department 69
COA
about 33, 34, 51
main account categories 39
main accounts, classifying 34, 35
main accounts, controlling 40
nontransactional accounts, using 37
transactional accounts, using 36
configuration, inventory costing
about 247
Item groups 251, 252
Item model group 247-249
Product dimension groups 250
Storage dimension groups 250
Tracking dimension groups 251
configuration process 16
constant fields 209
controls, cash and bank management
credit limit 75
date activation 75
general ledger reconciliation 75
status activation 75
transaction currency 75
cost of goods sold (COGS) 166, 246, 259
credit limit 75, 76
currencies 51
Currency code validation option
list 48
optional 47
table 48
to be filled in 47
customer collections management, cash flow
accounts receivable 228
sales and marketing 228
customer credit limit management 182-191
customer hold activities 181
customer master data, characteristics
cash discount 177-179
customer price/discount groups 170-172
exploring 168, 169
payment methods 175
Sales order defaults fast tab 170

customer payment 167
customer price/discount groups
   about 170-172
   Payment fast tab 173
   Terms of payment field 174, 175
customer settlement 202, 203

D

daily transactions
   account alias 64
   performing 63
   recurring entries 65, 66
   voucher, saving 67, 68
database management 297
Data Import Export Framework (DIXF) 60
date activation 77, 78
Debit/Credit Controls group
   about 40
   Balance Control 43, 44
   Debit/Credit Proposal 41
   Debit/Credit Requirements 42
decision making, ERP reporting
   semi-structured 15
   structured 15
   unstructured 15
deferred cost of goods sold
      (deferred COGS) 259
depreciation method 208
depreciation profile 207
detailed transactions block 299
discount group, vendor master data
   about 111, 112, 170
   line discount group 112
   multi line discount group 112
   price group 112
   total discount group 112
dynamic fields 209

E

Enterprise Resource Planning (ERP)
   about 5, 33
   application consultant 7, 8
   characteristics 6
   common terms 16
   consultant, responsibilities 7, 8
   implementation team, discovering 6, 7

module integration 10
   reporting 13
   reporting needs, planning for 293, 294
ERP implementations, terms
   configuration 16
   customization 17
   installation 16
   modification 17
   personalization 16
   setup 16
ERP implementation intentions, samples
   business process 9
   controlling 9
   decision support 10
Excel Power View 295
exchange rate type 51
executive decisions block 301

F

fields, bank reconciliation
   Matched bank documents 88
   Matched statement lines 88
   Open bank documents 88
   Open statement lines 88
finance controllership department
   about 68
   Human resources department 69
Finance department 69
financial dimension reporting
   about 285
   financial dimension sets 285-292
financial dimensions
   about 265, 266
   chart structure, building 267, 268
   considerations 266
   report filtration, parameters 289, 290
   system-defined dimension 272
   user-defined dimension 272
financial dimension sets
   about 285
   accessing 286-292
financial dimensions, standpoints
   data entry controls and validations 267
   reporting and analysis 267
   subledger and general ledger
      reconciliation 267

W

withholding tax
  about 58, 111
  price excludes sales tax rule 58
  price includes sales tax rule 58
work in progress (WIP) 259

Thank you for buying
Microsoft Dynamics AX 2012 R3
Financial Management

About Packt Publishing

Packt, pronounced 'packed', published its first book, *Mastering phpMyAdmin for Effective MySQL Management*, in April 2004, and subsequently continued to specialize in publishing highly focused books on specific technologies and solutions.

Our books and publications share the experiences of your fellow IT professionals in adapting and customizing today's systems, applications, and frameworks. Our solution-based books give you the knowledge and power to customize the software and technologies you're using to get the job done. Packt books are more specific and less general than the IT books you have seen in the past. Our unique business model allows us to bring you more focused information, giving you more of what you need to know, and less of what you don't.

Packt is a modern yet unique publishing company that focuses on producing quality, cutting-edge books for communities of developers, administrators, and newbies alike. For more information, please visit our website at www.packtpub.com.

About Packt Enterprise

In 2010, Packt launched two new brands, Packt Enterprise and Packt Open Source, in order to continue its focus on specialization. This book is part of the Packt Enterprise brand, home to books published on enterprise software – software created by major vendors, including (but not limited to) IBM, Microsoft, and Oracle, often for use in other corporations. Its titles will offer information relevant to a range of users of this software, including administrators, developers, architects, and end users.

Writing for Packt

We welcome all inquiries from people who are interested in authoring. Book proposals should be sent to author@packtpub.com. If your book idea is still at an early stage and you would like to discuss it first before writing a formal book proposal, then please contact us; one of our commissioning editors will get in touch with you.

We're not just looking for published authors; if you have strong technical skills but no writing experience, our experienced editors can help you develop a writing career, or simply get some additional reward for your expertise.

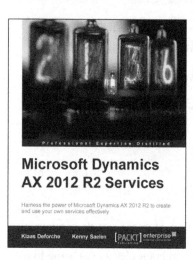

Microsoft Dynamics AX 2012 R2 Services

ISBN: 978-1-78217-672-5   Paperback: 264 pages

Harness the power of Microsoft Dynamics AX 2012 R2 to create and use your own services effectively

1. Learn about the Dynamics AX 2012 service architecture.

2. Create your own services using wizards or X++ code.

3. Deploy your services in a variety of ways using High Availability.

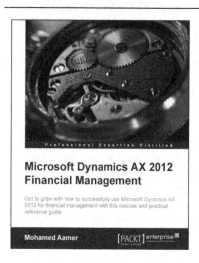

Microsoft Dynamics AX 2012 Financial Management

ISBN: 978-1-78217-720-3   Paperback: 168 pages

Get to grips with how to successfully use Microsoft Dynamics AX 2012 for financial management with this concise and practical reference guide

1. Understand the financial management aspects in Microsoft Dynamics AX.

2. Successfully configure and set up your software.

3. Learn about real-life business requirements and their solutions.

4. Get to know the tips and tricks you can utilize during analysis, design, deployment, and operation phases in a project lifecycle.

Please check **www.PacktPub.com** for information on our titles

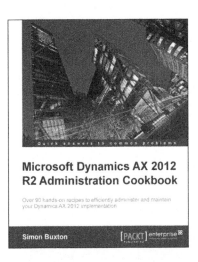

Microsoft Dynamics AX 2012 R2 Administration Cookbook

ISBN: 978-1-84968-806-2   Paperback: 378 pages

Over 90 hands-on recipes to efficiently administer and maintain your Dynamics AX 2012 implementation

1. Task-based examples for application and third-party interactions through the AIF.

2. Step-by-step instructions for performing user and security management operations.

3. Detailed instructions for performance and troubleshooting AX 2012.

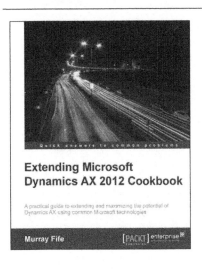

Extending Microsoft Dynamics AX 2012 Cookbook

ISBN: 978-1-78216-833-1   Paperback: 314 pages

A practical guide to extending and maximizing the potential of Dynamics AX using common Microsoft technologies

1. Extend Dynamics in a cost-effective manner by using tools you already have.

2. Solve common business problems with the valuable features of Dynamics AX.

3. Follow practical and easy-to-grasp examples, illustrations and coding to make the most out of Dynamics AX in your business scenario.

Please check **www.PacktPub.com** for information on our titles

Made in the
USA
Monee, IL